THE PRICELESS JEWEL

For forty years Sangharakshita has been playing an important part in the spread of Buddhism throughout the modern world. He is head of the Western Buddhist Order (Trailokya Bauddha Mahasangha), and is actively engaged in what is now an international Buddhist movement with centres in thirteen countries worldwide. When not visiting centres he is based at a community in Norfolk. His writings are available in eleven languages.

Also by Sangharakshita:

A Survey of Buddhism

Flame in Darkness

The Enchanted Heart

The Three Jewels

Crossing the Stream

The Essence of Zen

The Thousand-Petalled Lotus

Human Enlightenment

The Religion of Art

The Ten Pillars of Buddhism

The Eternal Legacy

Travel Letters

Alternative Traditions

Conquering New Worlds

Ambedkar and Buddhism

The History of My Going for Refuge

The Taste of Freedom

New Currents in Western Buddhism

A Guide to the Buddhist Path

Learning to Walk

Vision and Transformation

The Buddha's Victory

Facing Mount Kanchenjunga

The FWBO and 'Protestant Buddhism'

The Drama of Cosmic Enlightenment

Wisdom Beyond Words

The Meaning of Orthodoxy in Buddhism

Mind—Reactive and Creative

Going For Refuge

The Caves of Bhaja

My Relation to the Order

Hercules and the Birds and Other Poems

Buddhism and the West

Forty-Three Years Ago

SANGHARAKSHITA

THE PRICELESS JEWEL

•

WINDHORSE PUBLICATIONS

Published by Windhorse Publications
3 Sanda Street
Glasgow G20 8PU

© Sangharakshita 1993

Printed by The Cromwell Press
Melksham, Wiltshire

Cover design Dhammarati

British Library Cataloguing in Publication Data.
A catalogue record for this book is available from the British Library

ISBN 0 904766 58 6

CONTENTS

Publication History

'The Priceless Jewel'
The Middle Way, Vol 61, No.3, The Buddhist Society, London, November 1986, pp.157–164.
'Aspects of Buddhist Morality'
from *Studia Missionalia, Vol 27*, Rome 1978, pp.159–180.
'Dialogue Between Buddhism and Christianity'
Concilium, No.136, Nigmegen, Holland, June 1978.
The Journey to Il Convento
Windhorse, Glasgow 1984.
St Jerome Revisited
Windhorse, Glasgow 1985.
Buddhism and Blasphemy
Windhorse, London 1978.
Buddhism, World Peace, and Nuclear War
Windhorse, Glasgow 1984.
'The Bodhisattva Principle'
Published as *The Bodhisattva: Evolution and Self-Transcendence*, Windhorse, Glasgow 1983.
The Glory of the Literary World
Windhorse, Glasgow 1985.
'Dharmapala: The Spiritual Dimension'
Dhammamegha No.47, Triratna Grantha Mala, Poona 1992.
'With Allen Ginsberg in Kalimpong (1962)'
From *Best Minds: A Tribute to Allen Ginsberg*, Lospecchio Press, New York 1986, pp.246–248.
'A Note on *The Burial of Count Orgaz*' and 'Criticism East and West'
have not been pubished before.

Preface

At one point I was minded to call the essays and addresses brought together in this volume 'Chips from a Western Buddhist Workshop', in memory of F. Max Müller's *Chips from a German Workshop*, which I had read many years earlier, but in the end I decided that such a title would be too cumbersome. Nonetheless, the contents of this slim volume of mine, as of his four substantial ones, are chips in the sense that their production has been secondary to that of larger literary undertakings. Not that they are therefore of only minor significance. Written between 1978 and 1991, some of them contain definitive statements on issues I regard as being of the highest importance, and it is for this reason that I have brought them together under the title of *The Priceless Jewel*, which is also the title of the opening item of the volume.

Originally known as 'The Jewel in the Garment', 'The Priceless Jewel' was delivered as a sermon in the chapel of King's College, Cambridge, on the morning of Sunday 15 July 1987, to a congregation consisting mainly of American tourists who had come, presumably, to hear the famous choir rather than to listen to a Buddhist discourse of instruction. I gave the sermon at the invitation of the chaplain, the Rev. Stephen Coles, who conducted the service.

'Aspects of Buddhist Morality' was written at the beginning of 1978 as a contribution to a special volume, on morality in world religions, of the Roman Catholic journal *Studia Missionalia*. It was written at the invitation of the editor, the Rev. Father Dhavemony.

'Dialogue Between Buddhism and Christianity' was written for the 'Bouddhisme et Christianisme' issue of the Revue Internationale de

Théologie *Concilium*. When it was reprinted in the Ola Leaves series the Editor's Foreword noted: 'The actual headings of this essay represent themes for discussion laid down by the editor of *Concilium*. Left to his own devices, the author would probably *not* have chosen to discuss the subject under these headings at all.' The essay was written in the first half of 1978.

Both 'The Journey to Il Convento' and 'St Jerome Revisited' are addresses I gave at Il Convento di Santa Croce in Tuscany, Italy, in the autumn of 1984. They were given at the FWBO's fourth three-month pre-ordination course for men.

'Buddhism and Blasphemy' was written in 1978, the 'Year of the Blasphemy Trial', and was my contribution to the debate surrounding the trial and conviction of Denis Lemon and Gay News Ltd for the crime of blasphemous libel. On its publication as a booklet this essay attracted more attention in non-Buddhist circles than any of its companions in this volume. Twice reprinted, it became part of a submission to the Law Commission, which took the views expressed in 'Buddhism and Blasphemy' into consideration when making its proposals for the reform of the criminal law. It was also quoted from in a debate in the House of Commons, and drew favourable comment from well known figures in the fields of literature, science, and the performing arts.

'Buddhism, World Peace, and Nuclear War' was originally delivered as a lecture in July 1984 at the Croydon Arts Centre and again at Conway Hall, London. On its publication it, too, attracted attention in non-Buddhist circles, though to a lesser extent than 'Buddhism and Blasphemy' had done, particular interest being shown in my comments on the breakdown of the notion of objective truth.

'The Bodhisattva Principle: Key to the Evolution of Consciousness, Individual and Collective—a Buddhist View' is an address I gave in March 1983 at the invitation of the Wrekin Trust as part of their sixth annual Mystics and Scientists Conference, entitled 'Reality, Consciousness and Order', held at King Alfred's College, Winchester. Whether the capacity in which I was invited to participate was that of a Mystic or Scientist was not clear. In any case, the rather unwieldy title was not entirely of my own devising, and I had to bend my talk a little to fit.

'The Glory of the Literary World' was given as a paper in August 1985 at Friends House, London, to mark the publication of my new book, *The Eternal Legacy: An Introduction to the Canonical Literature of Buddhism*.

Unlike the other essays and addresses in this volume, 'A Note on *The Burial of Count Orgaz*' was written simply to please myself, in the sense that I did not write it in response to an invitation. It was written in the summer of 1991, at Guhyaloka, near Alicante, the FWBO men's retreat centre in Spain, a year after I had visited Toledo and seen the famous painting.

'Criticism East and West' was written in the spring of 1988. It was to have been read at a weekend school on 'Criticism in Crisis' organized by the Manchester University's Department of Extra-Mural Studies. In the event the school had to be cancelled and my paper has remained unpublished until now.

'Dharmapala: The Spiritual Dimension' was written in the summer of 1991, at Guhyaloka, at the request of the Maha Bodhi Society of Sri Lanka for inclusion in its 100th Anniversary Souvenir. Due to the troubles there, however, the Souvenir could not be published.

In 1984 I was invited to contribute to the Festschrift that was being brought out as a tribute to Allen Ginsberg on the occasion of his sixtieth birthday. A year later, in the autumn of 1985, while on retreat at Il Convento di Santa Croce, I wrote 'With Allen Ginsberg in Kalimpong (1962)'.

May these 'chips' of mine serve to feed the flame of devotion to the Dharma in the hearts of all readers of this book.

Sangharakshita
Padmaloka
Norfolk
29 July 1993

THE PRICELESS JEWEL

World-Honoured One! It is as if some man goes to an intimate friend's house, gets drunk, and falls asleep. Meanwhile his friend, having to go forth on official duty, ties a priceless jewel within his garment as a present, and departs. The man, being drunk and asleep, knows nothing of it. On arousing he travels onward till he reaches some other country, where for food and clothing he expends much labour and effort, and undergoes exceedingly great hardship, and is content even if he can obtain but little. Later, his friend happens to meet him and speaks thus: 'Tut! Sir, how is it you have come to this for the sake of food and clothing? Wishing you to be in comfort and able to satisfy all your five senses, I formerly in such a year and month and on such a day tied a priceless jewel within your garment. Now as of old it is present there and you in ignorance are slaving and worrying to keep yourself alive. How very stupid! Go now and exchange that jewel for what you need and do whatever you will, free from all poverty and shortage.'

The parable of the priceless jewel within the garment, as it may be called, occurs in the eighth chapter of the *Saddharma-Puṇḍarīka* or 'White Lotus of the Real Truth' Sūtra, one of the most important and influential of all the Buddhist scriptures. This scripture, commonly known as the *White Lotus Sūtra*, opens with the Buddha entering into deep meditation and emitting from between his eyebrows a ray of light that illumines the entire universe. On emerging from this meditation, he explains to his disciples, who are present in large numbers, that truth in its fullness can be understood only by those who are spiritually enlightened. Others must approach it gradually, step by step, through a series of progressive stages. For this reason, he says, he has hitherto confined himself to giving teaching of a more elementary nature. Now, however, the time has come for him to disclose the higher teaching. Now he will reveal the final truth. To many of the disciples this announcement comes as quite a shock. They are convinced that what the Buddha has so far taught them is the whole truth and that they have nothing more to learn. Some of them, indeed, are so convinced of this that they actually withdraw from the assembly, unwilling to hear what the Buddha has to say. Those that remain are, however, in the majority, and it is to them that the Buddha proceeds to reveal the final truth.

He begins by explaining that the different spiritual ideals which he has hitherto taught are only temporary expedients, made necessary by the temperamental and spiritual differences existing among the disciples themselves. In reality there is only one spiritual ideal, the ideal which he himself exemplifies, the ideal of absolute spiritual altruism or Supreme Buddhahood. This ideal, which is the highest ideal, is the ultimate ideal for all the disciples, and in it all lesser ideals therefore eventually merge. These lesser ideals are the different forms of spiritual individualism, to which the disciples who have withdrawn from the assembly still adhere and which they are unwilling to give up. Spiritual individualism is the attitude of being concerned with the attainment of Enlightenment, or salvation, *for oneself alone*, without caring whether others attain Enlightenment or not. Absolute spiritual altruism, on the other hand, is the attitude of being concerned with the attainment of Enlightenment, or salvation, not simply for one's own benefit but for the benefit of all living beings. Such unbounded altruism does not, however, consist in devoting oneself first to one's own spiritual welfare and then to the spiritual welfare of others. Rather does it consist in the spontaneous compassionate activity that manifests when the very distinction between self and others is transcended or when, to speak less metaphysically, one realizes that one's own spiritual development is bound up with that of other people, even as theirs is bound up with one's own.

The Buddha's revelation that in reality there is only one spiritual ideal, the ideal of absolute spiritual altruism, and that this is the ultimate ideal for all, initially meets with a fully positive response from only one member of the assembly. This is Śāriputra, the wisest of the Buddha's disciples, whose only regret is that hitherto he has devoted himself to the lesser ideal of spiritual individualism. As though to console him, the Buddha explains that in a previous existence he had actually dedicated himself to the ideal of absolute spiritual altruism but that, forgetful of this fact, he had in his present existence wrongly imagined spiritual individualism to be the highest ideal. In a future existence, he assures him, he will realize the ideal of absolute spiritual altruism or Supreme Buddhahood and will lead countless other beings to the same lofty realization. This prediction the assembly receives with great rejoicing. Śāriputra then tells the Buddha that twelve hundred disciples who have realized the ideal of spiritual individualism, and who were under the impression that they had nothing more to learn, are greatly perplexed by what they have just heard. Would the Buddha please speak to them and explain the reason for the discrepancy between the old teaching and the new?

In response to Śāriputra's request, the Buddha not only reaffirms the provisional and instrumental nature of his teaching, the sole purpose of which is to lead living beings in the direction of absolute spiritual altruism, but also makes his meaning clear with the help of a lengthy parable, for, he says, 'intelligent people through a parable reach understanding.' This parable is the famous parable of the burning house, according to which the Buddha induces living beings to forsake mundane existence in much the same way that a loving father induces his heedless children to come out of the house that is on fire—that is, by promising to give them the very things of which they happen to be most fond. Such is the effect of the parable that four leading elders realize that it is not too late for them to give up the lesser ideal of spiritual individualism and dedicate themselves to the higher ideal of absolute spiritual altruism, and one of them, the ascetically-minded Mahākāśyapa, explains the joy that they all feel by relating a parable of his own that is, in fact, the Buddhist equivalent of St Luke's parable of the prodigal son. The Buddha then relates five more parables, three of which serve to make the provisional and instrumental nature of his teaching still more clear, while the others are in answer to questions raised by Mahākāśyapa.

By this time the whole assembly is feeling the effect of the Buddha's words, and more and more disciples announce their acceptance of the new teaching. Among them are five hundred disciples who have realized the ideal of spiritual individualism and therefore thought that they had nothing more to learn. Now they have realized their mistake and the Buddha predicts that in a future existence they will all realize the ideal of absolute spiritual altruism or Buddhahood. Overjoyed, they bow down at his feet and like Mahākāśyapa give expression to their feelings in a parable. This parable is the parable of the priceless jewel within the garment, with which we are concerned this morning. Having related the parable, the five hundred 'converted' disciples explain that they themselves are the man who went to his friend's house, got drunk, and fell asleep, that the priceless jewel within their garment is the ideal of absolute spiritual altruism or Buddhahood, and that the friend who tied it there is the Buddha himself. In a previous existence he had taught them the ideal of absolute spiritual altruism, subsequently they had forgotten it, and he has just taught it to them again and reminded them of their original commitment. Now they no longer need trouble themselves with lesser ideals.

Such is the parable of the priceless jewel within the garment in the context of the *White Lotus Sūtra*. But, like most parables, the parable related by the five hundred 'converted' disciples has a more general—even a more universal—significance, both in the context of Buddhist tradition and in the context of the religious experience of mankind. To begin with, the parable taken as a whole is an expression of the overwhelming joy, wonder, thankfulness, and awe we experience on encountering a truth, a reality, that far transcends anything we have previously thought of or felt or imagined. At first, of course, we may shrink from that truth, or that reality, just as the Buddha's disciples did: we may even run away from it; for instinctively we feel that to encounter it will oblige us to give up our most cherished attitudes and beliefs or, at the very least, to modify them drastically. But if we can allow ourselves to encounter the new truth, or the as yet unimagined reality, if we can allow ourselves to accept it and embrace it, then our horizon will expand immeasurably, fresh vistas will open up for us in all directions, and we shall find that we have gained infinitely more than we gave up. Nor is that all. As the parable taken as a whole also makes clear, the new truth, though new, is at the same time strangely familiar. It is as though we have heard it before, known it before, accepted it before. Indeed, we feel that we *have* heard it before, *have* known it before, *have* accepted it before, just as the five hundred 'converted' disciples realize that the ideal of absolute spiritual altruism had in fact been their ideal for many previous existences, even though in their present existence they had, out of forgetfulness, wrongly thought otherwise for a while.

This paradoxical feeling of absolute newness and, at the same time, complete familiarity, is what many Western Buddhists experience, to a greater or a lesser extent, on the occasion of their first contact with Buddhism, whether that contact takes the form of reading a Buddhist book, seeing an image of the Buddha, or paying a visit to a Buddhist spiritual community. They feel not just that they have gained something infinitely precious but that they have *re*gained it. They feel that, after many wanderings, they have not only arrived at last at the gates of a glorious palace but also that, incredible as it seems, they have 'come home'. Some of them seek to account for this feeling of complete familiarity by saying that to them Buddhism represents what they have, in fact, always believed, though without fully realizing it. Others seek to account for it by saying, with varying degrees of conviction, that they must have been Buddhist in a previous existence. However they may account for the feeling, or even if they choose not to account for it at all, such Western Buddhists are naturally astonished when somebody tells them, as somebody occasionally does, even today, that he—or she—is unable to understand how it is possible for one born and brought up in the West, as a member of Western society and in the midst of Western culture, to accept an Eastern religion like Buddhism or, in other words, to accept a religion that is foreign and exotic. But such a thing *is* possible, as daily is becoming more evident, and the reason why it is possible is that the system of spiritual teaching and training that we call Buddhism is, in reality, neither Eastern nor Western, any more than man himself, in the depths of his being, is either Eastern or Western. When, therefore, the so-called Englishman or American or Spaniard accepts the so-called Eastern religion of Buddhism he accepts it, even as he encounters it, on a level where the terms Eastern and Western no longer have any meaning.

If a few words of personal confession may be permitted, this was very much my own experience forty-five years ago when, at the age of sixteen, I had my first real contact with Buddhism. That contact took place when I read two short but exceptionally profound Buddhist scriptures of great historical and spiritual significance. These were the *Diamond Sūtra*, a work belonging to the 'Perfection of Wisdom' corpus, and the *Sūtra of Wei Lang*, a collection of discourses by the first Chinese patriarch of the Ch'an or Zen school, who is better known as Hui Neng. Reading these two works and realizing that, although in one sense the truth they taught, or the reality they disclosed, was new to me, in another sense it was not new at all but strangely familiar. I certainly did not feel that I was accepting an Eastern religion, or a religion that was foreign and exotic. Rather I felt that contact with Buddhism was, at the same time, contact with the depths of my own being: that in knowing Buddhism I was knowing myself, and that in knowing myself I was knowing Buddhism.

But from personal confession we must return to the parable of the priceless jewel within the garment, and in particular to the principal motifs or symbols of the parable. There are three of these: (1) the motif of drunkenness or sleep; (2) the motif of the other country; and (3) the motif of the priceless jewel. These are all universal motifs or symbols and, though at present we are concerned with them mainly in their Buddhist form, it would be strange if we were not sometimes reminded, however distantly, of the forms which they assume in other spiritual traditions.

The first motif to appear as the parable unfolds is that of drunkenness or sleep, which is one of the most important motifs in the whole range of Buddhist thought. Drunkenness or sleep, like blindness, represents the state of spiritual *un*awareness or ignorance. It represents a state in which we have no knowledge of any higher truth, or reality, or ideal, and in which we do not, perhaps, acknowledge the theoretical existence of such a truth or even regard it as a possibility. In other words, it represents a state of profound spiritual alienation. This state is, so to speak, the natural condition of man. Here we must not allow ourselves to be misled by an over-literal reading of the parable. In the parable, which of course is a kind of story, the drunkenness and the sleep have a definite point of origin. A man goes to an intimate friend's house, gets drunk, and falls asleep. The actions all take place in time. There is a period before he goes to the friend's house, a period before he gets drunk, a period before he falls asleep, and then there is a period after he has done these things. According to Buddhism, however, there is no point of ultimate origin for the state of spiritual unawareness or ignorance in which we are enthralled. However far back in time we may go, through however many births and deaths and rebirths, we shall never arrive at the point at which unawareness or ignorance began and prior to which 'we' existed in a state of pure awareness or knowledge. No such point can be perceived. Because no such point can be perceived (that is, perceived within the temporal order) the state of unawareness or ignorance is a primordial state, and because it is a primordial state it is spoken of as the natural condition of man.

But though unawareness or ignorance is a natural condition of man that condition is not necessarily a permanent one. The fact that the ultimate point of origin of the state of unawareness or ignorance cannot be perceived does not mean that the state cannot be transcended. We transcend that state and achieve a state of pure awareness or knowledge when we 'wake up', here and now, to the higher truth, or reality, or ideal, and when we wake up to it—in the existential rather then the theoretical sense—as a result of following a progressive spiritual path that leads us from ethics to concentration and meditation and from concentration and meditation to clear vision or wisdom. Possible though it is to transcend the state of unawareness or ignorance, however, so long as it is *not* transcended there can be no escape from the suffering which is the inevitable concomitant of such a state. This brings us to the motif of the other country to which the man in the parable travels after leaving his friend's house and where 'for food and clothing he expends much labour and effort, and undergoes exceedingly great hardship, and is content even if he can obtain but little.'

The other country represents the objective counterpart of the state of spiritual alienation in which we eventually find ourselves as a result of our spiritual unawareness or ignorance. It represents the kind of world in which we live when we have no knowledge of any higher truth, or reality, or ideal, and do not, perhaps, acknowledge the theoretical existence of such a truth. Since the higher truth is the living water that nourishes the very roots of our being and enables us to grow—another of the *White Lotus Sūtra's* parables likens the Buddha's teaching to the rain—in the absence of that truth our world is a dry and barren place in which, scorched as it is by the heat of the passions, there is hardly any sign of spiritual life. Thus the other country is the Waste Land, the land made desolate by the sickness or infirmity of its king, as well as the 'far country' into which the prodigal son takes his journey, where he wastes his substance with riotous living, and where, when he has spent all, there arises a mighty famine and he begins to be in want. Moreover, the world in which we live when we have no knowledge of any higher truth, or reality, or ideal, is a world in which we devote ourselves to inferior goals and in which, therefore, we experience no deep or lasting satisfaction. In the language of the parable, we expend much labour and effort for food and clothing, undergo exceedingly great hardship, and are content even if we can obtain but little—that is, little in comparison with what we could obtain if we followed the spiritual path and 'woke up' to the higher truth and all that it can give us. This is not to say that in devoting ourselves to our inferior goals we are doing what we really want to do. It is not to say that we are acting from a condition of genuine freedom. Rather do we expend much labour and effort, and undergo the exceeding great hardship, because we are slaves to the compulsion of our own unaware and ignorant desires. For this reason the other country is not only a Waste Land, not only a far country stricken by famine, but also a land of slavery and oppression. In other words the other country is Egypt. It is the Egypt of the biblical story of Israel's bondage and liberation, and it is the Egypt of Gnostic symbolism. It is the land of sorcery into which, in the so called

'Hymn of the Pearl', the son of the King of the East goes down in order to bring the One Pearl which lies in the midst of the sea and where the Egyptians cunningly mix drink for him, and give him a taste of their meat, so that he forgets that he is a king's son, and forgets the Pearl.

Since the other country is Egypt, it naturally follows that it is the foreign country; that is, the country that is not simply other than our own, in a neutral sense, but which is actually inimical and hostile to us. Thus the world in which we find ourselves living as a result of our spiritual alienation is a world in which we are foreigners and aliens, and the reason we are foreigners and aliens, even though we may wrongly think of ourselves as actually belonging to that world, is that without knowing it we have in our possession the means of overcoming the alienation and 'waking up' to the higher truth, or reality, or ideal, of achieving a state of pure awareness or knowledge, and of restoring ourselves to a world of spiritual abundance. This brings us to the priceless jewel, the third of the three motifs of the parable with which we are concerned this morning. The priceless jewel represents the higher truth, or reality, or ideal, as this is potentially existent within us. As such it is also the jewel-in-the-lotus of the famous Indo-Tibetan Buddhist mantra; it is the Grail of Arthurian legend, whether that Grail be a crystal cup, a stone dish, or a magic cauldron; it is the Philosopher's Stone, that transmutes everything into gold. It is also, perhaps, the piece of silver that the woman in the Lucan parable lost and for which she sought diligently until she found it. In the content of the parable of the priceless jewel itself, of course, the priceless jewel represents the higher ideal of absolute spiritual altruism or Buddha-hood to which the Buddha's disciples had originally dedicated themselves and which they had forgotten.

As in the case of the motif of drunkenness or sleep, however, we must not allow ourselves to be misled by an over-literal reading of the parable. The fact that the priceless jewel is tied within the man's garment does not mean that the truth, or reality, or ideal, which is potentially existent within us lies just below the surface of consciousness and is immediately accessible. It does not mean that a merely theoretical recognition of the fact that it is possible for us to achieve a state of pure awareness and knowledge is sufficient to make us actually 'wake up' to that state. In the parable itself the man's intimate friend tells him that the priceless jewel that he formerly tied within his garment is still present there. The 'ex-changing' of the jewel represents the lengthy process of transforming the truth, or reality, or ideal, as potentially existent within us into that same truth as actually existent in all our thoughts, words, and deeds. It presents the process of following the spiritual path until such time as we succeed in 'waking up' as distinct from merely dreaming about waking up. The exchanging of the priceless jewel thus corresponds to the actual going in quest of the Grail by the knights of the Round Table, to the alchemist's actual production of the Philosopher's Stone, and to the woman's actually lighting the candle and sweeping the house and searching diligently till she finds the lost piece of silver. Without this exchanging, this going in quest, this production, this searching diligently, there can be no '[doing] whatever you will, free from all poverty and shortage,' no achievement of the Grail, no transmutation of everything into gold', no finding of the lost piece of silver. Thus it is not enough for us simply to tell ourselves that we have the priceless jewel within our garment. We also have to exchange the jewel. It is not enough for us simply to believe that we are spiritually enlightened already, as some modern works on Zen Buddhism, with their ringing declarations of 'Look within; thou art Buddha!' would appear to suggest. We also have to follow the spiritual path which, leading from ethics to concentration and meditation and from concentration and meditation to clear vision or wisdom, will enable us eventually to achieve a state of pure awareness or knowledge.

But if we must not allow ourselves to be misled by an over-literal reading of the parable of the priceless jewel, neither must we allow ourselves to be confused by an over-literal understanding of its profound modern analogues. In particular, we must beware of the confusion arising from an over-literal understanding of the highly secularized version of the jewel motif that has appeared among us in recent times (say within the last two hundred years) and which forms the basis of a good deal of modern thought, and it is to one aspect of this confusion that I would like to devote a few words before we conclude. According to this secularized version of the jewel motif man is by nature fundamentally good, in the sense that he has a natural inclination to goodness and health and happiness. Provided we do not understand the terms 'good' and 'good-ness' in too superficial and one-sided a manner (that is, in a manner that takes no account of man's distinctively spiritual possibilities), not much harm is done and our secularized version of the jewel motif will still bear some resemblance to its traditional prototype. Confusion arises when from the fact that man is by nature fundamentally good we conclude that it is only circumstances which prevent him from actually being so, particularly circumstances in the form of the social, economic, and politi-cal conditions under which he lives. This is to suggest, in effect, that just as in the parable the garment is external to the jewel tied within it, so the factors that prevent man from actually being good are external to him. The truth of the matter is that man comprises both jewel and garment, so to speak, and that—though the parable itself fails to mention this detail—the garment must be untied, that is, the jewel must be removed from the garment or the garment from the jewel before it is even possible for the man in the parable to take the jewel and exchange it for what he needs. The garment within which the priceless jewel is tied is, of course, the unawareness and ignorance that must be overcome before we can achieve the state of pure awareness or knowledge which, in a metaphysical rather than a psychological sense, we are or which, less misleadingly, is us, and we untie the jewel from the garment when we engage in the ethical and spiritual practices that will enable us to overcome unawareness and ignorance.

This is not to say that external factors are of no importance. It is not to say that the social, economic, and political conditions under which we live do not affect our mental state or do not have some bearing on the way in which, or even on the extent to which, we are able to follow the spiritual path. For the vast majority of people such is undoubtedly the case, and it is for this reason that Buddhism seeks not only to transform the individual but also seeks, through its ideals of spiritual community, right livelihood, and ethical government, to transform the social, economic, and political conditions under which the individual lives and, in this way, to transform the world. Depending on the kind of person we are, as well as on the kind of situation in which we find ourselves, the external factors which prevent us from being good—from being spiritually enlightened—will appear of greater or less significance both in themselves and in relation to the internal factors. Whatever the position may be, one thing is clear. In order to overcome internal and external factors alike, we shall have to be prepared to encounter a truth, or a reality, that far transcends anything we had previously thought or imagined. We shall have to regain the higher spiritual ideals which we perhaps have, individually and collectively, forgotten. We shall have to recover from the state of drunkenness, wake up from the state of sleep, and, retracing our steps from the other country to our own country, recognize the precious object that will enable us to do whatever we will, free from all poverty and shortage. Sitting here in this ancient and beautiful building, on this peaceful Sunday morning, let us resolve to spare no effort until we actually find the priceless jewel which, even now, is within our garment.

ASPECTS OF BUDDHIST MORALITY

IN 1949, SHORTLY AFTER MY ORDINATION as a *sāmanera* or 'novice monk' at Kuśinagara, the site of the Buddha's 'Great Decease', I fared 'with bowl and robe' from the plains of northern India through the forests of the Terai and so up into the foothills of Nepal. The purpose of the journey was to visit the Newar Buddhists of Butaol and Palpa-Tansen, who were lay disciples of my own preceptor. On the way I not only had to stop and beg my food but also ask for directions. At one village at which I stopped the villagers not only fed me and put me on the right road but, thinking that I was a Hindu like themselves, warned me that the Newar Buddhists were very strange people. 'They don't like to hear about God,' they explained. 'They don't like to hear about the glorious exploits of his *avatāras*, or about *bhakti*. All they want to hear about is dull, dry morality.' It is with this same 'dull, dry morality' that the present article is concerned. I hope to show that, while morality occupies as important a place in Buddhism as my story suggests, for Buddhists at least it is not so dull and dry a topic as my Hindu hosts supposed.

The Indian Buddhist term that is translated, generally, by the Western-Christian 'morality' or 'ethics' is, of course, *śīla* (Sanskrit) or *sīla* (Pāli). The extent to which *sīla* is an integral part—though only a part—of the Buddha's Dharma is sufficiently attested by the fact that it is included in some of the most ancient and important formulations of the Buddhist spiritual path, as well as among some of the most important sets of spiritual practices. Thus *śīla* is the first of the three *śikshās* (Pāli *sikkhās*) or 'trainings' to be undergone by the disciple, the second and third of them being *samādhi* or 'concentration' and *prajñā* (Pāli *paññā*) or 'wisdom'. It is these three 'trainings' which were, according to the *Mahā-parinibbāṇa Sutta*, the substance of the Buddha's farewell address to his disciples—an address which he repeated in eleven out of the fourteen places which he visited on his final tour. 'Such and such is morality (*sīla*),' he is reported as saying, 'such and such is meditation (*samādhi*), such and such is wisdom (*paññā*). Great becomes the fruit, great the advantage of meditation, when it is set round with morality. Great becomes the fruit, great the advantage of wisdom, when it is set round with meditation. The mind set round with wisdom is set quite free from the biases (*āsavas*), that is to say, from the bias towards sensuous experience (*kāma*), towards conditioned existence (*bhava*), towards speculative opinions (*diṭṭhi*), and towards ignorance (*avijjā*).'[1] *Sīla* is also one of the three 'items of meritorious action' (Pāli *puñña-kiriya-vatthuni*, Skt *puṇya-kriyā-vastūni*), coming after *dāna* or generosity and before *bhāvanā* or 'development (of higher states of consciousness)', i.e. 'meditation'. In addition to featuring in these two important triads, *sīla* or morality is reckoned as one of the three, four, five, or seven *ariyadhanas* or 'spiritual treasures' of man. Moreover, 'purification of morality' is the first of the seven successive 'purifications' (*visuddhi*) described in the *Rathavinīta Sutta*[2] and 'recollections of morality' the fourth of the ten 'recollections' (*anussati*) commented on by Bhadantacariya Buddhaghosha in the *Visuddhimagga*.[3] Although *sīla* does not occur as one of the 'members' of the Āryan Eight-membered Way, the fact that the eight members of the Way are traditionally included in the three 'trainings', with right speech, right action, and right livelihood being grouped together under the heading of *sīla*, means that *sīla* is, in fact, part of this well known formulation too.[4] All the formulations of the Path and sets of spiritual practices so far mentioned belong, if not to the earliest, at least to the very early days of Buddhism, and are the common property of Hīnayāna and Mahāyāna alike. The six or ten 'perfections' or 'transcending virtues' (*pāramitās*) are as a group—though only as a group —of somewhat later origin.[5] As the special practices of the Bodhisattva, the spiritual hero of the Mahāyāna, who aims not just at his own liberation from suffering but at Supreme Enlightenment for the benefit of all sentient beings, they constitute the principal formulation of the Path for all the Mahāyāna schools and are, therefore, the common foundation of their entire spiritual life and spiritual practice. *Śīla* or morality is the second of these 'perfections', although strictly speaking it becomes such only when united with 'wisdom' (*prajñā*), which is really the only *pāramitā*. From these examples, which are no more than 'a handful of sinsāpa leaves', it is obvious that *sīla* or morality is, in fact, an integral part of the Buddha's Dharma, and that throughout Buddhist history it has occupied a prominent place in the teaching of all schools. Indeed, illuminated and illustrated as it has been by a glorious succession of sages and saints—as well as upheld by an ocean-wide variety of ordinary folk, living under all kinds of conditions—it is one of the richest, most fruitful, and most fascinating fields of study in the entire range of Buddhism. In a short article like this it is quite impossible to do it anything like justice. I shall therefore confine myself to some of the more prominent aspects of the subject, and offer a few remarks on (1) The Nature of Morality, (2) Morality and the Spiritual Ideal, (3) Morality Mundane and Transcendental, (4) Patterns of Morality, (5) The Fruits of Morality, and (6) Determinants of Morality. While they are not arranged in any logical order, all these aspects are related, and some of them overlap.

1. The Nature of Morality

One way of approaching this aspect of the subject is by looking at the word *sīla*. In its primary sense *sīla* denotes 'nature, character, habit, behaviour' in general, as when a person of stingy or illiberal character is spoken of as *adānasīla*, or when one who is in the habit of speaking is said to be *bhaṇanasīla*. Its secondary sense, which is the one with which we are really concerned here, is 'moral practice, good character, Buddhist ethics, code of morality'. This is the *sīla* of one who is *susīla* or of 'good' nature, character, habit, behaviour, as opposed to *dussīla* or of that which is 'bad'. But what do we mean by 'good'? What do we mean by 'bad'? What is it, the presence or absence of which makes it possible for us to speak of morality or non-morality at all? The short Buddhist answer to these questions is to be found in the term *kusala* (Skt *kuśala*), and in its opposite *akusala* (Skt *akuśala*). When an action is accompanied by volitions and mental factors which are *kusala* it is said to be good and when it is accompanied by volitions and mental factors which are *akusala* it is said to be bad. The literal meaning of *kusala* and *akusala* is 'skilful' and 'unskilful', but as terms in moral discourse and ethics *kusala* signifies associated with disinterestedness (*alobha*), friendliness (*adosa*, Skt *advesha*), and wisdom (*amoha*) and *akusala* signifies associated with greed (*lobha*), hatred (*dosa*, Skt *dvesha*), and delusion (*moha*). What is meant by *sīla* in the sense of good action or good behaviour is now clear. It is that action or behaviour which is accompanied by, or is the expression of, volitions and mental factors which are *kusala*, that is to say, which are characterized by disinterestedness, friendliness, and wisdom. Buddhist morality is thus a morality of intention. This is not to say, of course, that it is a matter simply of 'good intentions', or that it consists in a semi-serious, semi-sentimental *wish* to do what is good or right. On the contrary, *sīla* or Buddhist morality is essentially a matter of volition and action, of action which, since the volition in question is *skilful*, cannot be in any way uncertain or inept. It must also be emphasized that *sīla* is a matter not just of the occasional good deed but of good behaviour: it is *habitual* good action. This habitual good action is not bodily only but, in accordance with the well known Buddhist threefold division of man into body, speech, and mind, also vocal and mental. *Buddhist morality can therefore be said to consist in the habitual performance of bodily, vocal, and mental actions expressive of volitions associated with disinterestedness, friendliness, and wisdom.* More specifically, it consists in the observance of the ten *śīlas*, or of the ten 'ways of skilful action' (*kuśala-karma-pathāḥ*). In respect of bodily action, one abstains from the taking of life, from theft, and from sexual misconduct; in respect of vocal action, one abstains from untruthfulness, from harsh speech, from idle gossip, and from tale-bearing and backbiting; in respect of mental action, one abstains from indulgence in greed, hatred, and wrong views. One also practises the corresponding positive virtues. One cherishes life, is generous, and remains content with one's own married or celibate state; one speaks what is true, speaks with affection, speaks what is useful and timely, and speaks in such a way as to promote harmony and concord; and one cultivates thoughts which are disinterested, friendly, and based on right views.

The nature of morality is also made clear in various 'scholastic' discussions of the subject. According to the *Paṭisambhidāmagga*, 'There is morality (*sīla*) as volition, morality as consciousness-factor, morality as restraint, morality as non-transgression.'[6] As Buddhaghosha explains, morality as volition and morality as consciousness-factor consist in the ten 'ways of skilful action' considered in the one instance as acts of abstention (from unskilful ways) and in the other as states of abstaining. Morality as restraint (*saṁvara-sīla*) should be understood as fivefold: restraint by the 'monastic rules' (*pāṭimokkha*), restraint by mindfulness, restraint by knowledge, restraint by patience, and restraint by energy. Morality as non-transgression is the non-transgression of the precepts of morality that have been undertaken (i.e. by way of 'ordination', whether as a 'lay' disciple or as a 'monk').[7] Of these four kinds of morality—or senses of the term morality—the first and second have been dealt with in the previous paragraph, while the fourth will be touched upon in the section on 'Patterns of Morality'. According to the *Bodhisattvabhūmi*, as quoted (in Tibetan translation) by Gampopa: 'One must know that the essence of ethics and manners [i.e. *śīla*] comprises the following four qualities: (1) to accept properly from others; (2) to be inspired by pure motivation; (3) to mend one's own ways once one has fallen from one's code [of morality]; and (4) to avoid falling by being mindful and devoted.' As Gampopa explains, the first of these qualities consists in acceptance, i.e. the acceptance of the precepts of morality from a teacher in the traditional manner, and the remainder in preservation, i.e. the preservation of what has been thus accepted.[8]

2. MORALITY AND THE SPIRITUAL IDEAL

Morality does not exist in isolation. As the fact of its being included as a separate stage in various formulations of the Buddhist spiritual path—as well as included among different sets of spiritual practices—is sufficient to indicate, it exists as part of a larger and more complex whole. The whole is the Path or Way itself, considered as the sum total of all stages and all practices whatsoever, whether elementary or advanced, mundane or transcendental. From the standpoint of common sense at least, a path is something that proceeds in a certain direction, or towards a certain fixed point: a path that does not lead anywhere is a contradiction in terms. As complement or counterpart of the Path or Way, therefore, there also exists the Goal. The Goal is generally known as nirvāṇa (Pāli *nibbana*), or the complete cessation of thirst or craving (Pāli *taṇhā*, Skt *trishna*) and, therefore, of suffering (Pāli *dukkha*, Skt *duḥkha*)—though as I have pointed out elsewhere, cessation is far from being the last word of Buddhism.[9] As realized by an individual human being, particularly as realized by the historical 'founder' of Buddhism, this Goal is known as Enlightenment (*bodhi*) or as Perfect Enlightenment (*sambodhi*), and the 'founder' himself as the Buddha or the Perfectly Enlightened One. Since for Buddhism it is axiomatic that what one human being has realized can be realized by other human beings too, if they only exert themselves in the right way, the Buddha, by virtue of his Enlightenment, i.e. by virtue of his having realized the Goal, becomes the great exemplar for all those who wish to realize the Goal for themselves as he realized it for himself. In other words, the Buddha becomes the Spiritual Ideal. Because he is the Spiritual Ideal—the supreme object of spiritual endeavour—the Buddha is also the ultimate Refuge, that is to say, he is the supreme object of that Going for Refuge which is the central and definitive act of the Buddhist life. In the words of Gampopa, 'He is the ultimate refuge because He possesses the *dharmakāya* and the devotees of the three paths [i.e. the three *yānas*: *śrāvakayāna, pratyekabuddhayāna,* and *bodhisattvayāna*] also find their fulfilment in Him by obtaining the final pure *dharmakāya.*'[10] Though there are commonly said to be three Refuges, i.e. the Buddha, the Dharma, and the Sangha, inasmuch as the Dharma is revealed by the Buddha, and the Sangha made up of those who have realized the Path by following the Dharma, in the ultimate sense there is only one Refuge, i.e. the Buddha.

The connection between morality and the Spiritual Ideal is now clear. Morality is one of the three great stages of the Path, the others being meditation and wisdom, and consists in the habitual performance of bodily, vocal, and mental actions expressive of skilful volitions. Since the Buddha, by virtue of his having realized the Goal, is the Spiritual Ideal, and therefore the sole Refuge, and since Morality is one of the three great stages of the Path, it follows that, inasmuch as the Path has for its object the Goal, the indirect object of the skilful volitions in the expression of which morality consists is the Buddha. Thus morality does not exist in isolation not only because it is connected, as one of the stages of the Path, with the Goal, but because as skilful volition it is connected with the Spiritual Ideal, with the Buddha, i.e. has the Buddha as its ultimate object. It is, in fact, only those actions of body, speech, and mind which are expressive of skilful volitions that have the Buddha, as Spiritual Ideal, as their object, which can properly be said to constitute Buddhist morality. Actions which have as their ultimate object a good rebirth, whether here on earth or in some higher heavenly world, or which are performed solely for reasons of social propriety or legal obligation, do not constitute Buddhist morality, even though *as actions*, externally considered, they may appear to be no different from the actions which make up Buddhist morality, i.e. which are expressive of skilful volitions having the Buddha as object.

The fact that *sīla* or morality has the Buddha as its ultimate object is illustrated by what takes place at the most important of all Buddhist ceremonies, that of 'Going for Refuge', when the threefold refuge formula is repeated thrice after whoever is presiding on the occasion. Immediately after the 'Going for Refuge' (*śaraṇagamana*) there follows the 'Taking of Moral Precepts' (*śīla-grahaṇa*), five or more in number. In other words, in the act of Going for Refuge one has made the Buddha the object of one's (skilful) volitions, that is to say one has committed oneself to the realization of the Spiritual Ideal. Such a commitment involves the following of the Path, and this consists—broadly speaking—in the practice of the three successive stages of morality, meditation, and wisdom and the perfecting of them one by one in that order. Only a total commitment, faithfully sustained over a period of many years, will enable one to do this. One is, however, expected to do at least something at once: one is expected to practise *sīla* or morality. The positive volitions of which one has made the Buddha the object should be sufficiently powerful to find expression at least in terms of bodily and vocal action, even if not in terms of mental action. If they are not powerful enough to do this then it is doubtful if one has really made the Buddha the object of one's volitions—has really gone for Refuge. The ceremonial Going for Refuge is therefore followed by the Taking of Moral Precepts as an integral part of the proceedings. Morality, far from existing in isolation, is the initial expression of one's commitment to the Spiritual Ideal.

3. Morality Mundane and Transcendental

In the days when it was taken for granted that Buddhism could be described in terms of Western thought, there was a good deal of discussion as to whether it was a monism or a pantheism, a form of absolutism or a form of relativism, and so on. The discussion came to an end—in intellectually responsible circles at least—when it was recognized that Buddhism could not really be described in any such way because, in the well known words of Dr Suzuki, its point of view was one from which terms like monism and the rest had no meaning. Yet although Buddhism cannot be described in terms of Western thought, it would not be wrong to say that for practical purposes at least it is a form of dualism, or at any rate is dualistic in character, that is to say, that it postulates two 'ultimate' principles and sees the spiritual life as consisting in a process of transition from the one to the other. That this is so is evident from what the Buddha says in the *Ariyapariyesana Sutta* about the two quests (*pariyesana*), the noble (*ariya*) and the ignoble (*anariya*). The ignoble quest is when one who is himself subject to birth, ageing, decay, dying, sorrow, and stain, goes in search of what is likewise subject to birth, ageing, decay, dying, sorrow, and stain. The noble quest is the opposite of this, i.e. it is when one who is himself subject to birth, ageing, decay, dying, sorrow, and stain, goes in search of that which is not so subject.[11] Here it is the conditioned (Pāli *saṅkhata*, Skt *saṁskṛita*) and the Unconditioned (Pāli *asaṅkhata*, Skt *asaṁskṛita*) that are the two 'ultimate' principles, and it is they that make possible the two different processes of transition. In the case of the ignoble quest the process of transition is from the conditioned to the conditioned, and in the case of the noble quest it is from the conditioned to the

Unconditioned—saṁsāra to nirvāṇa. The worldly life is based on the first process, the spiritual life on the second.

Although the conditioned and the Unconditioned, saṁsāra and nirvā ṇa, are both absolutes, in the sense that neither can be derived from, or reduced to, the other, they are nevertheless connected. What connects them is the Path. The Path consists of a number of different stages, variously reckoned as three, five, seven, ten, thirteen, or fifty-two in all, and these, whatever the total number happens to be, always fall into two groups, or two sections, respectively known as the mundane path and the transcendental path. These two paths, when placed as it were end to end, make up the Path in its entirety. The mundane path is so called because the skilful volitions and mental factors that make up the various stages of which it consists are still subject to the deeply-rooted—indeed primordial—tendencies known as the *āsavas* (Skt *āsravas*), the 'cankers' or 'biases', i.e. the cankers of, or biases toward, sensuous experience (*kāma*), conditioned existence (*bhava*), speculative opinions (*diṭṭhi*), and ignorance (*avijjā*). Because of the continued presence of the 'biases', regression from the mundane path to the unskilful volitions and mental factors is always possible. For this reason the mundane path is part of saṁsāra. Nevertheless it is only in dependence on the mundane path that the transcendental path—from which no regression is possible—can arise. More specifically, it is only in dependence on 'meditation' that 'wisdom' can arise. The mundane path is, therefore, also part of the Path. The transcendental path is so called because the 'skilful' volitions and mental factors which make up its various stages are either partly or, in the case of the last stage, wholly free from the 'biases'. Just as the mundane path forms part of saṁsāra, therefore, so part of the transcendental path forms nirvāṇa. Thus the Path in its entirety embraces both saṁsāra and nirvāṇa, or, in other words, includes both its own starting point and its own Goal.

The bearing of this on morality is obvious. As we have seen, morality consists in the habitual performance of bodily, vocal, and mental actions expressive of skilful volitions. Since these volitions may belong either to the mundane path or to the transcendental path, i.e. may be either subject or not subject to the 'biases', it follows that there are two kinds of morality, mundane morality and transcendental morality. In the words of Buddhaghosha, 'All morality subject to āsavas is mundane (*lokiya*); that not subject to āsavas is transcendental (*lokuttara*). Herein, the mundane brings about improvement in the future becoming and is a prerequisite for the escape from becoming.... The transcendental brings about escape from becoming and is the plane of "reviewing knowledge" (*pacca-vekkhana-ñāṇa*).'[12] From this it is evident that, much as mundane morality and transcendental morality may resemble each other externally, they are very different in their effects. As we shall see in detail in a later section, mundane morality brings about an improvement in one's future conditioned existence, i.e. one's existence within saṁsāra, besides helping to provide a basis for the development of the successive stages of the transcendental path and, therefore, a means of escape from saṁsāra. Transcendental morality, on the other hand, brings about escape from saṁsāra and is itself an aspect of the Goal. There are other differences. Inasmuch as it is expressive of skilful volitions and mental factors that may, at any moment, be overwhelmed by a sudden upsurge of the *āsavas*, mundane morality requires for its maintenance a constant deliberate effort. Transcendental morality requires for its maintenance no effort at all. As the natural expression of volitions which, in the absence of the *āsavas*, cannot be anything but 'skilful', it maintains itself. Mundane morality is a matter of discipline, of conscious adherence to a prescribed pattern of behaviour, or code of conduct. Transcendental morality is completely spontaneous. Mundane morality is the flawed and imperfect morality of the average man or 'worldling' (Pāli *puthujjana*, Skt *pṛthag-jana*) which, to the extent that it is not a matter of *habitual* good action— and in the case of mundane morality good action requires constant effort—strictly speaking is not morality at all. Transcendental morality is the pure and perfect morality of the 'saint' (Pāli *ariya*, Skt *ārya*), especially that of the Arhat, in whom the *āsavas* have been completely destroyed through wisdom and in whom, therefore, there exists no 'bias' toward any form of unskilful behaviour. On the level of formulations of the Path, mundane morality is the morality that *precedes* meditation and wisdom. Transcendental morality is the morality that *succeeds* them. From this it follows that, since they come immediately after Perfect Vision and Perfect Emotion—the first and second 'members' of the Āryan Eight-membered Way, which are equivalent to wisdom—Perfect Speech, Perfect Action, Perfect Livelihood—the third, fourth, and fifth 'members' of the Way— are equivalent not to mundane morality but to transcendental morality, a point which is often overlooked.

4. PATTERNS OF MORALITY

Morality is a 'many-splendoured thing', as rich and varied in its manifestations as life itself. Yet basically it is a very simple thing. It consists in no more than the habitual performance of bodily, vocal, and mental actions expressive of volitions which, whether subject to the 'biases' or not, are associated with disinterestedness, friendliness, and wisdom. These actions can, however, be performed in many different ways, by many different kinds of people, under all sorts of conditions, and for all sorts of reasons. Seen not in the abstract but concretely, that is to say, seen not in terms of immutable moral principles but in terms of the actual moral behaviour of millions of individual Buddhists through the ages, morality therefore presents itself as an ever-shifting panorama of actual skilful actions of every conceivable variety, from the most ordinary to the most extraordinary—the humblest to the most heroic and exalted. It is, indeed, a sort of living tapestry, a tapestry glowing with colour and made up of innumerable tiny threads, each thread being a particular skilful action. Looking at it in different ways—from different angles—one perceives in this tapestry various configurations of colours and threads—various configurations of skilful actions. These configurations are the different 'patterns of morality'. They are patterns both in the sense of archetypes or exemplars, and in the sense of complex wholes, characterized by a definite arrangement of parts. Although all the patterns are made up of skilful actions of one kind or another, the particular sort of pattern that skilful actions make is determined by various factors. Broadly speaking, the patterns of morality differ according to the degree of spiritual development, and the socio-ecclesiastical status, that they involve, as well as according to the precise nature of the spiritual ideal toward which the volitions of which their constituent 'skilful' actions are the expression are directed. Only a few of the more important and representative patterns need be mentioned here.

One of the best examples of the way in which the pattern of morality differs according to *the degree of spiritual development* is provided by the so-called 'tract on sīla'. This is an ancient document which occurs, in whole or in part, with or without variations, in many places in the Pāli Canon. In it the Buddha describes three grades of morality. The lesser morality (*cūḷa-sīla*) consists in the abstention from the taking of life, from theft, from unchastity, and from false, malicious, disagreeable, and useless speech. In other words, it consists in the observance of the first seven out of the ten 'ways of skilful action', the only difference being that here abstention from sexual misconduct (*kāmesu micchā-cārā*) is replaced by abstention from unchastity (*abrahmacariyā*). This is the pattern of morality of one whose skilful volitions are sufficiently strong to find expression in bodily and vocal action, but not in mental action. The middle morality (*majjhima-sīla*) is more advanced. According to J. Evola's useful summary, its precepts 'deal with a kind of spartanization of life: reduction of needs, cutting away the bond formed by a life of comfort, with particular reference to eating, sleeping, and drowsing. There are also precepts which come under the heading of a "departure", of a physical or literal leaving of the world: for example, avoidance of business or undertakings, non-acceptance of gifts, abandonment of possessions and refusal to assume fresh ones, and so on. Included in this part of "right conduct" is abstention from dialectical discussions and speculation....'[13] This is the pattern of morality of one whose skilful volitions are so powerful that they not only find expression in mental action but bring about a complete transformation in his whole way of life. Most advanced of all is the greater morality (*mahā-sīla*). To quote Evola again, it concerns 'not only abstention from practising divination, astrology or mere magic, but also from abandoning oneself to the cult of some divinity or other. One can therefore speak in some measure of surmounting the bond of religion in the sense of a bond that makes one lead the saintly life [i.e. the spiritual life] with the notion "By means of these rites, vows, mortifications, or renunciations I wish to become a god or a divine being."'[14] This is the pattern of morality of one whose skilful volitions are the most powerful of all. They are sufficiently powerful, indeed, to cut through the whole dense and luxuriant undergrowth of ethnic religious beliefs and practices. Some of these beliefs and practices are as prevalent nowadays as they were in the Buddha's time. As Evola points out, 'The precepts dealing with astrology, divination, and the like, could easily refer to the modern debased practices of like nature in the form of "occultism", spiritualism, and so on. Measured with the ideal of Awakening [i.e. *bodhi*] all this has thus the character of a dangerous straying.'[15]

The pattern of morality also differs according to socio-religious status. By socio-religious status is meant one's technical standing in the Buddhist community as determined by one's sex, whether male or female, and mode of life, whether that of a householder or one who has 'gone forth' from home into the homeless state. One who goes for Refuge, or is 'ordained' (the expressions are synonymous) within the context of a household life is known as a 'lay' disciple or *upāsaka* (fem. *upāsikā*), while one who goes for Refuge, or is 'ordained' within the context of homelessness is known as a 'monk' (Pāli *bhikkhu*, Skt *bhikshu*) or 'nun' (Pāli *bhikkhunī*, Skt *bhikshuṇī*). The pattern of morality of the lay disciple, male or female—the particular configuration of skilful bodily and vocal actions created by the conditions of household life—is represented by the so-called Five Precepts (Pāli *pañca-sīla*, Skt *pañca-śīla*). These are the first four out of the ten 'ways of skilful action', considered as 'factors in (moral) training' (Pāli *sikkhāpada*, Skt *śikshāpada*), plus abstention from intoxicants. On full moon and new moon days a particularly intense moral effort, incompatible with the normal demands of household life, modifies this pattern, and the Five Precepts become the Eight Precepts. The Eight Precepts are the Five Precepts, with abstention from sexual misconduct changing into abstention from unchastity, plus (6) abstention from untimely meals, (7) abstention from dancing, singing, music, and unseemly shows, from the use of garlands, perfumes, and unguents, and from things that tend to beautify and adorn the person, and (8) abstention from using high and luxurious seats and beds. The pattern of morality of the lay disciple is also represented by the provisions of the *Sigālovāda Sutta*, popularly known as 'the householder's code of discipline' (*gihi-vinaya*).[16] Here the whole duty of man, so far as the lay disciple is concerned, is shown to consist in the proper observance of six relationships, i.e. those with parents, teachers, wife and children, friends and companions, servants and work people, and spiritual teachers and brahmins. The pattern of morality of the monk—the particular configuration of skilful actions created by the conditions of monastic life—is represented in its earlier, more eremitical, form, by the *prātimoksha* (Pāli *pātimokkha*) or 150-clause 'Rule', and in its later, more coenobitical form by the *skandhaka* (Pāli *khandhaka*) or 'Chapters', which together constitute the complete Vinaya or Code of (Monastic) Discipline. The pattern of morality of the nun is similar to that of the monk. Besides abstaining from the taking of life, from theft, from unchastity, and from falsely laying claim to higher spiritual attainments, both the monk and the nun live on alms, possess virtually no personal property other than their three robes and their begging-bowl (though they are entitled to share in the corporate property of the monastic community), and devote themselves exclusively to the study, practice, and teaching of the Dharma. In its specifically Ch'an or Zen form, the pattern of morality of one who has 'gone forth' is represented by the 'pure standards' of the great T'ang Dynasty master Pai-Chang, who was the first to make manual work for the benefit of the community an integral part of monastic life, declaring, 'A day of no working is a day of no eating.'

Finally, the pattern of morality differs according to the precise nature of the Spiritual Ideal. This does not mean that there is more than one Spiritual Ideal—there could not be more than one, for there is only one historical Buddha—but only that for practical purposes the Spiritual

Ideal can be thought of in different ways, or in different terms. In particular it can be thought of in terms of supreme wisdom or in terms of infinite compassion, that is to say, in terms of spiritual individualism or in terms of spiritual altruism. When thought of in terms of spiritual individualism it is known as the Arhat Ideal. When thought of in terms of spiritual altruism it is known as the Bodhisattva Ideal. The Arhat Ideal represents the spiritual ideal of the Hīnayāna, according to which one should aim at liberation from all suffering for oneself alone. The Bodhisattva Ideal, on the other hand, represents the spiritual ideal of the Mahāyāna, according to which one should aim at Supreme Enlightenment for the sake of the mundane and spiritual advancement of all living beings. The Mahāyāna attitude finds expression in the Bodhisattva Vow, one of the shortest and best known versions of which is:

However innumerable beings are, I vow to save them;
However inexhaustible the passions are, I vow to extinguish them;
However immeasurable the Dharmas are, I vow to master them;
However incomparable the Buddha-truth is, I vow to attain it.

Yet striking as the contrast between the two ideals undoubtedly is, spiritual individualism and spiritual altruism are by no means mutually exclusive. Liberation from suffering, even for oneself alone, cannot be achieved without the eradication of craving, and craving cannot be eradicated without recourse to generosity—which is a form of altruism. Similarly, it is hardly possible to gain Supreme Enlightenment, even for the sake of others, without paying attention to one's own spiritual development—which is a form of spiritual individualism. In the long run the two ideals coincide: wisdom and compassion are one, or rather, are not two. Even so, in the early stages of the Path the difference between the two spiritual ideals is sufficient to modify the patterns of morality of their respective followers to a considerable degree. The pattern of morality of those who make the Arhat Ideal the supreme object of their spiritual endeavour—the special configuration of skilful actions created by the following of the Hīnayāna—is represented by the literalistic, not to say legalistic, observance of the Code of (Monastic) Discipline, as when a monk refused to pull his own mother up out of a pit into which she had fallen, because this would have involved coming into physical contact with a woman. The pattern of morality of those who make the Bodhisattva Ideal the supreme object of spiritual endeavour—the special configuration of skilful actions created by the following of the Mahāyāna—is represented by the observance of the Five or the Eight Precepts, or the ten 'ways of skilful action', or the Code of (Monastic) Discipline, and so on, of the Hīnayāna, not just in a 'liberal' manner, but *in the spirit of the Mahāyāna*. In practice this eventually meant the virtual rewriting of the Monastic Code. This resulted in the emergence of a special Mahāyāna code of discipline, a code which represented a pattern of morality in which the nature of the Bodhisattva Ideal found direct expression, in its own terms, rather than indirect expression, in terms of the Hīnayāna, i.e. in terms of a pattern already created by a particular socio-ecclesiastical status. There are several versions of this code. According to one version, it consists in abstaining from eighteen major and forty-six minor offences. The first two major offences are: (1) To glorify oneself and disparage others for the sake of gains and honours, and (2) To withhold the wealth of the Dharma from others. The first two minor offences are: (1) Not to worship the Three Jewels three times a day, and (2) To follow after desires.[17] Besides being thought of in terms of wisdom and compassion, the one Spiritual Ideal can also be thought of in terms of silence, magical potency, and so on. In addition to the Arhat Ideal and the Bodhisattva Ideal, therefore, there are various other spiritual ideals. Among these are the archaic Muni Ideal, the later Siddha or Vidyādhara Ideal of the Vajrayāna, and the Zen Rōshi Ideal, each of which modifies the pattern of morality of its followers in its own way.

5. THE BENEFITS OF MORALITY

The benefits accruing from the practice of morality are both worldly and spiritual, mundane and transcendental. Moreover, they can be experienced both in the present life and in some other state of existence after death. The most immediate of these benefits in non-remorse (Pāli *avippaṭisāra*), which consists in the consciousness that one's bodily, vocal, and mental actions are all skilful and that one has nothing with which to reproach oneself regarding morals. Buddhism attaches great importance to this state. Not only does non-remorse lead to a higher degree of integration and, therefore, to greater harmony and balance of character, but also, properly reflected upon, it leads to the experience of delight and rapture which, in turn, leads to concentration (*samādhi*)—to insight—to wisdom—to freedom—to nirvāṇa. For the moral householder there are five benefits in the perfecting of morality: (1) increase of wealth due to non-heedlessness, (2) a good reputation, (3) social confidence, (4) a peaceful death, and (5) rebirth in a happy, heavenly world.[18] So great and

glorious are the benefits of morality that Buddhaghosha, having dealt
with them in scholastic fashion, and feeling no doubt that something
more was needed, bursts into song as it were and eulogizes them in some
enthusiastic verses of his own devising:

> *The true religion gives to noble sons*
> *No other stay than virtue* [sīla]. *Who can tell*
> *The limit of her power? Not Gangā stream*
> *Nor Yamunā nor babbling Sarabhū,*
> *Nor Aciravatī nor Mahī's flood,*
> *Can purify on earth the taints of men.*
> *But virtue's water can remove the stain*
> *Of all things living. Necklaces of pearl,*
> *Rain-bearing breezes, yellow sandalwood,*
> *Gems, nor soft rays of moonlight can destroy*
> *Heart-burnings of a creature. She alone—*
> *Virtue—well-guarded, noble, cool, avails.*
> *What scent else blows with and against the wind?*
> *What stairway leads like her to heaven's gate?*
> *What door into Nibbāna's city opens?*
> *The sage whose virtue is his ornament*
> *Outshines the pomp and pearls of jewelled kings.*
> *In virtuous men virtue destroys self-blame,*
> *Begetting joy and praise. Thus should be known*
> *The sum of all the discourse on the power*
> *Of virtue, root of merit, slayer of faults.*[19]

Gampopa, more soberly, says that the results of (the perfection of)
morality are: '(i) fulfilment and (ii) effectiveness in our situation in life.
The first is unsurpassable Enlightenment.... Effectiveness in our temporal life means that we experience the most perfect happiness of
Saṃsāra, even if we do not want it.'[20]

Besides conferring benefits within the human or the divine order, or
both, mundane morality—the habitual performance of skilful actions
subject to the 'biases'—also contributes to the actual maintenance of those
orders in existence. This is made clear by the classification of the ten 'ways
of skilful action' and the ten 'ways of unskilful action' according to
whether they are performed to a great, to a moderate, or to a slight extent.
Performed to a great extent, the ten 'ways of unskilful action' lead to
rebirth as a tormented being, i.e. to rebirth in hell, performed to a

moderate extent to rebirth as a hungry ghost, and performed to a slight extent to rebirth as an animal. Similarly, performed to a slight extent the ten 'ways of skilful action' lead to rebirth as a human being, performed to a moderate extent to rebirth as a desire-world god, and performed to a great extent to rebirth as a form- or formless-world god. If the ten 'ways of skilful action'—if mundane morality—is not practised even to a slight extent, men will not be reborn again as human beings and the human order of conditioned existence will come to an end. Morality is therefore necessary to the maintenance of the human state. It is necessary to the maintenance of a human society, i.e. a society with human values. Describing the terrible state of affairs that prevails when the moral basis of society has disintegrated, and predicting to the monks that a time will come when human beings will be short-lived and when only an inferior kind of food will be available, the Buddha says:

> *Among such humans the ten moral courses of conduct [i.e. the ten 'ways of skilful action'] will altogether disappear, the ten immoral courses of action will flourish excessively; there will be no word for moral among such humans—far less any moral agent. Among such humans, brethren, they who lack filial and religious piety, and show no respect for the head of the clan—'tis they to whom homage and praise will be given, just as today homage and praise are given to the filial-minded, to the pious, and to they who respect the heads of their clans.*
>
> *Among such humans, brethren, there will be no [such thoughts of reverence as are a bar to intermarriage with] mother, or mother's sister, or mother's sister-in-law, or teacher's wife, or father's sister-in-law. The world will fall into promiscuity, like goats and sheep, fowls and swine, dogs and jackals.*
>
> *Among such humans, brethren, keen mutual enmity will become the rule, keen ill-will, keen animosity, passionate thoughts, even of killing, in a mother towards her child, in a child towards its mother, in a father towards his child, and a child towards its father, in brother to brother, in brother to sister, in sister to brother. Just as a sportsman feels towards the game that he sees, so will they feel.*
>
> *Among such humans, brethren, there will arise a sword-period of seven days, during which they will look on each other as wild beasts; sharp swords will appear ready to their hands, and they, thinking 'this is a wild beast, this is a wild beast,' will with their swords deprive each other of life.*[21]

Here it is interesting to see that one of the things that accompanies the disintegration of the moral basis of society and, therefore, the collapse of society itself in the truly human sense, is sexual promiscuity including incest. If such indeed is the case, we could expect to find that the reverse process, the creation by man of a truly human—a morally based—society, would be accompanied by the institution of the incest taboo. According to Darlington, this is exactly what we find. 'Some races of animals prefer to mate with their likes; others with unlikes. In these circumstances, human stocks which varied towards the rejection of incest would have, not at once but after a few hundred generations, an advantage over those who favoured or allowed incest. For they alone would be variable and adaptable [i.e. because they practised out-breeding and not in-breeding]. They alone would do new things and think in new ways. The future would be with them.'[22] In other words, human society cannot develop unless man is variable and adaptable, and he cannot be variable and adaptable without the incest taboo. Morality, at least to the extent of the incest taboo, is necessary to the very existence of human society. Even genetically speaking, morality is part of the very definition of humanity.

Morality is even more necessary to the existence of divine society, that is to say, to the existence of the world or worlds of the gods, and even more part of the definition of divinity. If a slight practice of the ten 'ways of skilful action' is necessary for rebirth as a human being, and thus for the maintenance of the human order of existence, for rebirth as a god and the replenishment of the divine order of existence—from which beings decease as soon as the stock of merit that caused them to be reborn there is exhausted—the practice of the ten 'ways of skilful action' at least to a moderate extent is required. The gods, we are told, rejoice when a Buddha appears in the (human) world. They rejoice because, as a result of his teaching, there will be a more intensive practice of morality on earth and, therefore, a greater number of men being reborn after death as gods. As a result of this increase in their numbers, the gods will become more powerful. Being more powerful they will be able to overcome the āsuras or 'titans' in battle. Morality is therefore not just necessary to the maintenance of human society. It is necessary to ensure the preponderance of the forces of good over the forces of evil throughout the universe. Morality is of cosmic significance.

6. DETERMINANTS OF MORALITY

Morality is an integral part of Buddhism. It consists in the habitual performance of skilful actions expressive of skilful volitions, i.e. disinterestedness, friendliness, and wisdom. It is the initial expression of one's commitment to the Spiritual Ideal, may be subject or not subject to the 'biases', i.e. may be mundane or transcendental, and contains a number of different patterns of observance. Moreover, morality confers benefits both mundane and spiritual, and besides being essential to the maintenance of the human order contributes to the triumph of the forces of good in the universe.—So much we have learned. So much may anyone learn who studies Buddhism. But a theoretical knowledge of morality, even if it covers all aspects of the subject instead of only a few, is a very different thing from the actual habitual performance of skilful actions. How, then, do we make the transition? What is it that induces us to start cultivating skilful rather than unskilful volitions and to lead a moral rather than a non-moral life? In a word, what are the determinants of morality? According to Buddhaghosha, morality is of three kinds, according to whether it arises out of, or gives precedence to, one or another of three factors. '...That practised out of self-regard by one who regards self and desires to abandon what is unbecoming to self is virtue [*sīla*] *giving precedence to self*. That practised out of regard for the world and out of desire to ward off the censure of the world is virtue *giving precedence to the world*. That practised out of regard for the Dhamma (Law) and out of desire to honour the majesty of the Dhamma is virtue *giving precedence to the Dhamma*.'[23] I shall conclude these remarks on Buddhist morality with a few words of explanation on each of these.

The fact that the Buddha reached the Goal and gained Enlightenment shows that Enlightenment can be gained by all men, if only they make the effort. The Buddha is therefore the Spiritual Ideal. All men are potentially Enlightened—because they are men. This potentiality is not a mere abstract possibility but the living seed of Enlightenment actually present in the depths of the human heart, not as a sort of foreign body but as the essenceless essence of human nature itself. It is the presence of this seed that enables the individual human being to develop, i.e. to progress from stage to stage of being and consciousness. Indeed, it is in the unfolding of the seed into shoot, bud, and finally perfect flower, that such progress consists. What is termed morality *giving precedence to self* is thus morality practised out of consciousness of oneself as an evolving being for whom, as an evolving being, some things are appropriate and others not. Here it is the individual's own potentiality for Enlightenment that is the determinant of morality. In addition to being practised out of self-regard, however, morality can be practised out of other-regard. The seed of Enlightenment is present in all men. This means that others are evolving beings as well as oneself. What is termed morality *giving precedence to the world* is thus morality practised out of other-regard or out of consciousness of others as evolving beings. Here it is others' potential for Enlightenment—or even their actual Enlightenment—that is the determinant of morality. In this context 'world' (*loka*) means not the ordinary human world but the moral and spiritual community, the members of which are not only one's moral exemplars but also sources of inspiration and spiritual guidance. Above the self-regarding and the other-regarding practice of morality there is the Dharma-regarding. Enlightenment is not only immanent in self and world but transcends them. Outside time, and beyond the duality of subject and object, there is the Dharma in the sense of the Goal and the stages of the transcendental path. The Dharma is of such overwhelming greatness that, when one encounters it, one's sole desire is that it should be honoured in a fitting manner. What is termed morality *giving precedence to the Dhamma* is thus morality practised out of the fullness of this desire. Here it is Enlightenment itself—the Unconditioned itself—that is the determinant of morality.

Buddhaghosha's morality *giving precedence to self, to the world*, and *to the Dhamma*, could perhaps be correlated with the pseudo-Aśvaghosha's conception of the spiritual life as due to 'Permeation through Manifestation of the Essence of Suchness', to 'Permeation through Influences', and to 'The Influences of Suchness'.[24] But consideration of this topic, interesting as it is, will have to be deferred. If we were to go into it now it would make this article far too long. Even without going into it, however, it should by this time be apparent that Buddhist morality is not so dull or so dry a subject as people sometimes think.

Dialogue Between Buddhism and Christianity

Buddhism and Christianity are both universal religions. They are not, like the old ethnic religions, limited to a particular part of the earth's surface or to a particular breeding group within the human population, nor, strictly speaking, is it possible to be born into them. Although for purposes of communication they adopted—in fact had to adopt—the outward forms of the culture (Vedic-Sramanic and Judaeo-Hellenic respectively) in the midst of which they originally appeared, and although they subsequently gave birth to distinctive cultures of their own, neither of them can be identified with even the most highly developed culture; nor can they, with justice, be discussed in exclusively 'cultural' terms. In principle, the message of both Buddhism and Christianity is addressed not to man as a member of a group (family, tribe, etc.) but to man as an individual who is capable of responding as an individual and either attaining nirvāṇa, realizing Buddhahood, etc., or saving his own soul, winning the Kingdom of Heaven, etc. An individual becomes a Buddhist, or becomes a Christian, in the one case through the act of Going for Refuge to the Three Jewels (Buddha, Dharma, and Sangha), in the other by undergoing the rite of Baptism. Those who have gone for Refuge, or who have been baptized, form a spiritual community (sangha, church) that is in reality quite distinct from any mundane group to which the Buddhist or the Christian may also belong even when all the other members of that group happen to be Buddhists or Christians.

Although Buddhism and Christianity are both universal religions, and although as universal religions they resemble each other more closely than they resemble any of the ethnic religions, they are, at the same time, about as different from each other as it is possible for them to be. One might in fact say, paradoxically, that it is possible for them to be so different just because they are both universal religions. The differences between them are both intrinsic and extrinsic. Buddhism is not only non-theistic, but the most important representative of the non-theistic group of religions, to which also belong ethnic religions like Taoism and Confucianism, as well as Jainism, which even though it has remained confined to the Indian subcontinent is in principle a universal religion. Christianity is of course theistic, and the principal representative of the theistic group of religions, in which are included Judaism, which is an ethnic religion, and Islam, which is a universal religion with strong ethnic features. In fact, on account of its subtle and complex Trinitarian doctrine Christianity may be considered the theistic religion *par excellence*. On the practical side, Buddhism emphasizes the importance of the part played by meditation and contemplation (*śamathā* and *vipaśyanā*) in spiritual development, whereas Christianity insists on the indispensability of the sacraments for the living of the Christian life. In profane historical-phenomenological terms, Christianity is the principal Semitic faith, Buddhism the leading Indo-Aryan teaching. Christianity has dominated the history of Europe, while Buddhism has profoundly influenced the history of Asia. Christianity is the religion of the West. Buddhism is the religion of the East.

Despite the fact that these two great spiritual phenomena grew up in the same world—indeed occupied opposite ends of the same great Eurasian land mass, until very recent times there was no real contact between them. Nestorian Christians and Mahāyāna Buddhists did, of course, have a certain amount of contact in Central Asia, perhaps in China too; a life of the Buddha found its way into medieval Europe as the biography of a Christian saint; Desidiri made his way to Lhasa, and wrote a book in Tibetan in which he refuted Buddhism, and St Francis Xavier argued with a Zen monk—and that was about all. Only in very recent times has there been anything like sustained or significant contact be-tween the two religions, and as time goes on such contact is likely to increase rather than diminish. Indeed, it can be expected to play an ever more important part in the spiritual life of mankind.

THE NATURE OF DIALOGUE

According to the dictionary, a dialogue is a conversation between two people. It might therefore be expected that a dialogue between Buddhism and Christianity would be simply a conversation, in the sense of an exchange of views, between the two religions. But in fact this is not so. In the modern ecumenical context—whether as between sects within one and the same religion or as between different religions—the term dialogue has come to possess not only a more specialized but also a richer meaning. This meaning is not unconnected with the fact that many of the sects and religions that nowadays are parties to dialogue, but especially the religions, have hitherto developed in complete isolation. This is particularly so, as we have seen, in the case of Buddhism and Christianity, which for by far the greater part of their careers have remained in almost total ignorance of each other's existence. Because they developed in mutual isolation, and because they moreover met with no decisive spiritual challenge from any other universal religion, both Buddhism and Christianity tended to see themselves as religious absolutes, within whose all-embracing synthesis a place, and an explanation, could be found for all the spiritual facts of existence—including, in theory at least—the teachings of all other religions.

In this respect the position which the two religions adopted on the spiritual plane (and on the earthly plane too, in the case of the medieval papacy) was analogous to the position adopted on the sociological plane by the civilizations of Ancient India and Ancient China. Jambudvīpa was synonymous with the inhabited earth, the Middle Kingdom equivalent to the whole civilized world. When China, in the middle of the nineteenth century, first came in contact with the Western powers, it was forced to recognize that these were not, in fact, outlying dependencies of the Celestial Empire that could be overawed by a few well chosen words from the Dragon Throne, but independent sovereign states with whom she was obliged to treat on equal terms. In much the same way, Buddhism and Christianity have been brought face to face, and forced to recognize each other's existence as separate spiritual universes. Christianity can no longer put Buddhism in its place, as it were, by speaking of it as a mere ethical system, or as a form of natural mysticism. Buddhism can no longer relegate Christianity to the *devayāna* with a good-natured comment on the spiritual inadequacies of theism. From now onwards Buddhism and Christianity must take each other more seriously than that. From now onwards they must try to communicate.

But for communication to be possible there must be a medium of communication: there must be a common language. Since the two religions developed in complete independence of each other, however, no such common language exists. Both of them developed, of course, a powerful and flexible 'theological' or 'Buddhological' language which is as adequate to the expression of their own ultimate content (Divine Revelation, Enlightenment) as a language of this sort can by its very nature be, but in each case the language is completely understandable—or fully 'transparent'—only to the members of the spiritual community within which it arose and who habitually use it as their means of communication with one another. What is said in one 'language' cannot be translated into the other without very serious distortion. Even to speak in terms of 'Buddhology', as though there was something in Buddhism corresponding to the Christian notion of theology—even, in fact, to speak of Buddhism as a religion—is already to introduce an element of distortion into the discussion. There is also no question of Buddhism and Christianity alike being translated into some neutral(?) 'universalist' Esperanto and left to communicate with each other through this medium. Were this to be done, the possibility of distortion, and therefore of mutual incomprehension, would be increased to such an extent that even if communication were achieved it could hardly be regarded as a communication between Buddhism and Christianity. Having been brought face to face, and forced to recognize each other's existence, Buddhism and Christianity are in the position of having to communicate without a medium of communication, without a common language. In the ecumenical context, it is in this communication without a medium of communication that the essence of dialogue consists. Less paradoxically, dialogue is that form of communication in which the means of communication has to be created in the course of the process of communication itself.

The Principal Obstacle to Dialogue

Obstacles to a fruitful dialogue between Buddhism and Christianity are of many kinds. Even in these days of improved communications, Buddhists and Christians may not always find it easy to meet. There may be difficulties arising out of the special nature of one's vocation, whether as parish priest, meditation master, or social worker. Moreover, the members of one's flock, or one's religious superiors, may not approve of contact between the followers of the two religions. Even when one is face to face with one's partner in dialogue there are still psychological obstacles to be surmounted. Suspicion and prejudice enter only too easily into any human heart, and one may at times be deficient in honesty, in patience, in charity (*maitrī*), in even in common courtesy. More formidable still, there is the inherent difficulty of grasping the real meaning of concepts with which one is totally unfamiliar, as well as of appreciating the significance of symbols that one finds strange and even bizarre. But the principal obstacle to fruitful dialogue consists in confusing dialogue with certain other activities which, though they superficially resemble it, are really quite different. Dialogue can be confused with discussion, with debate, and with diplomacy. Above all, it can be confused with monologue. As long as this confusion persists, no dialogue is possible. Indeed, by creating the illusion of dialogue when, in fact, no dialogue is taking place, it actually postpones the achievement of dialogue indefinitely.

The nature of discussion, debate, and diplomacy, is not difficult to understand. For our present purpose, discussion may be defined as the exchanging of ideas, debate as arguing for victory, and diplomacy as the strategy by which a pseudo-religious power structure seeks to ensure its own survival and aggrandizement, and the destruction of its competitors, by secular means other than that of open violence. A discussion between Buddhism and Christianity, or between Buddhists and Christians, differs from a dialogue in its being conducted, more often than not, on an abstract, not to say an academic, basis, and in its not going deep enough to come up against the fact that they are speaking two different languages and are not, in fact, really intelligible to each other. Similarly, a debate differs from a dialogue inasmuch as because both religions see themselves as absolutes neither victory nor defeat is possible for either. Debate is thus based on a false assumption. As for diplomacy, this is, in reality, not a form of religion sunk from being a spiritual community (sangha, church) to being a secular group among secular groups, that is to say a political and/or socio-economic power structure among power structures.

Since the broad sense in which discussion, debate, and diplomacy are not dialogue is obvious enough, nothing more need be said about them. But in what sense of the term, exactly, is monologue not dialogue? Apart from the purely formal opposition between the two terms, this is not so obvious, and because it is the confusion of dialogue with monologue, in particular, that is the principal obstacle to dialogue, in this case a few words of explanation are required. As we have already seen, both Buddhism and Christianity tend to see themselves as religious absolutes. Each is a universe in itself. Each speaks its own theological or 'Buddhological' language, as it were, and what is said in one language cannot really be translated into the other. In communicating with each other, therefore, both religions are likely to misunderstand and both are likely to be misunderstood. This may not always be realized. In fact, both parties may be under the impression that they are communicating, and that dialogue is taking place, when this is not so at all. What has happened is that A has taken a word, or a concept, used by B, has attached to it the meaning that it bears for A, and then replied to B as though B had used it in the sense which it would have had for A had A used it. A is therefore not replying to something that B has said but to something that A has said. A is therefore not communicating with B at all. A is communicating with A. What is taking place is not a dialogue but a monologue. Buddhism, for example, may attach to the word God, as used by Christianity, the same meaning that it is accustomed to associate with its own Mahābrahma, and may try to continue the communication on those terms. Similarly, Christianity may attach to such words as voidness (*śūnyatā*), trance (*dhyāna*), and wisdom (*prajñā*), meanings quite different from those which they traditionally hold for Buddhism. Misunderstandings of this sort are much less likely to arise—or if they do arise are much more likely to be corrected—when the two religions meet in the persons of an individual Buddhist and an individual Christian, communicating in the flesh. When they meet only on paper, with the Buddhist or the Christian author trying to communicate with a Christianity or a Buddhism that exists nowhere but in his own brain, the result will be not dialogue but monologue.

THE PROBABLE BEST METHOD OF STARTING DIALOGUE

If dialogue is not to be confused with discussion, debate, or diplomacy, and if Buddhism and Christianity meet in the persons of an individual Buddhist and an individual Christian, the question of the best method of starting dialogue can probably be left to look after itself. Provided that the two parties to the dialogue are open to each other, and provided each really listens to what the other has to say, there is no reason why dialogue should not take place—no reason why they should not be able to communicate even without a medium of communication, that is to say, without a common language, without a mutually acceptable system of concepts, symbols, and values. When dialogue takes place, however, both parties should realize that it is bound to be of a very piecemeal nature, and that they should not expect too much from it. Indeed, they should not expect anything at all from it except the possibility of continued dialogue. If they expect an accession of interesting new ideas, it will become discussion. If they expect victory, or even just the enrichment of, or a positive contribution to, their own (Buddhist or Christian) religious experience, it will become debate. If they expect an accommodation with regard to the practical interests of the secular power structure with which, on their 'institutional' side, they may happen to be identified, it becomes diplomacy.

More important than the question of the best method of starting dialogue is that of the best person to start it. The 'what?' is at bottom a 'who?'. In deciding who is the best person, however, we must be careful not to overlook the obvious fact that a dialogue between Buddhism and Christianity is a dialogue between Buddhism and Christianity. It is dialogue, that is to say, between these two religions in their central, 'classical' forms—not a dialogue between them in any diluted, de-mythologized, rationalized, and secularized, modern version. Buddhism and Christianity can, in fact, engage in dialogue only in the persons of the fully committed Buddhist and the firmly believing Christian, and it is these, therefore, who are the best persons to start—and carry on—dialogue between the two religions. On no account can Buddhist–Christian dialogue be regarded as a fashionable exercise for the uncommitted academic, or for those Buddhists or Christians who, uncertain of their own faith, are looking for an intellectually stimulating and professionally rewarding career in the field of 'comparative' religious studies. This does not mean that those who engage in dialogue may not be equipped with a scientific knowledge of Buddhism or of Christianity as, for example, a sociological phenomenon. It means that a scientific knowledge of a religion is not, in itself, a qualification for engaging in dialogue on its behalf.

Religious Experience as Characteristic of Buddhism as a Starting Point in Dialogue with Buddhism?

It would seem that, from the Christian point of view, religious experience as characteristic of Buddhism is quite acceptable as a starting point in dialogue with Buddhism. But even if not taken as an actual starting point, once dialogue had really begun the subject of religious experience could hardly fail to be brought up sooner or later. Presumably it would also be possible to take 'religious experience as characteristic of Christianity' as a starting point in dialogue with Buddhism. From a Buddhist point of view, however, the expression 'religious experience' is ambiguous and, therefore, misleading. It could, for instance, be taken to refer either to the experience of concentration and meditation (*śamathā*), or to the experience of insight (*vipaśyanā*); to the act of Going for Refuge to the Three Jewels, to the arising of the bodhicitta, or to the 'turning about' (*parāvṛitti*) in the deepest seat (*āśraya*) of consciousness (*vijñāna*). Even if it is taken in the restricted sense of the experience of suffering, and we focus attention on that, serious objections can still be raised against the taking of religious experience as characteristic of Buddhism as a starting point in dialogue at all. Indeed, the identification of 'religious experience' with the experience of suffering and liberation from suffering may serve to reinforce these objections.

Whatever form of communication we engage in, progress is from the simple to the complex, from the shallow to the profound, the peripheral to the central. This is all the more so in the case of the form of communication we call dialogue, wherein religious absolutes confront each other without the benefit of a common language. It would therefore seem that for Christianity to take religious experience as characteristic of Buddhism, especially the experience of liberation from suffering, as a starting point in dialogue with Buddhism, is not really feasible. Indeed, by coming to premature conclusions about the nature of this experience it might even make dialogue between the two religions impossible. Religious experience is an extremely difficult thing to communicate, even when a medium of communication exists, and the experience of liberation from suffering is not an 'experience' in the ordinary sense, not even a 'religious experience'. For Buddhism it is not just liberation from ordinary human wretchedness, but from everything conditioned (*saṁskṛita*) and mundane (*laukika*). As such, it is identical with the attainment of nirvāṇa or Enlightenment (*bodhi*) or, in other words, with the ultimate goal of Buddhism—a goal that must be realized by one's personal spiritual exertions and which is, we are expressly told, beyond the sphere of reasoning (*attakkavacara*).

This brings us to a second ambiguity, not one of language but identity. When religious experience as characteristic of Buddhism is put forward as a possible starting point in dialogue with Buddhism, it is not clear whose religious experience is meant. Is it the experience of the Buddhist who is party to the dialogue? (I assume, perhaps wrongly, that his Christian counterpart will have no Buddhist religious experience.) Or is it the experience of some other Buddhist, living or dead, who does not himself actually participate in dialogue? Is it, even, not any particular person's experience at all that is meant, but some general concept of religious experience—a concept which, so far as any actual parties to the Buddhist–Christian dialogue are concerned, may be no more than a matter of words? These questions are raised, not in any hair-splitting spirit of pedantry, much less still in order to make dialogue more difficult, but simply as a means of emphasizing the fact that the starting point of dialogue with Buddhism should be something about which at least one of the two parties can speak from personal knowledge. There is a world of difference between taking religious experience as characteristic of Buddhism as a starting point in dialogue and taking as starting point the words and concepts which traditionally reflect that experience.

In view of these facts it would therefore appear that some more peripheral topic than 'religious experience', or the experience of liberation from suffering, is needed as a starting point for dialogue with Buddhism, i.e. some point of doctrine, or religious practice, or liturgical observance, that is intelligible to, and within the imaginative grasp of, both parties. Religion need not be identified exclusively with 'religious experience'. Indeed, the exaggerated value which is sometimes attached to 'religious experience' in the narrower, more subjective, sense, is not a feature of Buddhism. Even if, for some reason, religious experience as characteristic of Buddhism has to be taken as a starting point in dialogue with Buddhism, there can be no question of anyone embarking on a confident exposition of that about which even the Enlightened hesitate to speak. Rather should some more modest, everyday type of religious experience be taken as a starting point. If this is done, and if on both sides there is sufficient openness and sufficient awareness of their own limitations, then there may be some hope that there will begin between Buddhism and Christianity a truly fruitful dialogue, that is to say, a dialogue that will not degenerate into monologue but which will continue.

The Journey to Il Convento

WE HAVE ALL MADE THE JOURNEY to Il Convento. Most of you made it for the first time, a few for the third or even the fourth time. Of those who have made the journey for the first time most have made it in the hope of being ordained during the three months we shall be together here, and it is to them in particular that these remarks are addressed, even though what I have to say will also be applicable to those who have made the journey to Il Convento not in the hope of being ordained, for they are already ordained, but in order to help others to prepare themselves for ordination.

Addressing myself, then, to those of you who have made the journey to Il Convento for the first time, and have made it in the hope of being ordained, I wonder to what extent you realize the significance of this journey, and the real nature of its connection with your being ordained here. Initially, when you received your invitation to this pre-ordination course, it might have seemed to you that the journey to Il Convento was no more than a means to an end, the end being, of course, to participate in 'Tuscany 84', and, hopefully, to be ordained. The actual process of getting here, it might have seemed, had no special significance. It was, perhaps, something to be got through as quickly and cheaply as possible, the main idea being that one should transport oneself from London or Glasgow or wherever to Il Convento with the minimum of fuss and bother. On the other hand, when you received your invitation it might have occurred to you that the journey to Il Convento presented an opportunity of enjoying something you had not, perhaps, been able to enjoy for a long time, especially if you had been working in an FWBO co-op, i.e. a holiday, either with one of your spiritual friends or, less mindfully, in company of a rather different type. But even if you were concerned simply to get here, or simply to enjoy a little holiday *en route*, it will almost certainly have dawned on you, sooner or later, that the journey to Il Convento was more than just a means to an end, more than just an agreeable interlude, and that it had a significance of its own that it was not easy to formulate in conceptual terms. Indeed, for some of you it might have seemed that the more familiar you became with those magic words Il Convento, Batignano, Grosseto, and the more mantra-like the way in which they rolled off your tongue, the more the phrase 'the journey to Il Convento' came for you to assume overtones of a mysterious and even archetypal nature.

That this should be so is not surprising. On more than one occasion I have spoken in terms of our acting out, in the course of our lives, what I have called our personal myth, and the various journeys we make are often an important part of that myth. The journey is, in fact, a myth in its own right, so to speak, or rather it is an archetype which finds expression in many myths and symbols, many legends and stories, though without being exhausted by them and without being identical with any or all of them. Thus we have the voyage of the Argo, or Jason's journey in quest of the Golden Fleece; Odysseus's ten-year journey from 'the ringing plains of windy Troy' back to his home in rocky Ithaca; the Chosen People's still more protracted journey up from Egypt into the Promised Land; Monkey's journey to the West, i.e. from India, from which he and his companions returned to China with the *false* scriptures, the ones that had writing on them; the prophet Mohammed's Night Journey from Mecca to Jerusalem up through the heavens; Dante's journey through the Inferno, Purgatorio, and Paradiso; Christian's journey from the City of Destruction to the Heavenly Jerusalem; Basho's journey from the Far North, and many other journeys by land and sea, through the air and through worlds and even universes. All these journeys possess, some of them more obviously than others, a significance that is not exhausted by their literal, surface meaning. This being the case it is only to be expected that a journey as crucial as the journey to Il Convento, that is to say, the journey to the venue of ordination, with all that ordination implies, should be imbued with a very special significance, even though that significance might not be immediately apparent.

To begin with, the journey to Il Convento is a journey from West to East. Most of you started your journey in England, and even those of you who did not actually start it there spent some time in England before setting out on the journey to Il Convento. The East is, of course, the source of light, for that is where the sun rises, and from time immemorial a journey towards the East has been a journey towards the light, or a spiritual journey. In medieval Iran there was even a school of mystic philosophers known as the Orientals (*ishrāqīya*), in the sense of those who were 'oriented' or who turned themselves in the direction of, and travelled towards, the 'Orient' or world of supersensitive realities, and who spoke of entry into that world in terms of arriving at an 'oriental' knowledge (*'ilm ishrāqī*). In more recent times a distinguished German author has spoken of a mysterious 'Journey to the East' undertaken not by one person only but by a number of people, and has even written a book with that title. Thus the journey to Il Convento is significant in that inasmuch as it is a journey to the East, it is, at the same time, a spiritual journey, or a pilgrimage. One might, of course, object that Il Convento is not very far east of England and that a real journey to the East would take one not to Italy but to India, not to Batignano but to Bhaja. That would be quite true, in a sense, and perhaps there is something to be said for our holding these pre-ordination courses further afield than we do, so that it would be a question not of a journey to Il Convento, or even a journey to Bhaja, but of a journey to Sārnāth or Buddha Gayā. Nevertheless it must not be forgotten that the journey to the East does not really terminate at any particular point, either in the literal or the metaphysical sense. All that is really necessary is that our journey, whether long or short, should be a journey to the East, i.e. in the direction of the East, and that it should be a journey to the East in the *real* sense of the term. Whether it is a journey to Il Convento, or to Buddha Gayā, or even to Padmaloka, is of quite secondary importance.

Though the journey to Il Convento is a journey from west to east, it is also, at the same time, a journey from north to south. It is a journey from the Protestant north to the Catholic south, or even, to some extent, to the pagan south. It is a journey from cold to warmth, from gloom to sunshine, from pink complexions and blond hair to swarthy complexions and black hair, from pine forests to olive groves, from barley fields to vineyards, from the grim figures of Thor and Wotan to the more pleasing ones of Ceres and Dionysius. It is a journey from skies and seas that are nearly always grey to seas and skies that are rarely anything but blue. In another sense it is a journey from the surface of things to the depths, from the conscious to the unconscious mind, from brain-cells to bloodstream (as D.H. Lawrence might say), from the modern to the archaic, from the present to the past, from the rational to the irrational. In order to go forward we have to go back, or rather, we have to go forward and back at the same time. In order to move in the direction of the east we have to move in the direction of the south. In order to travel towards the region of light and life we have to travel towards—and through—the region of darkness and death.

Besides being a journey from west to east, and from north to south, the journey to Il Convento is not a straight journey but a crooked or zigzag journey. Not only have most of you not come here by the most direct route possible, but you have made all sorts of detours, so that if all your different routes were to be plotted on a map of Europe it would show not a single beaten track but a complicated network of lines all of which eventually converged on Il Convento. Leaving aside those who came here by the shortest and quickest route they could find—as well, perhaps, as those who treated themselves to a holiday—the reason for this is, obviously, that you took advantage of the journey to Il Convento to do a little sight-seeing and that, with a certain amount of overlapping, you did your sight-seeing in different places. But why did you decide to see something of Rome and Naples (I am taking hypothetical examples, since I do not know exactly where each one of you went), rather than something of Venice and Ravenna? What was it, precisely, that drew you to the red-ribbed dome of the Santa Maria di Fiore in Florence, as it seemingly floats above a sea of red roofs? Why were you so keen to see the Leaning Tower of Pisa? What sort of mental picture did you have of these places, or what did they mean to you, that you decided to visit one rather than another of them, or allow yourself to be drawn away from the direct route in this direction rather than in that? Practical considerations played a part, no doubt, to some extent, but in the ultimate analysis the deciding factor must have been subjective or even largely unconscious. Nor is that all. In Rome and Naples, as in Venice and Ravenna and any of the innumerable other places you may have visited, there will have been many churches and palaces, many art galleries and museums, many gardens and grottoes. What was it that led you to one rather than to another of them, or caused you to linger in front of this painting or piece of sculpture rather than in front of that? Last year an Order member who saw Michaelangelo's David in the Academy at Florence afterwards reported that he was so overwhelmed that he felt like prostrating himself before it. Why did he not (apparently) feel like prostrating himself before Orcagna's Tabernacle—or, for the matter of that, before Donatello's David? In making your way from one city or town of Italy to another, from one church or museum to another, and from one painting or sculpture to another, you were no doubt directed not so much by logic as by what may be described as a sort of irrational wisdom, in the sense of an obscure awareness of an inner need, and it was because you were so directed that your journey to Il Convento was not straight but crooked in both the literal and the metaphysical sense, for as Yeats tells us:

Wisdom is a butterfly
And not a gloomy bird of prey.

It is a butterfly because a butterfly floats from flower to flower, or flutters aloft in the air, in zigzag fashion, as you must have observed in the course of your walks in the vicinity of Il Convento, where the butterflies are apparently more abundant than they are in most parts of England, as well as sometimes being of an unfamiliar species. In this connection I remember reading somewhere that in China the streets were formerly built not straight but crooked, with many sudden bends, because people believed that evil spirits moved only in straight lines, and could not go round corners. In modern times, of course, many Western cities have been laid out on a grid plan, with one perfectly straight avenue crossing another exactly at right angles. Paris, for instance, was rebuilt on this kind of plan in the middle of the nineteenth century, the reason being that in the event of an armed uprising the broad, straight avenues would enable the government to bring is artillery to bear on the revolutionary masses with maximum effect. Bullets and artillery shells, like evil spirits, cannot go round corners.

But to return to the journey to Il Convento. In the course of your sight-seeing, in the case of those of you who did any, you will have been led to one building rather than to another, and have lingered in front of this sculpture or painting rather than in front of that, not so much because you found it of special historic or artistic interest (though this may, of course, actually have been the case at times), but rather because you were deeply moved by it and because it possessed, for you at least, a significance that you were at a loss to explain. For reasons that are, perhaps, obvious, you will probably have been affected in this way more by sculptures and paintings than by buildings, and more by individual sculptured or painted figures than by groups of figures or by landscapes. Be that as it may, the likelihood is that a certain work of art moved you so deeply because it represented an image or symbol, and because this image or symbol embodied an archetype—though it is important not to make too hard and fast a distinction either between the image or symbol and the sculptured or painted form by which it is represented, or between the archetype and the image or symbol in which it is embodied. Moreover, if you were sufficiently receptive to what you saw, and sufficiently sensitive, the irrational wisdom that directed you to a particular sculpture or painting in the first place will, by virtue of your contact with that work of art, have been clarified and strengthened to such an extent as to be transformed into imagination, by which I do not mean fancy but a faculty for the perception of images, in the sense of archetype-images or images that are the embodiments of archetypes. That faculty once developed, you will have moved from one work of art to another, or from one image to another, finding each work of art, and each image, more deeply moving and more highly significant than the last. Thus the journey to Il Convento is not only a crooked journey from one image to another. In fact, it is a journey through a world of images, or through an imaginal world, and herein lies its greatest significance. Now all this obviously requires explanation, and you may well be thinking that I am moving ahead far too rapidly. You may even be thinking that your own journey to Il Convento does not correspond very closely to the journey to Il Convento as described by me. At this point perhaps the best thing I can do, therefore, is to give you one or two examples, from my own experience, of the sort of thing about which I have been speaking.

These examples are not drawn from any of my own journeys to Il Convento, but they are at least drawn from a journey to Italy. This journey took place in the summer of 1966, when I passed through Italy on my way to Greece, entering the country by way of the Gothard Pass and leaving it from the port of Brindisi. It was my first visit to Italy, and since I had been intensely interested in Italian art, especially Italian Renaissance art, ever since my childhood, I wanted to make the fullest possible use of my opportunity. Wherever I went I tried to see every church, palace, museum, and art gallery, and every sculpture and painting that each one of these contained. In this way I traversed northern Italy, passing through Milan, Bergamo, Verona, Vicenza, Venice, Padua, and Ravenna. Probably I saw hundreds of buildings and thousands of sculptures and paintings. As the days went by, however, I became aware that I was being drawn to some paintings (for instance) much more than by others, and that the attraction often had more to do with the theme of the paintings than with the quality of their execution or the reputation of the artist. One of the themes, or subjects, by which I was most drawn was that of St Jerome. St Jerome is one of the four Fathers of the Latin Church. He lived in the latter half of the fourth and the first quarter of the fifth century, and was a contemporary of St Augustine, another of the Fathers of the

Latin Church, with whom he had an acrimonious correspondence. When he was already middle-aged St Jerome left Rome and went to live in the Holy Land, at Bethlehem, and it is at this stage of his career that he is usually depicted in Christian art. In the course of that journey in 1966 I must have seen two or three dozen St Jeromes, and I have seen many others since, either in the original or in reproduction. He is usually represented either in the desert, or in his cell, and either on his knees in front of a crucifix, or at his desk. I was drawn most of all by those paintings which represented him in his cell, or study, with an hourglass in front of him, a lion (which he had tamed) sleeping at his feet, his red cardinal's hat hanging on the wall (due to his association with the reigning pope he was traditionally regarded as a cardinal, though cardinals as such did not come into existence until many centuries later), a large volume open before him, and a quill pen in his hand. St Jerome was, of course, responsible for the production of the Vulgate, the standard Latin version of the Bible, which was in use throughout the Middle Ages, and when represented in his study he is generally understood to be engaged in this great work. Incidentally, he is represented as a very old man, with a long white beard. Sometimes his cell-study is practically bare, sometimes furnished with every scholarly comfort and convenience. Somehow this theme, or image, took hold of my mind. St Jerome was the Wise Old Man, and, as you know, the Wise Old Man is one of Jung's Archetypes of the Collective Unconscious. That he was engaged in the work of translation, especially that of rendering the word of God into ordinary human speech, meant that something hidden in the depths was being brought to the surface, or brought from darkness into light. Thus St Jerome was the Alchemist—another embodiment of the Wise Old Man. His cell-study (sometimes depicted as a cave) was the Alchemist's laboratory. Indeed, it was the Alchemist's alembic, in which the Red King united with the White Queen, or his crucible, in which lead was transmuted into gold. In this way the image of St Jerome in his study tended to merge with other images, not only of the Alchemist in his laboratory, but also of the Philosopher in his study—especially Rembrandt's Philosopher, as he sits with the staircase spiralling up through the darkness behind him.

No doubt I was drawn to the image of St Jerome partly because of my personal situation at the time. I was living in the desert. I had left the 'Rome' of collective, official, even establishment, Buddhism, and was seeking to return to the origins of Buddhism in the actual life and experience of the Buddha and his immediate disciples. Not only that. I was trying to teach Buddhism in the West, which meant I was trying to communicate the spirit of the Dharma in terms of Western rather than in terms of Eastern culture. I was thus a translator, with all that that implies in the way of seeking to fathom the uttermost depths of what one is trying to translate so that one may translate it faithfully, i.e. bring its meaning to the surface, or from darkness into light. Thus I was drawn to the image of St Jerome, and was able to see that image as an embodiment of the archetype of the Wise Old Man as 'Translator' and Alchemist, because I had a personal affinity with that image, or because there was something in me that corresponded to that image. In other words, I had possessed, or had developed, a faculty for the perception of that kind of image. I possessed an imagination or, since the word imagination is often used in a pejorative sense, I possessed at least the rudiments of what has been termed the imaginal faculty. This imaginal faculty enabled me to see in the figure of St Jerome more than what was given by the paintings themselves, whether considered as 'works of art' in the modern sense or as examples of traditional religious iconography. It enabled me to see the figure of St Jerome—who in a sense was no longer St Jerome—as in fact belonging to a completely different plane. It enabled me to see him as an image that had its existence in a world of images or in an imaginal world—a world to which one has access by virtue of the imaginal faculty.

Another image to which I was drawn at that time was the image of the Angel, though I was not drawn to it as much as to the image of St Jerome. Indeed, I must have been drawn to this particular image quite early in life, for I can remember executing a whole series of pencil drawings of angels when I was thirteen or fourteen. These angels I depicted as hovering in, or flying through, the air, and since one of them carried a sword he was, I suppose, the archangel Michael. Some years later, during my stay in Kalimpong, I was deeply impressed by the image of the Angel as he appears in Rilke's *Duino Elegies*. More recently, having allowed my interest in angels to lapse for a number of years, I have taken up the study of this image again and have even devoted a certain amount of thought to it. Some of you may recall that thanks to reproductions of the well known painting in the National Gallery, London, the image of Tobias and the Angel is now well established in the FWBO as an image of *kalyāna mitratā* or spiritual friendship. You may have encountered other versions of the same subject in the course of your journey to Il Convento, as I myself did in the course of both my 1966 visit to Italy and my four journeys to Il Convento. That you should see paintings of Tobias and the Angel on the way to Il Convento is, of course, wholly appropriate, for your journey to Il Convento parallels Tobias's journey to Rages, and like him you need to be accompanied by an Angel, whether in visible or invisible form. Indeed, unless you are accompanied by an Angel the journey to Il Convento is not the journey to Il Convento at all, but only a journey.

Now both the image of St Jerome and the image of the Angel are Christian images, and you may be wondering to what extent these can be of significance to a Buddhist. The difficulty is more apparent than real, and is perhaps best resolved by a reference to Jung's Archetypes of the Collective Unconscious. As I think is well known, in studying the dreams of his patients Jung discovered that these often reproduced, quite spontaneously, themes and motifs that play an important part in the various mythologies of mankind, as well as in the teachings of the different religions. Some patients, for instance, described, and even painted, circular figures which bore a remarkable resemblance to Buddhist mandalas. From all this Jung eventually concluded that there were various basic psychic patterns, or archetypes, which were common to the whole human race, both past and present, and which found expression in myths, in religious beliefs, in dreams, and in works of art. These common psychic patterns he termed the Archetypes of the Collective Unconscious. Though the patterns or archetypes were common to the whole human race, however, the various forms in which they expressed themselves were not. The forms were culturally determined, and therefore extremely varied. Thus although the images of St Jerome and the Angel are Christian images, they are Christian images only in the sense that in them an archetype which is of universal significance and value has been clothed in a Christian, Italian, Renaissance form—even in a form peculiar to a particular artist. It is for this reason that it is possible for a Christian image to be of significance to a Buddhist. What the Buddhist is drawn to is not so much the Christian form of the image as the archetype of which that image is an embodiment, and it is therefore really the archetype that is of significance to him. In some cases, of course, the form taken by a Christian image, e.g. the Crucifixion, will be so repugnant to Buddhist sentiment as to render it quite impossible for a Buddhist to be drawn to the image and, therefore, in this instance at least, to the archetype of which it is the embodiment. In other cases, such as the images of St Jerome and of the Angel, the fact that the form taken by the image is conditioned by, or belongs to, a culture with which the (Western) Buddhist happens to be familiar, and with which he feels a definite emotional connection, may even mean that he is drawn to it to a greater extent than he is drawn to its traditional Buddhist counterpart, where such exists, so that he is in the uncomfortable position of finding the Christian image of significance to him on account of its being the embodiment of an archetype of which he has a better intellectual understanding, and even a keener spiritual appreciation, in specifically Buddhist terms. In yet other cases, both the Christian image and its Buddhist counterpart may be of significance to a Buddhist, and it may be clear to him that both images are embodiments, within their respective cultures, of one and the same archetype, even though he is at the same time fully aware that in Buddhism the archetype is incorporated within a much broader and more meaningful context.

For me this was especially so with regard to the image of the Angel, which was probably one of the reasons I was drawn to it. The image of the Angel, though Christian, not only has its immediate antecedents in Classical antiquity, but also its counterparts in practically all other religions and cultures, as a glance at the illustrations to Peter Lamborn Wilson's well known book, *Angels*,[25] will be sufficient to show. In the case of Buddhism, the principal counterparts of the image of the Angel are the deva and the Bodhisattva, as represented in traditional Buddhist art. Indeed, the Buddhist may well feel that the image of the Bodhisattva is the embodiment *par excellence* of the particular archetype in question. Indeed, he may feel that the archetype of which the Bodhisattva is the embodiment, and which the image of the Angel reflects in a different cultural context and on a lower spiritual level, is in fact nothing less than the Archetype of Enlightenment, as it may be termed, and as such immeasurably transcends the archetypes that were the subject of Jung's discoveries. This of course implies an enlargement of the meaning of the term 'archetype' far beyond the significance it possesses for any current system of psychology. It also implies a stratification, so to speak, of images, in accordance with the degree to which they are the embodiments of a particular archetype, and even, perhaps, a stratification of the archetypes themselves. This in turn implies a stratification, in the sense of an arrangement in a progressive, hierarchical order, of the faculty by which the images themselves are perceived, or rather, a stratification of the successive stages of its unfoldment or manifestation. Thus one arrives at the conception of a hierarchy of levels of the imagination, or imaginal *faculty*, corresponding to a hierarchy of levels of images and archetypes, or imaginal *world*. In Buddhism this imaginal world is known as the world—or worlds—of the gods, access to the different planes and sub-planes of which can be obtained through the cultivation of the corresponding mental state, in the form of a particular 'concentration' (*dhyāna*) or sublime abode (*brahma vihāra*).

But though I have spoken of the imaginal faculty, the expression should not, in a sense, be taken too literally. The imagination, or image-perceiving faculty, is not so much a faculty among faculties as the man—the spiritual man—himself. It is spoken of as a faculty because, in the case of the vast majority of people, it exists in such a rudimentary form that it appears to be simply a 'faculty' like, for instance, reason or emotion, or because it has not yet been developed or manifested at all. The imaginal faculty is, in reality, the man himself, because when one truly perceives an image one perceives it with the whole of oneself, or with one's whole being. When one truly perceives an image, therefore, one is transported to the world to which that image belongs and becomes, if only for the time being, an inhabitant of that world. In other words, truly to perceive an image means to become an image, so that when one speaks of the imagination, or the imaginal faculty, what one is really speaking of is *image perceiving image*. That is to say, in perceiving an image what one really perceives is, in a sense, oneself.

By this time you may be thinking that I have got rather a long way from the journey to Il Convento, but that is not really the case. Buddhism sees mundane existence as stratified into three great planes or 'worlds', each with its subsidiary worlds or sub-planes. These three worlds or planes (*loka, dhātu*) are those of (1) desire for sensuous experience (*kāma*), (2) archetypal form (*rūpa*), and (3) no archetypal form (*arūpa*) or, perhaps we should say, extremely subtle archetypal form. 'Beyond' these three worlds there lies the Unconditioned or transcendental. In terms of spiritual cosmography the spiritual life consists of a journey from the world or plane of sensuous desire, through the worlds or planes of archetypal form and extremely subtle archetypal form, to the Unconditioned or transcendental, and it is of this archetypal journey that the journey to Il Convento is an image or symbol. Thus when you start your journey by leaving England you are not just leaving grey skies. What you are really doing is leaving your old interests and activities, your old habits and attachments, your old way of life, and even your old self. What you are really doing is leaving the world of sensuous desire. Similarly, when you visit this or that town or city *en route*, and do your sight-seeing, you are not just looking at churches and palaces, museums and art galleries, gardens and grottoes, not just admiring buildings, sculptures, and paintings. What you are really doing is moving from one image, i.e. archetype-image, to another, or travelling through a world of images. What you are really doing is traversing the world or plane of archetypal form. (The world or plane of extremely subtle archetypal form really falls outside the scope of the comparison—except, perhaps, in the case of those who spent some time in the Alps.) In the same way, when you arrive at Il Convento you arrive at the threshold of the transcendental, for you have made the journey to Il Convento in the hope of being ordained or, in more traditional language, of being able to go for Refuge to the Three Jewels, and not only are the Three Jewels essentially transcendental but the act of going for Refuge to them is, ultimately, transcendental too.

Thus the journey to Il Convento is not only a journey from west to east, and from north to south, not only a crooked or zigzag journey, not only an opportunity for sight-seeing. It is also an inner journey, an inner exploration, that takes one through the three great worlds or planes of mundane existence up to the very threshold of the transcendental. Of course, I hardly need tell you that however successfully you might have accomplished the journey to Il Convento in the literal sense—and the fact that you are here at all means that you have done at least that—in the metaphorical sense you have probably accomplished the journey only in the most rudimentary fashion. In particular, your journey through the world of images will probably have been of a very sketchy nature and have taken place at a comparatively low level. Indeed, it may have consisted in little more than a series of brief forays into unfamiliar regions where images loomed as though through mist rather than revealing themselves in brilliant sunshine against skies eternally blue. But even if this should not have been the case it does not, in a sense, matter very much. The real journey to Il Convento has to be made not once but many times. Each time you make the journey you make it in a more thorough-going fashion or, so to speak, at a higher level. It is like making your way up a mountain by a spiral path. Each time you circle the mountain you circle it at a higher level, but it is the same mountain that you are circling. Thus each time you make the journey to Il Convento and leave the world of sensuous desire, traverse the world of images, and arrive at the threshold of the transcendental, you do so in a fuller and more effective manner than you did before. Your old way of life, and your old self, is increasingly abandoned, while far from being a series of brief forays into unfamiliar regions, your journey through the world of images is a more and more protracted sojourn among archetype-images of ever increasing refinement, richness, beauty, and sublimity among which you feel more and more at home. Christian images will, no doubt, eventually be left far behind, and perhaps Buddhist images too, and one will find oneself in the presence of the archetypes which those images embody, and even in the presence of the archetypes of the archetypes.

But before that happens one will perhaps have realized that images are not, in fact, such fixed and definite things as one originally thought. Images are fluid. They can change, which means that their significance can change. Perhaps I can best illustrate what I mean with the help of a short story. In the course of my life I have written only six or seven short stories, though I have had ideas for many more, and the short story to which I refer has not actually been written down. The idea of it came to me a few weeks ago as a result of the sightseeing Prasannasiddhi and I had been doing in Pisa in the course of our latest journey to Il Convento. As you know, sightseeing can be quite tiring, especially when one is getting on in years, and I think the idea of the story must have come to me as a result of the feeling of tiredness I experienced one day after we had visited the National Museum of St Matthew, the Cathedral and Baptistery, the Leaning Tower, the Museum of the Sinopias, and several churches. The story began with two people coming to Italy on a sort of cultural tour. I imagined them visiting all the famous Italian cities, and seeing the great churches and palaces, the museums and art galleries, much as I had done in 1966. One day they happen to find themselves inside a particularly fine cathedral (and this is where the story really begins), equipped with the usual Crucifixions, Madonnas (both with and without Child), Annunciations, Saints, and Martyrs (being grilled, beheaded, sawn in two, broken on the wheel, shot full of arrows, torn with pincers, skinned alive, etc.), Nativities, Ascensions, Assumptions, and Last Judgements, together with sundry cherubs and putti. Since the place is so vast, and there is so much to see, the two friends spend several hours looking round the cathedral. Moreover, they are so interested in all the paintings and sculptures, which are of excellent quality, that they fail to notice that the place has gradually emptied and that the sacristan, thinking that everyone had left, has locked the massive bronze doors for the night. The younger of the two friends therefore goes in search of a side entrance that might still be open, while his older companion, feeling in need of a rest, sits down on a bench at the foot of one of the enormous Gothic pillars of the nave. By that time it is practically dark, and he has not been sitting there for more than a few minutes when he hears a confused sound of footsteps and voices. It is almost as though a party of sightseers had entered the cathedral. But it is not a party of sightseers. On lifting his head he sees in the dim light that now pervades the whole building an extraordinary sight. The sculpted and painted figures at which he and his friend had gazed so intently only a short while ago are now stepping down from their marble pedestals, and out of their carved and gilded frames, on to the floor of the cathedral. There are hundreds of them, and after a momentary pause some of them seem to have started moving down the aisle in his direction. The sound of footsteps and voices grows gradually louder as they approach.

What followed was the main part of the story, and was to have taken up the greatest amount of space, but since I have not worked it out in detail I can give you only a rough sketch of what happened. No doubt this will be enough for my present purpose. The idea was that once they had stepped down from their pedestals, and out of their picture-frames, the figures should all start behaving in a way that was not completely in accordance with their official character, so to speak. They were off duty, now that the cathedral was closed, and were free to behave as they liked. So Christ stretches his arms and says that he is glad to get down from that crucifix for a few hours, while the Virgin Mary complains that the Child gets heavier every day and she does not know how much longer she will be able to stand here holding him. As for the Child himself, he is playing with some of the more mischievous-looking putti, and they are actually trying to use one of the cherubs, who is of course all head and wings, as a football. The Archangel Michael is also there. He lays aside his sword and his scales, takes off his shining armour, and starts doing press-ups in the middle of the nave. God the Father then comes along, having stepped down out of an enormous fresco of the Last Judgement. He is rather worried, and mutters into his beard, saying that he is fed up with judging people, and in any case thinks he has made quite a few mistakes. As if to confirm his suspicions, a crowd of figures out of the same fresco surround him and indignantly complain about the treatment they have received. Some of those who have been sent to heaven complain that it is a dull and boring place, and ask to be sent somewhere more interesting, while some of those who have been sent to hell complain that the devils do not give them any attention. They could stand anything except that, they say. Even poor old St Jerome is there. His back is stiff from spending so many hours at his desk, and he is glad to have a respite from that endless work of translation. As for the lion, having woken up, shaken his hide, and followed St Jerome out of the picture-frame, he takes a leisurely stroll down the aisle, pausing to rub himself against the legs of various Saints and Martyrs, all of whom have something to contribute to the proceedings. St John the Baptist remarks that it is nice to have his head back on again, while a female saint whose name I have forgotten makes a similar remark about her breasts. St Lawrence hopes that no one will mind him mentioning the fact that his gridiron is in need of repair, St Agnes confesses to St Mary Magdalene that she is tired of looking after all those lambs, while St Mary Magdalene confides to St Agnes that she thinks hair shirts don't really suit her any more. Salome, who is of course neither a saint nor a Martyr, asks her mother whether she ought not to learn a new dance, since Herod seems to be getting tired of the old one after all these years.

How the story developed from that point onwards I found it difficult to decide. Perhaps the complaints that the figures from the Last Judgement make to God the Father become so loud that the elder of the two friends, sitting there on his bench in the nave, gives a start, rubs his eyes, and finds that the sculpted and painted figures have returned to their pedestals and picture-frames, and that the place is again practically dark. Or perhaps the figures suddenly all become aware of his presence and make a concerted rush at him, or try to drag him up on to a pedestal, or into a picture-frame. Anyway, it has all been a dream, and he is now awake. His young friend is standing beside him, shaking him vigorously by the shoulder. He has found a side entrance still unlocked, he says, and they must hurry or it will be too late. Thus the short story ends. It is not, of course, a very original story. I have read one novel, and at least two short stories, in which the statues in a museum all come to life and have various adventures, and these may well have influenced me. Moreover, to make one's principal character undergo some highly unusual experience which, in the end, turns out to have been a dream, is a rather hackneyed device. Nonetheless, I hope that despite its shortcomings this latest short story of mine has been able to illustrate the point that images are not such fixed and definite things as one might have thought, and that their significance can change. Images and their significance are, in fact, changing all the time. The Angel as represented in Italian Gothic art is very different from the Angel as represented in Italian Renaissance art, and both are very different from the Angel as represented in Italian Baroque art, besides which there are within each of these periods great differences as between the Angel as represented by one artist and the Angel as represented by another. Thus over the period of a few hundred years the image of the Angel, together with the significance of that image, is seen to undergo a whole series of developments and transformations even within the limits of a single national culture.

Images can not only change; they can also be broken. They are 'broken' when they have lost all significance for us, a process which begins when we no longer perceive them with the imaginal faculty or, what amounts to much the same thing, when we no longer respond to the particular archetype they embody. In the literal sense, images are broken when the paintings and sculptures which are their embodiments are smashed or burned. This usually happens when the images themselves no longer have significance for us, as was the case with the Puritans when they smashed and burned the 'superstitious' paintings and sculptures that adorned the cathedrals and churches of England, or when their meaning is completely misunderstood, as was the case with the Muslim invaders of India who smashed and burned the 'idols' they discovered in the Buddhist temples and monasteries. Perhaps it is not without significance that the journey to Il Convento should be a journey to what was formerly a Christian monastery. Il Convento di Santa Croce, to give the place its full title, until a little less than two hundred years ago was occupied by a community of brown-robed Franciscan friars who in theory, at least, had 'come together'—the literal meaning of the word from which convent is derived—in order to live in accordance with the ideal of Christian perfection as exemplified by St Francis, the founder of their order. How long Il Convento di Santa Croce had by that time been in existence I do not know. It may have dated back to the Middle Ages, or it may have been a recent foundation. Whichever may have been the case, the friars were expelled, and the building itself badly damaged, about two hundred years ago, during the Napoleonic Wars—presumably at the time of Napoleon's conflict with the Papacy.[26] Whether the friars returned to their monastery after the downfall of the great tyrant I do not know, but if any of them did return, and if they did so without delay, it must have given them great satisfaction to look—as we can still look today—from the olive groves of Il Convento down to the great coastal plain, and from there to the island of Elba, lying a dim grey shape on the horizon, behind its strip of blue sea, and to think that Napoleon was confined there: though it must have given them still greater satsifaction when, after the escape from Elba and the Hundred Days, he was finally confined to the island of St Helena, a much less pleasant place. On the other hand, human nature being what it is, they may have lamented his fall, and even offered up prayers on his behalf, for he had eventually made his peace with the Church and signed a concordat with the Pope, as many a tyrant had done before him, and as tyrants have done since.

In this connection, i.e. in connection with the subject of Napoleon, I remember that last year my own journey to Il Convento included four days in Paris. Among the places I went to see with Prasannasiddhi, as well as with Subhūti and Śīlabhadra, who were giving us their company so far as the French capital, was the Tomb of Napoleon. As might have been expected, this was a large and imposing structure in extremely bad taste and it was seemingly dedicated not just to the glorification of Napoleon Bonaparte but to the glorification of the spirit of militarism or, to put it more crudely, the spirit of war. To walk round inside the Tomb, with its clumsy neo-classical sculptures, and its vulgarly expensive marbles, was to make a foray into the world of the *āsuras* or anti-gods, or into that world of aggression, competition, and conflict, that has to be left behind by anyone engaged on the journey to Il Convento. To make matters worse, a shop next door to the Tomb was doing a brisk business in Napoleonic postcards and souvenirs of every kind, including swords, suits of armour, and model soldiers. After visiting the Tomb I felt a strong urge to write an open letter to President Mitterand pointing out that if he really was a Socialist, and really believed in peace, he should close down the Tomb of Napoleon forthwith, since it was the negation of everything for which he stood. However, I did not write the letter, since I found it difficult to believe that anything so contrary to French national sentiment would be allowed to reach him. All the same, I am unwilling to give up the idea entirely, and may yet find a way of carrying it out. But that is another story.

The reason why it is not without significance that the journey to Il Convento should be a journey to what was formerly a Christian monastery is that that monastery is in a state of disrepair and dilapidation. What happened to it after the monks returned, if they ever did, I am unable to tell you. At some time during the last two hundred years the place was a glass factory, as the lumps of green vitreous material that strew the surrounding area testify, but for how long it was a glass factory I do not know. More recently it was used for agricultural purposes until it passed into the hands of the present owner, who uses the place, during the summer months, for putting on small-scale productions of seventeenth century Italian operas and other works—a fact which is also not without significance, though what that significance is I shall leave you to discover for yourselves. Yet despite having been put to such a variety of uses, Il Convento remains in much the same condition as, I imagine, it was left by Napoleon's troops after the expulsion of the friars. What was once the church is hardly even a shell, the roof having been ripped off, and the façade reduced to a heap of rubble. Though the cloister is more or less intact, several of the brick pillars are damaged, while hardly a trace remains of the frescoes that once covered the walls. The journey to Il

Convento is thus a journey to a place of broken images. In the literal sense there are, indeed, not even any broken images, though on the occasion of my first journey to Il Convento I did see, before someone put it away in a cupboard, a cracked wooden figure of St Anthony of Padua that looked as though it was badly in need of a coat of paint. Since the journey to Il Convento is a journey to a place of broken images, the Going for Refuge which is the whole purpose of that journey takes place—and this is the point I really want to make—in the midst of broken images. We become Buddhists, in fact, in the midst of the ruins of Christian civilization and culture, and though the images of that culture may still draw us, to some extent, in their specifically Christian sense they no longer have any significance for us. That is in fact why we go for Refuge. That is why in the midst of the ruins of Christian culture, in the midst of the broken images, we set up our own Buddhist images, which will, we hope, eventually take over and reconstruct the whole place.

One more thing and I have done. As I have said more than once, the journey to Il Convento is a journey that takes us from the world of sensuous desire, through the world of archetypal form, to the threshold of the transcendental. The real journey to Il Convento is therefore a journey that must be made not once but many times, each time at a higher level. So much, perhaps, has already been made clear. What also needs to be made clear is that it is possible to make the journey to Il Convento without coming to Il Convento in the literal sense at all. We can make it without leaving England, without seeing Italy, for since the journey to Il Convento is an inner journey it is a journey that we can make staying in our own house and sitting in our own room. As Lao Tzu says, 'Without looking out of the window, one can see the Way of Heaven.' But although this is true it is no more than half the truth, or even less than half. Man has not only an inner but an outer being; he consists not only of mind but also of speech and body. Consequently, if one really wants to make the journey to Il Convento—if one really wants to leave the world of sensuous desire, traverse the world of images or the imaginal world, and arrive at the threshold of the transcendental—then one will want to do so in the most complete and total manner possible. One will not be content to 'go forth' metaphorically. One will want to 'go forth' literally too. Thus one's inner journey will be paralleled by an outer journey, and this outer journey will not necessarily be a journey from London or Glasgow to Il Convento. It may be a journey from Bombay to Bhaja, or from Manchester to Padmaloka. But wherever it begins and wherever it ends it will be a journey to a place where one can be ordained, a place where one can go for Refuge to the Three Jewels with body, speech, and mind.

Yet even though one's outer journey does not necessarily take one to Il Convento, there is no doubt that at the present juncture in the history of the FWBO those who are in a position to make the journey to Il Convento in the literal sense are particularly fortunate. I am therefore glad that this year fifteen of you have been able to make that journey for the first time, and to make it in the hope, now about to be fulfilled, of being ordained here. I hope that you will be able to make the real journey to Il Convento many, many times. I hope that each time you make the journey you will be able to make a more decisive break with the world of sensuous desire. I hope that each time you make it you will be able to explore the world of images at ever higher and more refined levels. Above all, I hope that as you truly arrive at the threshold of the transcendental your Going for Refuge will be transformed into a transcendental Going for Refuge. When that happens, the purpose of the whole journey to Il Convento will be fulfilled.

Saint Jerome Revisited

In the course of the paper on 'The Journey to Il Convento' which I read to you a few weeks ago I spoke of our being drawn to one image or symbol rather than another, often without understanding why, and by way of illustration I described how in the course of my journey to Italy in 1966 I was myself drawn by two images. One of these was the image of St Jerome. Since I described him at some length in the paper, and moreover tried to explain why the image of St Jerome—especially St Jerome in his study, translating the Bible into Latin—should have been of significance to me at that time, I was under the impression that for the time being at least I was finished with that particular image and could forget all about it. But this did not turn out to be the case. Within a few days of reading the paper I found myself thinking about St Jerome quite a lot, and the more I thought about him the more significant the image of the old man bending over his desk in his cell, or study, or cave, seemed to be. It was as though an archetype-image, once activated, possesses a life of its own, and forces itself upon your attention, so to speak, whether you like it or not, and insists on continuing the conversation which, so far as you are concerned, is finished. I therefore decided that the best thing I could do would be to write another paper, devoted exclusively to the image of St Jerome, in the hope that once I had written it, and perhaps read it, I really would be finished with this particular image for the time being.

At first I thought I would write the paper when I was back at Padmaloka, and comfortably settled in my own study again. At Padmaloka I have all my books, and I would be able to look up all sorts of references to St Jerome, as well as to the various images and symbols with which the figure of the saint is traditionally associated. In the end, however, I decided to write the paper here at Il Convento, partly because the image of St Jerome refused to leave me in peace and partly because the thought occurred to me that it might, in fact, actually be an advantage if I was not able to look up any references, since then I would have to rely entirely on my memory and my imagination, which might mean that my imagination would be able to play a more active part in the writing of the paper than otherwise would have been possible. True, I might make mistakes, e.g. mistakes in matters of historical fact, but that would not matter very much. There are one or two mistakes in 'The Journey to Il Convento'. After writing the paper I realized that although in my short story I had described the figure of God the Father stepping down from the fresco of the Last Judgement I had not, in fact, seen any such fresco. In all the frescoes of the Last Judgement which I had seen the judge was not God the Father but Christ, in accordance with the words of the Apostle's Creed, 'From whence he (i.e. Christ) shall come to judge the quick and the dead.' Similarly, after I had read the paper one of you questioned whether Il Convento di Santa Croce was originally occupied by Franciscan friars or Augustinian canons, since he had seen a reference to Augustinian canons on the back of one of the present-day Il Convento's opera programmes. Whether God the Father or Christ should have been described as stepping down from the fresco, and whether Il Convento was originally occupied by Franciscans or Augustinians, does not of course affect the validity of the points I was trying to make, so that so far as the paper itself is concerned the 'mistakes' have no significance. They may, however, have a psychological, or even a spiritual, significance of their own, but that is a matter into which I do not propose to enter on the present occasion. Instead, now that those of you who made the journey to Il Convento in the hope of being ordained have had your hope fulfilled, let us go back over some of the ground that we have already covered and examine it more thoroughly. Let us revisit St Jerome.

As I mentioned last time, St Jerome is usually represented either in the desert or in his cell—that is to say, when he is represented in his own right, so to speak, and not simply as one saint among many in an altarpiece or predella—and it is in his cell, or study, that we shall be visiting him. Before doing so, however, let us pay a short visit to St Jerome in the desert. Paintings of St Jerome in the desert exhibit a much greater variety than do paintings of St Jerome in his study, almost as though the traditional iconography was not so definitely fixed and the artist had

greater freedom, at least in certain respects. Paintings of this sort sometimes represent, according to the title, not St Jerome in the desert but
St Jerome performing penance. What they all really represent, however,
is simply St Jerome in a landscape, and this is in fact the best and most
accurate way of describing them. Since the landscape was, of course, that
of the Holy Land, to which St Jerome had retired from Rome, what the
artists of the Italian Renaissance should have depicted was, presumably,
the kind of landscape that Holman Hunt depicts in *The Scapegoat*—a
dreary expanse of salt marshland with the bottle-green streak of the Dead
Sea in the distance backed by a low range of weirdly glowing pink and
mauve foothills. In order to paint this landscape the Pre-Raphaelite artist
had to make a journey to the Holy Land, but the artists of the Italian
Renaissance made no such journey, and never thought of making it. They
simply painted whatever landscape lay nearest to hand. The result is that,
more often than not, St Jerome is seen not in the desert, or what the King
James Bible calls the wilderness, but in the midst of an extremely beautiful, typically Tuscan or Umbrian landscape, with plenty of luxuriant
Mediterranean vegetation and an abundance of picturesque rock forma-
tions. The landscape is, of course, not cultivated but wild, but it is wild
with the wildness not of the desert but of Paradise before the Fall.
Sometimes St Jerome is shown actually performing penance. In such
cases he is dressed in a sort of loincloth, often tattered, and either kneels
before, or clasps, a rude crucifix. Sometimes, again, he sits on a rock, his
head resting on his hand, as though deep in meditation. More often than
not, his faithful lion can be seen somewhere in the picture, usually fast
asleep, though in some of the more naïve representations of the scene he
appears to be sharing in St Jerome's devotions. In quite a number of
paintings of what I have termed 'St Jerome in a landscape' the figure of
the saint was, I noticed, quite tiny in comparison with the rest of the
picture. In a few such cases it actually took one a minute or two to find
the figure of St Jerome, which in relation to the surrounding countryside
then appeared not only tiny but insignificant. What the artists had in fact
depicted was not St Jerome in the desert, or St Jerome doing penance, or
even St Jerome in a landscape, but simply man in the midst of nature, and
in these paintings, I further noticed, nature, in her richness and abundance and beauty, appeared serenely indifferent to the existential anguish
of man—an anguish which she was, in fact, incapable of comprehending.
Man and nature were strangers to each other. Though he lived in the
midst of her, he was not *of* her. She knew him, if she knew him at all, only
as a physical body, and as a physical body he was infinitely smaller than

she was, and infinitely less powerful. What these representations of man in the midst of nature seemed to be saying was that viewed from the outside, or simply as a material object among material objects, man is a very insignificant creature. In order to appreciate his greatness, or what an Italian Renaissance philosopher calls 'the dignity of man', it is necessary to view him from the inside, from within, as a spiritual being among other spiritual beings, or at least among objects of spiritual significance. In other words, it is necessary to turn from St Jerome in the desert to St Jerome in his study.

St Jerome's study, or cell, is of course often depicted as a cave. The mouth of this cave can sometimes be seen in paintings of St Jerome in the desert, or performing penance, either situated quite near at hand or up on the mountainside, depending on the scale of the painting. This cave constitutes a kind of link between the two different representations of St Jerome or, one might even say, between the two different images of St Jerome, i.e. St Jerome in the desert, or performing penance, and St Jerome in his study translating the Bible. Now I have said that in order to appreciate the greatness of man it is necessary to view him from the inside, from within, as a spiritual being among spiritual beings. But it is only man himself who can view man in this way. Nature cannot do it. *She* is able to view him, if she views him at all, only from the outside: she sees him only as a physical body. In order to see himself as a spiritual being man has to stop viewing himself only as a physical body, as nature does, and *enter into the cave of the heart*. To begin with the heart will appear to him as an object, even as a physical object or physical organ. That is why in paintings of St Jerome in the desert the cave can be seen, but it is seen from the outside, since there it is part of nature, part of the material universe. When man, as represented by the figure of St Jerome in a landscape, enters the cave, the cave is no longer object but subject. Man has turned himself inside out, as it were. St Jerome is no longer in the desert. He is in his study, and we are there in his study with him.

The first thing we notice about the study is that except for a few spiritually significant items such as a red hat, an hourglass, and a human skull, it is completely bare. (I am speaking of what may be termed the 'typical' representation of St Jerome's study in Italian Renaissance art.) In particular, it does not contain—apart from one important exception, which I shall mention in a minute—any natural object. There are no flowers in vases, for instance, and no food—not so much as a crust of bread or a cruse of wine. Moreover there are no windows and therefore no view, so that St Jerome cannot look out at the surrounding desert when he gets tired of translating the Bible and the Greek and Hebrew characters start dancing in front of his eyes. In the cave of the heart man cannot see nature, and nature cannot see man. There must, of course, be a door, but it cannot be open, for no sunlight streams through it into the cave, which is filled with a mysterious glow of its own. (Sometimes St Jerome is depicted working by the light of a candle.) What the typical representation of St Jerome in his study really gives us is a cross-section of an inner world. In this inner world man is not insignificant, as he is when viewed from the outside, as part of the material universe, and this is why in paintings of St Jerome in his study the figure of St Jerome himself looms extremely large. Indeed, it sometimes practically fills the entire painting. If in the case of St Jerome in a landscape, or in the midst of nature, there is hardly room for St Jerome, in the case of St Jerome in his study there is hardly room for nature. As I have already said, with one exception St Jerome's study, or cell, does not contain any natural object, that is to say, any living natural object, for presumably his desk is made of wood that was once part of a tree and the pages of the Bible he is translating of parchment that was once part of a sheep. One might even say that St Jerome's study contains nothing but St Jerome, for every one of the spiritually significant items, as I have called them, is in a sense an extension of the saint's own personality—as is even the one natural object that the study contains.

This natural object is the lion. He is always with St Jerome in his cell, or study, just as he is nearly always with him in the desert, or when he is doing penance. Like the cave, he is a kind of link between the desert and the study, the objective world and the subjective world, matter and spirit. How St Jerome came to be associated with the lion, or the lion with St Jerome, I do not recollect ever reading. Tucked away in an obscure corner of the legendary life of the saint there is, in all probability, an episode of the type made familiar to us by the story of Androcles and the Lion—an episode, that is to say, in which St Jerome removes a thorn from the paw of a lion who, out of gratitude, thereafter stays with him as his attendant. Even if there is such an episode, however, the artists of the Italian Renaissance do not seem to have represented it in any way. It is as though they felt that the lion's presence in the painting—whether of St Jerome in the desert or St Jerome in his study—needed no explanation. He was simply there, and he was there not for biographical reasons but for psychological and spiritual reasons that were perfectly obvious to anyone in whom the imaginal faculty was awake and who could understand the language of images and symbols. Translated from the language of images and symbols into the language of concepts the significance of the lion is not difficult to appreciate. The lion is the king of beasts. Apart from man, who in reality belongs to a different order of existence, the lion is the highest of all natural objects. Just as the vegetable kingdom is higher than the mineral kingdom, so the animal kingdom is higher than the vegetable kingdom, and in the animal kingdom the lion is supreme. In the lion, therefore, all the energies and powers of the natural world are gathered together and given their highest and most perfect embodiment. Thus the lion is nature *par excellence*, which in fact means that the lion represents not so much nature herself as nature as she exists in man. The lion accompanies St Jerome because he is part of St Jerome. He is St Jerome's lower nature, so to speak. He is the Lower Evolution as taken up into, and incorporated with, the Higher Evolution. Thus the lion not only stays with St Jerome in the desert, where he is a natural object among natural objects, but also follows him into the cave—the cave of the heart—where he is a natural object among spiritual objects, or rather a natural object among objects of spiritual significance, and stays with him there.

In paintings of St Jerome in the desert the figure of the lion is often as tiny and as insignificant as that of St Jerome. Indeed, sometimes he disappears altogether, as though merged into the landscape, for since he represents nature, albeit nature *par excellence*, it is hardly necessary for him to be present in his individual capacity. In paintings of St Jerome in his study, however, the figure of the lion looms almost as large as that of the saint. True, as depicted in medieval Italian art he often looks more like a large yellow dog than a lion, but as depicted by the artists of the Italian Renaissance, who often studied him from life (Italian princes of the period like to keep lions in their menageries), he is in both form and feature the king of beasts indeed. Usually he is curled up quite close to St Jerome. When the figure of St Jerome threatens to fill the entire painting such proximity is a practical necessity, and the artist has to have recourse to some ingenious foreshortening to get them both in. Sometimes, indeed, the lion lies stretched out beneath St Jerome's desk, so that the saint is able to use him as a foot-warmer. Sometimes his eyes are wide open, and regard the spectator with a steady, level stare, but more often they are closed in sleep. But howsoever he is depicted, whether as more like a large yellow dog or more like a real lion, whether curled up or stretched out, awake or asleep, St Jerome's lion represents not only nature as a part of man but also nature as a part of man that has been tamed. Because he has been tamed the lion does not disturb St Jerome in his work of translation, and how important it is that St Jerome should not be disturbed we shall be able to appreciate only when we have a better understanding of the true nature of that work.

Meanwhile, we have by no means finished with the lion, or exhausted the significance of his association with St Jerome. When I first found myself thinking about St Jerome, shortly after reading my last paper, I did not pay much attention to the lion. But after I had decided that we should revisit St Jerome I found myself thinking about the lion almost as much as about St Jerome himself. Nor was that all. As I thought about St Jerome and the lion I found that I was thinking of other instances of close association between man and lion and that their images too were forcing themselves upon my attention. These instances came from both the Judaeo-Christian and the Classical traditions and involved images belonging to ancient myth and legend that were no less familiar to me, from art and literature, than the image of St Jerome himself, and imbued with hardly less significance. To begin with there were images of Samson slaying the lion and Daniel in the lion's den. Both these images came from the Bible, from the Old Testament, and I encountered them for the first time when, at the age of four or five or even earlier, I started spelling my way through Grandmother's Bible. This was a massive, leather-bound volume with huge gilt clasps that my father had inherited from his maternal grandmother. In the front it contained the names and dates of birth (and in some cases dates of death) of great-grandmother's and great-grandfather's children and grandchildren, to which, I believe, my father had added the names and dates of birth of myself and my sister. It also contained numerous full-page illustrations, all printed in the most vivid colours imaginable. Apart from Moses breaking the Tablets of the Law, the ones I remember most clearly are those of Samson slaying the lion and Daniel in the lion's den. In the first, a bright pink Samson wrestled with a bright yellow lion against an emerald green background. In the second, a Daniel in a deep blue robe knelt in prayer while a pale yellow light streamed down on to his head from the open heavens. Around him were strewn human skulls and bones (I particularly remember a set of ribs), while an enormous grey lion regarded him from the shadows. From the Classical tradition came the image of Hercules and the Nemean lion. The strangling of this enormous lion was the first of the famous Twelve Labours of Hercules, and after killing it the hero wore its skin as a sort of cloak, with the head forming a rough hood, and the paws dangling down in front like empty sleeves. In the case of all three images—Samson slaying the lion, Daniel in the lion's den, and Hercules and the Nemean lion—there is an association between a man and a lion, and in each case the man tames or subdues the lion. Samson tears the lion's jaws apart, Daniel renders the lion powerless by virtue of his faith in God, and Hercules strangles the lion to death. Thus in each case there is a close parallel with the association between St Jerome and the lion. At the same time, there are differences. In Samson's case, he actually destroys the lion. Daniel manages to keep the lion at bay. Hercules kills the lion and wears its skin. The three heroes may therefore be regarded as representing the three different attitudes which it is possible for man to adopt towards his own lower nature. He can destroy it, i.e. repress it completely, he can keep it at a safe distance, i.e. suppress it by religious and other means, or he can tame it and turn it into a companion, i.e. integrate it into his higher nature. The third possibility is represented by St Jerome and the lion, as well as by Hercules who, having strangled the Nemean lion, wears its skin on his shoulders. In all four cases, however, the lion is subdued. Man's lower nature is not allowed to disturb him as he pursues his distinctively human activities.

Once images of lions, and men in association with lions, had started forcing themselves on my attention in this way, there seemed to be no stopping them. Since we still have to consider the significance of the various items contained in St Jerome's study there is time for no more than a brief reference to a few of these images, with some of which you will already be familiar, though you may not have attached to them the kind of significance with which we are at present concerned. These more insistent images come from even farther afield than the images of men and lions which we have so far encountered. They come not from the Judaeo-Christian and Classical traditions but, originally, from the treasury of Indian Buddhist culture. The first such image is that of the Teaching Buddha and the two, sometimes four, lions which support his throne in the same way that elephants support the throne of the Earth-Touching Buddha and peacocks the throne of the Meditating Buddha, and so on. There are, of course, biographical and doctrinal reasons why the throne of the Teaching Buddha should be supported by lions rather than by animals of any other kind, but at present all I want to do is to draw attention to the association, in this case, between Enlightened Man and lion and to suggest that, on its own much higher level, it has the same general significance as the association between St Jerome and the lion or, for the matter of that, between the heroes of the Old Testament and of Classical legend and their respective lions. From the Buddha and his lions to Mañjuśrī, the Bodhisattva of Wisdom, and his, is no more than a short step. Lions support the throne of Mañjuśrī in exactly the same manner that they support the throne of the Teaching Buddha (those of you who are acquainted with the symbolism of the Five Buddhas will know the reason for this), but the best known and most typical example of the association between Mañjuśrī and the lion is that which represents the great Bodhisattva as using a single lion as his vehicle or mount. Such representatations seem to have been particularly abundant in Buddhist China, where Mañjuśrī was known as Monju-shi-li and where the Manchu or Ching dynasty—the last of the dynasties of China—supposedly took its name from him. In China, however, either there were no lions or Chinese artists did not care to study them from life, for in Chinese Buddhist art Mañjuśrī is represented as riding on an animal that looks much more like an enormous dog than like a lion. Indeed, under Manchu dynasty the Chinese actually succeeded in breeding a dog that looked like a lion. This was the famous 'lion-dog', in the West better known as the Pekingese, after its place of origin. These dogs were semi-sacred, and could be kept only by the emperor, who was regarded as an emanation of Mañjuśrī in much the same way that the Dalai Lama was regarded as an emanation of Avalokiteśvara. When the lion-dogs died their skins were made into chair-coverings for the imperial apartments, and I remember my father telling me that his step-father, who was present at the sack of the Summer Palace, had brought several of these chair-coverings back to England with him as souvenirs. Two or three decades earlier, however, the first pair of lion-dogs to be seen in the West had been sent—I believe by the celebrated Dowager Empress—as a present to Queen Victoria.

I had intended that these images of lions, and images of men in association with lions, should be the last that I would allow into this paper, but even as I was writing about them yet another image, from a completely different culture, positively forced itself upon my attention and insisted on finding a place here. Since it is high time we returned to St Jerome's study, and started considering the significance of the red hat hanging on the wall there, I shall do no more than mention this final instance of close association between man and lion. The image in question does not come from so far afield as the images from Indian and Chinese Buddhist culture, but it comes from a culture perhaps more alien in spirit. It is an image belonging to the myths and legends of ancient Assyria, as illustrated by the bas-reliefs preserved in the British Museum and elsewhere. The image is that of a powerfully built man, either a hero or a king, who stands with both arms extended to their full length, so that his body forms a Latin cross. In either hand he grasps a lion by the hind legs, so that it hangs down head foremost with its whiskers almost touching the ground. Once again man and lion are in close association, and once again man has subdued the lion. The red hat hanging on the wall of St Jerome's study is a cardinal's hat, that is to say, it is a round red hat with a broad brim over which red tassels hang down on either side. In more than one painting of St Jerome in his study it contributes a splash of vivid colour to what would otherwise be a sombre scene, sometimes piercing through the gloom with a rich ruby gleam. As I mentioned in the previous paper, due to his association with the reigning pope of his day, St Jerome was traditionally regarded as a cardinal, and when depicted in alterpieces and predellas along with other saints he usually wears not only his red cardinal's hat but also his red cardinal's robes, so that what with these and his long white or grey beard and the large, richly bound volume he holds clasped beneath one arm, he is a colourful and picturesque figure. In his study, however, St Jerome puts aside his cardinal's hat and robes. Indeed, the robes are nowhere to be seen. Only the red hat hangs there on the wall, where the warmth of its colour harmonizes with the warm orange-tawny hues of the lion asleep at St Jerome's feet, as though to suggest that there is some kind of connection between the two. A connection, indeed, there is. In the same way that the lion represents nature, or the natural order, so the red cardinal's hat represents human society, or the social order. This social order has not actually followed St Jerome into his cell, or study, or cave, as the lion has followed him, because unlike the lion it is not really part of St Jerome and it is possible for St Jerome to separate himself from it in a way that he cannot separate himself from the lion. But though St Jerome has separated himself from the social order—though he has left Rome and come to Bethlehem, to the desert—there is a sense in which the social order, while not exactly a part of him, is nevertheless present in him. It is present in him as his capacity to function within the social order—a capacity which he continues to possess even when he does not actually exercise it. It is his social self, or even his group self. The red hat represents not so much human society, or the social order, as it is in itself, as this social self. For the time being it hangs on the wall. St Jerome hung it there when he entered his study, or cell, or cave, and he can put it on again whenever he chooses to leave his study and resume his rightful place in the world.

Originally, a cardinal was a priest in charge of one of the Roman churches who, as well as running his own church, assisted the Bishop of Rome, i.e. the pope, in the administration of his diocese. (At that time, of course, the titles of cardinal and pope were unknown.) Later, when the pope had become the ruler of the whole Western Church, the cardinals assisted him in the administration of his vast ecclesiastical empire and, though they were no longer responsible for the running of the Roman churches, on his appointment every cardinal was attached to one of these churches in a titular capacity—a practice which I believe still exists. Thus the cardinals were 'princes of the Church'. With few exceptions they lived in sumptuous style, in magnificent palaces, possessed great personal wealth, and wielded enormous political influence. Most important of all, it was they who elected the pope, and they usually elected him from among themselves. By the time the artists of the Italian Renaissance came to represent St Jerome in his study a cardinal was a very important person indeed, so that to be presented with a red hat by the pope was the eventual aim of every ambitious cleric in Christendom. All that was well understood by the artists of the Italian Renaissance, and sometimes the red hat on the wall of St Jerome's study seems to glow with a sinister and lurid splendour. In theory the deep crimson of a cardinal's hat and robes symbolized his readiness to shed his blood in the service of the Church, but only too often it symbolized the blood he had had to shed in order to become a cardinal—not to speak of all the blood shed by the Church in the furtherance of its interests and the establishment of its power. Seen in the light of these developments, the red hat hanging on the wall of St Jerome's study represents not just human society, or the social order, not just St Jerome's social self. It represents the worldly ambition whose realization the social order makes possible. When he withdraws into the cave, when he devotes himself to the work of translating the Bible, or to bringing what was hidden in the depths up to the surface, or from darkness into light, St Jerome not only separates himself from the social order and keeps his social self in abeyance. He also renounces all worldly ambition, especially ambition which wears the cloak of religion and professes to sacrifice self for others when in reality it is sacrificing others to self. He renounces all thought of doing evil that good may come of it (the image of St Jerome as I see it does not necessarily correspond at all points with the Jerome of history), or seeking to achieve spiritual ends by worldly or unspiritual means. In other words, the red hat hanging on the wall of St Jerome's study represents the fact that having subdued his lower nature so that it does not disturb him as he pursues his distinctively human activities man separates himself from the social order and its temptations, at least for the time being, in order to pursue those activities in ever higher and more refined forms.

After the red hat come the hourglass and the human skull. These usually occupy a small shelf along the wall from the hat, though sometimes one or both of them stand on the top of St Jerome's desk, which is not a modern desk with a flat top but a sort of reading desk or lectern. According to the dictionary, an hourglass is a device consisting of two transparent chambers linked by a narrow channel, containing a quantity of sand that takes a specified time to trickle to one chamber from the other. When the chamber is empty and the lower chamber full the hourglass is reversed and the whole process is repeated. The significance of the hourglass is obvious. It represents time, just as the skull represents death. St Jerome is translating the Bible. The Bible is a very big book, and St Jerome is a very old man, and he has no time to lose if the work is to be finished before his death. Perhaps he has set himself to translate so many lines of Greek or Hebrew text for every reversal of the hourglass. Be that as it may, when I started thinking of the image of the hourglass, as it stands on a shelf in St Jerome's study, I found that images of hourglasses from other cultures were far from forcing themselves upon my attention in the way that images of the lion had done. The only images that came to mind were the semi-human hourglass in one of Hieronymus Bosch's paintings of hell and the vague and shadowy figure of Father Time—complete with hourglass and scythe—in various allegorical paintings by artists whose names I could not remember. This relative paucity of images may have been due to the fact that in modern times the hourglass has been replaced by the clock, so that we are familiar with it only in the miniature form of the eggtimer, which measures not the passing of the hours but the two or three minutes it takes to boil an egg. Or it may have been due to the fact that the hourglass was not really ubiquitous in the traditions and cultures of the world (in many cultures its place was taken by the clepsydra or water clock) and that it was therefore not a universal image. Since it was not universal, and to that extent not truly an image, it was unlikely that images would arise when I reflected upon its significance.

But if images did not arise ideas certainly did, and I was soon made aware that if the artists had not often depicted Time in their paintings the poets had often alluded to him in their poems. Within a matter of seconds half a dozen well known quotations from the English poets alone had floated into my mind. The first to come were the pathetic and haunting lines from Marvell's 'To His Coy Mistress', where after pointing out to the lady at some length that if they only had more time at their disposal her coyness would be less reprehensible, he exclaims:

But at my back I always hear
Time's wingèd chariot hurrying near,

thus conveying in an unforgettable manner the feeling we get, especially as we grow older, that time is actually overtaking us. This was followed by Shakespeare's memorable couplet:

Like as the waves make towards the pebbled shore,
So do our minutes hasten to their end.

and by Raleigh's solemn lines, supposedly written on the eve of his execution:

Even such is Time, which takes in trust
Our youth, our joys, and all we have,
And pays us but with age and dust;
Who in the dark and silent grave,
When we have wandered all our ways,
Shuts up the story of our days.

After a brief interval came the lines in which the young Milton gives touching expression to the mingled surprise and regret with which he realizes that he is now twenty-three:

How soon hath Time, the subtle thief of youth,
Stoln on its wing my three and twentieth year.

From a much lesser poet, but one whom Dr Johnson esteemed highly enough to recommend his inclusion in the series of English Poets for which he was writing his 'little prefaces', came the verse:

Time, like an ever rolling stream,
Bears all its sons away;
They fly forgotten, as a dream
Dies with the opening day.

This is, of course, a verse from the well known hymn, 'Oh God Our Help in Ages Past', by Isaac Watts, which I remember singing as a boy at school in morning assemblies. It might be interesting to speculate to what extent this verse helped to instil into me the Buddhist idea of universal impermanence.

No doubt many more quotations would have come if I had let them, and no doubt I would have tracked down still more, and not from the English poets alone, if this paper had been written at Padmaloka and I had been able to consult my books. But even the half dozen quotations which floated into my mind when I started thinking of the image of the hourglass, all but one of which I have reproduced here, should be sufficient to illustrate the extent to which allusions to death occur in the works of the poets. It will be noticed, however, that in two, possibly three, of the quotations I have given time seems to be personified or semi-personified, while in the two others he is compared with water in motion. Marvell imagines him as borne in a chariot equipped with wings instead of wheels, Milton as being himself a winged creature of some kind (at this point the image of a winged hourglass I have seen somewhere flashes into my mind), Raleigh as an invisible presence that takes everything from us and gives us nothing. As for Shakespeare and Watts, the one compares the minutes of which time consists to waves that come surging up the shingle, the other to a river in constant flow. (Though Watts's hymn is, I believe, a version of one of the Psalms, in the verse I have quoted there may be a submerged reference to the Cronos of Greek mythology, who devoured his own children as soon as they were born.)

Thus we find in these quotations not only ideas but also images. True, the images are not so vivid or so concrete as they would be if represented in painting, but that is because of the nature of time itself. According to Plato, time is the moving image of eternity, and it is because time is something that moves that it is impossible to depict it in painting in a satisfactory manner. The best the artist can do is to represent time as a winged old man with an hourglass and scythe; but the wings do not actually beat the air, the sands in the hourglass do not actually trickle down, and the scythe does not actually mow anything. What has been depicted is not time so much as the objects that symbolize time. In the case of poetry, however, the poet not only describes time as winged, or as borne in a winged chariot, but, in so describing it, makes use of syllables and words that are not simultaneous, like the different parts of a painting, but themselves successive. In other words, the poem itself moves with the movement it is describing. Thus Marvell's 'wingèd chariot hurrying near' actually does hurry: it is not merely depicted in a state of arrested motion. Moreover, with the word 'near' we actually hear the downward beat of its wings and feel their wind on the back of our necks. In the same way, though perhaps less successfully, Milton's 'subtle thief of youth' actually does perform the act of silently filching the poet's twenty-third year: he is not merely depicted frozen in the posture of performing it. Much the same is the case with Shakespeare's waves and Isaac Watts's stream, which actually make towards the pebbled shore, or actually rolls ever on, in accordance with the movement of the verse itself.

From these examples it should be clear that poetry is better adapted to the representation of movement than is the sister art of painting, and therefore better adapted to the representation of time. Perhaps the reason why so few images came to me when I started thinking of the image of the hourglass was that I expected them to come from the visual arts rather than from the performing arts or those arts which exist in time rather than in space and which include literature considered as that which is not only written but also read, whether aloud or to oneself. Such being the case, it was not surprising that following on the quotations from the English poets there should come into my mind ideas about time from Buddhist literature rather than images of time from the Buddhist visual arts. It indeed would appear that in the Buddhist visual arts images of time hardly exist (the demon who grasps the Tibetan Wheel of Life represents impermanence rather than time), and that in Buddhist culture time has not been personified even to the extent that it has been personified in the Classical and Judaeo-Christian cultures of the West. The only really noteworthy personification of time that came to me from Eastern sources came not from Buddhism at all but from Hinduism. It came from the twelfth chapter of the *Bhagavad Gītā*, in the course of which Śrī Kṛishna reveals himself to Arjuna as Time the All-Destroyer, down whose flaming gullet disappears not only the entire human race but everything in the universe. But however deficient Buddhism may be in images of time it is certainly not lacking in ideas about time. Buddhism itself could be described as a meditation on time, or on impermanence (it could perhaps be argued that in Buddhism these two concepts are not distinguished in quite the same way that they are in the West), or as a reflection on the shortness and preciousness of human life. Allusions to time occur even more frequently in Buddhist literature, both canonical and non-canonical, than they do in English poetry, and if I was to reproduce here all the quotations that came to me from this source as I thought of the image of the hourglass they would take up a quite disproportionate amount of space in this paper. Let me therefore quote just one passage, as an example of the kind of ideas to which I refer. It is a passage from the *Sūtra of Forty-Two Sections*, renowned as the first Buddhist scripture to be rendered into Chinese.

> *The Buddha said to a novice, 'How long is the span of a man's life?' 'It is but a few days,' was the answer. The Buddha said 'You have not understood,' and asked another novice, who replied, 'It is (like) the time taken to eat (a single meal).' To this the Buddha replied in the same way and asked a third: 'How long is the span of a man's life?' 'It is like the time taken by a (single) breath,' was the reply. 'Excellent,' said the Buddha, 'You understand the Way.'*

Translating this idea into the language of the images and symbols of St Jerome's study, one could say that the span of human life is not a few days, nor even like the time taken by the sands to trickle to one chamber of the hourglass from the other, but like the time taken by the falling of a single grain of sand. Man therefore has no time to waste. It is not enough for him to pursue his distinctively human activities, not enough for him to pursue them in ever higher and more refined forms. He must pursue them with full awareness that time is passing, and in the knowledge that unless he works unremittingly he will not be able to bring them to a successful conclusion. If the hourglass is not a universal image the skull most certainly is. With its empty eye-sockets and its grinning jaw it is indeed one of the most universal and most powerfully evocative of all images, and its significance can be understood immediately. Having come from Rome to Bethlehem, to the desert, and having taken up the work of translating the Bible into the vulgar tongue at a comparatively advanced age, St Jerome is not only acutely aware of the passing of time but also aware of the fact that, for mortal men, the passing of time inevitably brings death. Time and death are inseparable, and for this reason hourglass and skull usually stand side by side on the shelf in St Jerome's study, where he can see them all the time and from whence they admonish him, in the words of one of those Classical authors that he loved too well, that art is long, and human life short: *ars longa, vita brevis*.

Since the image of the skull is so universal, it was natural that when I thought of it as it stands in St Jerome's study, where it is depicted with such grim realism by the artists of the Italian Renaissance, there should have come to my mind images of skulls and skeletons of every kind, from the skeletons that decorate Christian tombs to the garlands of skulls that hang round the necks of Buddhist Tantric divinities, and from complex images such as that of the medieval Dance of Death, Holbein's woodcuts of which I knew and admired as a boy, wherein death in the form of a skeleton dances with lord and with lady, with prince and with prelate, and even with the very pope himself—indeed, with all sorts and conditions of men, to simple images such as those of the pairs of dancing skeletons depicted on Tibetan temple banners and the pyramids of skulls heaped on battlefields by conquerors like Tamerlane and at the feet of bloodthirsty gods by the priests of pre-Columbian Mexico. So many images of skulls and skeletons in fact came crowding into my mind from the different traditions and cultures of the world that it is quite impossible for me to describe them all, or even to enumerate more than a fraction of them. Instead, I shall describe just one image, and this can be taken as representing the rest. The image in question came from the fourteenth-century frescoes in the Campo Santo in Pisa, which I saw two months ago in the course of my journey to Il Convento. One of these frescoes, which is by an unknown master, depicts the Triumph of Death, who is represented as a kind of female devil with a scythe which she directs against a group of young men and women sitting in a grove, while ignoring the pleas of those who regard death as a deliverer. More interesting still, in the bottom left hand corner of the fresco a party of fashionably dressed men and women on horseback, out for a ride in the forest, suddenly come upon three open coffins, containing the bodies of three kings, one of whom has just died, one of whom is in an advanced state of decomposition, and one of whom is no more than a skeleton. Beside the coffin stands the figure of St Macarius the Hermit who, pointing to a long scroll, reads the party a lesson on the vanity of earthly existence. One cannot but be reminded, in the most forcible manner, of the well known story of how the youthful Buddha-to-be, on driving out from his palace in his chariot accompanied by his faithful charioteer, was successively confronted by an old man, a sick man, a corpse, and, finally, by a saintly ascetic. As if to underline the resemblance, above the figure of St Macarius other hermits are shown living among rocks and trees, in caves and cottages, occupying themselves with simple daily tasks, spiritual exercises, and religious discussion. The significance of the 'Four Sights' seen by the Buddha-to-be, as of the corpses of the three kings and the figure of St Macarius, is the same as that of the skull in St Jerome's study. Confronted by the fact of inevitable death, man has no alternative but to devote himself wholeheartedly to the pursuit of his distinctively human activities in their purest form.

From the fact that St Jerome's study contains an object symbolizing time and an object symbolizing death, one might have thought that it would also contain an object symbolizing human suffering, and in a sense it does. It contains a crucifix. As we have already seen, when depicted in the desert, or as performing penance, St Jerome is often represented as kneeling before, or clasping, a rude crucifix. But when at the hands of the artists of the Italian Renaissance the desert turns into a pleasant Tuscan or Umbrian landscape, and the figure of St Jerome shrinks into insignificance, the crucifix either becomes so small as to be unrecognizable or else disappears completely. It is as though the artists who depicted St Jerome's anguish as he performs his penance in the midst of the countryside, or man's existential anguish in the midst of an uncomprehending and indifferent nature, felt that this anguish was enough, and that it did not really need to be duplicated by the anguish of the figure on the cross. When St Jerome is depicted in his study, however, the scale of the painting changes, and to the extent that the figure of St Jerome becomes more prominent the crucifix becomes more prominent too. Nevertheless, the artists rarely give it the degree of prominence they might have done, considering the central importance of the Crucifixion in the Christian scheme of salvation, and sometimes they do not depict it at all. Again it is as though they were trying to universalize the image of St Jerome in his study, and therefore wanted to universalize the various images and symbols with which he is traditionally associated. When they do actually depict the crucifix, which usually either stands on the top of St Jerome's desk, or hangs on the wall facing him, what confronts the saint's gaze, when he lifts his eyes from the volume that lies before him, is not so much a representation of the crucified Saviour as an image of suffering humanity. In withdrawing into his cave, or study, St Jerome has in fact taken the sufferings of humanity with him, and it is in order to help alleviate those sufferings that he is translating the volume that lies before him. Even though man may separate himself from the social order and its temptations, and even though he may devote himself to the wholehearted pursuit of his distinctively human activities in their highest and most refined, as well as in their purest, form, it is impossible for him to forget the problem of human suffering. Indeed, it is to solve the problem of human suffering that man withdraws from the social order in the first place.

The volume that lies before St Jerome and which he is translating is, of course, the Bible, and together with the figure of St Jerome himself, as he leans over it with slightly knitted brows, it naturally constitutes the centre of interest of paintings of St Jerome in his study of every type. As depicted by the artists of the Italian Renaissance it is no mere pocket volume but an enormous folio of practically the same dimensions as the desk on which, or against which, it rests. Sometimes it is closed, as though St Jerome was on the point of opening it and beginning his day's work, or even as though he would never be able to open it and that it was, in fact, impossible to translate. Much more usually, however, it lies wide open, and we can see on either page the double columns of black text enclosed, more often than not, within a colourful border of interlacing foliage, flowers, and fruit, from which peep out strange figures of animals and men; we can see the illuminated capital letters, some of them of burnished gold; we can see the figures of prophets, saints, and angels. In short, from the size of the volume, and the extent to which it has been decorated, we can see its importance. 'What you love, you adorn,' a very wise friend of mine once said to me, many years ago (he was referring to my literary style, which some of my more austere friends considered much too 'flowery'), and the fact that the artists of the Italian Renaissance adorned the volume that lies on St Jerome's desk shows that they loved it. But what did they love? Technically, of course, the volume is the Christian Bible, beginning with the Book of Genesis and ending with the Revelation of St John the Divine, for it is the Christian Bible that St Jerome is translating. But the word 'bible' (from Byblos, the city where the papyrus used by the Greeks for the manufacture of books came from), means book, so that The Bible simply means The Book. What the artists of the Italian Renaissance depicted—what they loved and adorned—was therefore not so much the traditional Christian Bible as the Bible in a more universal sense. The volume that lies on St Jerome's desk is in reality the book *par excellence*. It is the archetypal book. But what is a book?

The answer to this question can be found, at least by implication, in an image or symbol with which you are all familiar: the image of the Wheel of Life, particularly as depicted in Tibetan Buddhist art. The Wheel of Life consists of four concentric circles, the third of which (reckoning from the hub outwards) is divided into five or six segments, one for each of the five or six principal classes of sentient beings. In each segment there appears a Buddha of a certain colour, who bears in his hands an object that is of special significance to the things of that class or 'world'. The Buddha who appears among the animals, or in the animal world, is light blue in colour, and bears in his hands a book. This book is not a Western-style volume but one of the Indo-Tibetan type, that is to say, it consists of a stack of loose oblong sheets held between two wooden boards of roughly the same dimensions. Sometimes the sheets are connected by strings passed through holes punched at either end, two or three inches from the edge. These details are not visible in actual paintings of the Wheel of Life, but the object the light blue Buddha bears in his hands is clearly a book of the Indo-Tibetan type just described, and he is clearly offering it to the different kinds of animals by whom he is surrounded. The book symbolizes knowledge, both sacred and profane, for it is knowledge that distinguishes man from the animals, so that if animals want to become human beings they must acquire knowledge. Here by 'animals' is meant not only animals in the literal sense but also those animal-like human beings whose interests are confined to food, sex, and sleep, and who are devoid of knowledge in the sense of having no consciousness other than that of the sense-objects that confront them in the present moment. The reason why it is the book that symbolizes knowledge, rather than any other object, is that it is by means of the book—which is essentially a device for the preservation and transmission of information—that we are enabled to extend our consciousness far beyond the limits imposed by our own individual experience. By means of the book we are enabled to transcend time and space and to communicate with human beings living in other ages and other climes, many of whom are far more highly developed than we are. We are enabled to enter into their experiences, and to share their knowledge. Thus the book is the golden key to the treasury of human culture. The book makes us more truly human. Hence it is not surprising that the object which the light blue Buddha offers to the animals should be a book, as representing the means by which they will rise to the human level and enter the human world. Similarly, it is not surprising that the mighty volume that lies on St Jerome's desk should be not so much the traditional Christian Bible as the Bible in a more universal sense, and not surprising that the artists of the Italian Renaissance, when depicting St Jerome in his study, should have adorned it to the best of their ability.

But if the volume that lies on St Jerome's desk is, in reality, the book *par excellence*, or the archetypal book, what is it that St Jerome is translating? In what sense can he be said to translate at all? According to Christian tradition, which in this case is based on the facts of history, St Jerome is translating the Bible, and on this level there is no difficulty. St Jerome is translating the Hebrew of the Old Testament and the Greek of the New Testament into the Latin of what came to be known as the Vulgate. But if the Bible means The Book, and if The Book symbolizes knowledge, what is it that St Jerome translates, or in what sense does he translate? In other words, how does one *translate knowledge*? What does one translate it into? Obviously, knowledge can be translated only into knowledge, just as one language can be translated only into another language, so that if knowledge is to be translated there must be another knowledge for it to be translated into, just as if a language, i.e. a text in one language, is to be translated there must be another language for it to be translated into. Thus translation implies plurality, whether of languages or of knowledges, and to speak of translating knowledge is therefore to speak of different kinds of knowledge. These kinds can be differentiated either horizontally or vertically. Differentiated horizontally, knowledge is either conceptual or symbolic, i.e. either a knowledge of concepts or a knowledge of symbols or images. Differentiated vertically, it consists of a knowledge of sense-objects, a knowledge of ideas or mental objects, a knowledge of archetypes, and a knowledge of ultimate spiritual realities. Knowledge of the highest kind is identical with its object. From all this it is clear that knowledge is translated either from one mode to another, as when what was expressed in terms of symbols and images is expressed in terms of concepts, or vice versa, or when it is translated from one degree to another, as when knowledge of ultimate spiritual realities is translated into knowledge of archetypes, or knowledge of archetypes into knowledge of ideas or mental objects. Since the Bible on St Jerome's desk is the book *par excellence*, it follows that the knowledge which it symbolizes will be knowledge *par excellence*, i.e. knowledge of ultimate spiritual realities. Thus St Jerome is translating in the sense that he is translating knowledge of ultimate spiritual realities into knowledge of the archetypes, and knowledge of the archetypes into knowledge of ideas or mental objects, so that those who have risen no higher than the level of ideas or mental objects will be given at least some intimation of the existence of those archetypes and those ultimate spiritual realities and be inspired to orient themselves accordingly.

To be a translator in *this* sense is to be more than a translator. It is to be an interpreter: an interpreter of one degree of knowledge, or one level of reality, to another. It is to be, even, a mediator between different planes of existence or different worlds. A parallel to the figure of St Jerome as translator in this more exalted sense is to be found within the Buddhist tradition in the slightly earlier figure of the great sage Nāgārjuna, the Second Founder of Buddhism, who after retrieving the 'Perfection of Wisdom' Sūtra from the kingdom of the nāgas, where the Buddha had deposited it, not only propagated it far and wide but also expounded its teaching in numerous works of his own, thus inaugurating a new era in the history of Buddhism. According to Buddhist tradition, the kingdom of the nāgas is situated in the depths of the ocean, and Tibetan Buddhist art loves to depict the saffron-robed figure of Nāgārjuna, wearing the pointed cap of a master of the Tripiṭaka or 'Three Collections' of Buddhist scriptures, seated on a raft in mid-ocean and receiving the massive Indo-Tibetan type volume of the 'Perfection of Wisdom Sūtra' from the hands of the mermaid-like nāga princess who has brought it up to him from the palace of the nāga king, where it has lain concealed for more than a thousand years (according to modern historical research, more than five hundred years). Since the ocean symbolizes deeper levels of knowledge (what is seen externally as 'higher' is seen internally as 'deeper'), the kingdom of the nāgas symbolizes the realm of ultimate spiritual realities, and the significance of Nāgārjuna's achievement consists in the fact that he has made the knowledge of those realities accessible to ordinary human consciousness by 'translating' it into knowledge of ideas or mental objects—at least to the extent that the limitations of that kind of knowledge permit. Thus Nāgārjuna is an interpreter of one degree of knowledge, or one level of reality, to another. He is a mediator between the plane or world of the nāgas and the human plane or world, or between the world of the Buddhas and the world of ordinary, unenlightened men and women. He is a human—as distinct from an archetypal—Bodhisattva, mysteriously hovering between the transcendental and the mundane.

Besides providing a parallel to the figure of St Jerome, the more remote and legendary figure of Nāgārjuna as the retriever and propagator of the 'Perfection of Wisdom Sūtra' enables us to appreciate, perhaps more deeply than would otherwise have been possible, the significance of the image of St Jerome as the translator not simply of the Bible in the traditional Christian sense but as the 'translator'—or the interpreter—of one degree of knowledge, or one level of reality, into another. There are, of course, within the Buddhist tradition, other parallels to the figure of St Jerome as translator in the more exalted sense with which we are at present concerned. There is the figure of Kumārajīva, who was almost the exact contemporary of St Jerome, and the figure of Yuan Chwang, who lived about two hundred years later, both of whom in addition to translating Buddhist scriptures from Sanskrit into Chinese explained them in Chinese for the benefit of Chinese audiences. To the best of my knowledge, the figure of Yuan Chwang in *his* study, after his return from India, is not depicted by the artists of the T'ang and Sung dynasties with nearly the same frequency that the image of St Jerome in his study, after his retirement from Rome to Bethlehem, is depicted by the artists of the Italian Renaissance. I did, however, once see a block print (as I think it was) of Yuan Chwang seated cross-legged behind a low desk across which lies a long scroll on which, with brush poised and a thoughtful expression on his face, he is inscribing row after vertical row of Chinese characters—presumably the text of one of the sūtras he has translated. Paintings of Yuan Chwang on his way back to China are fortunately more common. One of the best of them depicts the great translator in the guise of a pilgrim, with robes girt to the knee, and a staff in his hand. His whole body is bent forward, partly because of the weight of all the books and images he is carrying on his back, and partly because of his eagerness to complete his journey. Neither the block print of Yuan Chwang 'in his study' nor even the best of the paintings of Yuan Chwang as pilgrim give us, however, any reason to suppose that the artists of the T'ang and Sung dynasties ever saw in either of these figures anything that would have enabled them to transcend the facts of the immediate historical situation and to transform the figure of Yuan Chwang into an image of universal significance. Whether they ever saw anything in any of the other famous figures in Chinese Buddhist history that would have enabled them to transform them in this way, by concentrating on one crucial and representative episode in their career, it would be interesting to inquire.

But perhaps we have strayed too far away from the image of St Jerome in his study, or cell, or cave, as depicted by the artists of the Italian Renaissance, and in any case it is time we started drawing together the main threads of this investigation. Before we do so, however, there is one more point on which I would like to touch. Speaking of the different kinds of knowledge, I said that knowledge of the highest kind was identical with its object. By knowledge of the highest kind I meant, of course, knowledge of ultimate spiritual realities or, in other words, knowledge of nirvāṇa or knowledge of Enlightenment, which is identical with its 'object' because, at this level of reality, the difference between subject and object no longer obtains. But all knowledge is, in a sense, identical with its object, since otherwise knowledge would in fact be impossible. Thus when one 'translates' knowledge of one degree into knowledge of another degree, as when one translates knowledge of archetypes into knowledge of ideas or mental objects, one is not only 'translating' the archetypes as, so to speak, objects completely distinct and separate from oneself. One is also translating them as, to some extent, identical with oneself. In other words, one is translating what one has experienced on one level of consciousness into terms appropriate to another level of consciousness. One brings what one has experienced on the mountain top down into the valley or, to change the metaphor, one brings what one has experienced in the depths up to the surface, from darkness into light. It is in this bringing down, or bringing up, of what one has experienced on the heights, or in the depths, of one's own being, and giving it concrete form, as St Jerome does when be produces the Vulgate, that the essence of creativity consists. St Jerome is therefore not only the Translator and Interpreter but also the Creator and Artist, and because he is the Creator and Artist he is the Individual, that is to say, the True Individual; for the corollary of the fact that all knowledge is, in a sense, identical with its object, and that what one translates is one level of one's own being into another, is that all 'translation' is essentially an individual activity and, in a sense, even a solitary activity.

It is because the Translator is also the Individual, as well as the Interpreter and the Creator, that the artists of the Italian Renaissance, in depicting St Jerome in his study, depict him as having no companion except the lion, who in any case represents his own lower nature. The fact that they depict him in this way is all the more significant in that it is at variance with both ecclesiastical tradition and the facts of history. When St Jerome left Rome and went to live in the Holy Land he did not go alone but accompanied by a number of disciples, prominent among whom were a devout Roman matron and her daughter who, between them, were responsible for the construction of the small monastic establishment in Bethlehem where St Jerome eventually settled and where he translated the Bible. It would not have been difficult, therefore, for the artists of the Italian Renaissance to depict St Jerome with these two ladies, thanks to whose generosity he was able to carry on his work, as well as with the various personal attendants, research assistants, and amanuenses upon whose services he was likewise dependent. Yet they never did so. Instead, they chose to depict him in a study that, except for a few significant items such as a red hat, an hourglass, and a human skull, was completely bare, and they chose to depict him alone. From this it is obvious that in depicting the figure of St Jerome what they—or perhaps they and their patrons—were in fact doing was working, whether consciously or unconsciously, towards the creation of an image of universal significance. What the artists of the Italian Renaissance depict is, therefore, not so much St Jerome in his study, translating the Bible, as man in the cave of his own heart where, having subdued his lower nature and separated himself from the social order, he devotes himself to the pursuit of his distinctively human activities. What they depict is man as Interpreter and

Creator, bringing up into consciousness what he has experienced in the depths of his own being and giving it appropriate expression for the benefit of all. What they depict, and what I have tried in this paper to show them as depicting, is man as a spiritual being who, in the shadow of time and death, strives to fathom the mystery of existence.

Buddhism and Blasphemy

IN COMMON WITH MOST OTHER PEOPLE, Buddhists in Britain have always believed that they enjoyed complete freedom of expression in religious matters and that punishment for such 'crimes' as heresy and blasphemy was a thing of the past. This belief has now been rudely shattered. In July 1977 the editor and publishers of the newspaper *Gay News* were tried at the Central Criminal Court on a charge of blasphemous libel. Both were found guilty. The editor, Denis Lemon, was sentenced to nine months' suspended imprisonment and fined £500; the publishers, Gay News Ltd, were fined £1,000. In March 1978 their appeals against these convictions were dismissed, although Lemon's nine month suspended sentence was quashed. Shortly before this, Lord Willis had made an unsuccessful attempt to have a bill abolishing the offence of blasphemy passed by the House of Lords.

English law comprises statute law and common law. Statute law is law made by the 'sovereign power', i.e. the Crown in Parliament. Common law is customary law based upon precedent. The statutory offence of blasphemy having been abolished in the law reforms of 1967 and 1969, Lemon and Gay News Ltd were prosecuted under the common law of blasphemy and blasphemous libel (written blasphemy), developed by judges between the years 1676 and 1922, which like the rest of the common law the reforms of the sixties had left untouched. The last successful prosecution for blasphemy had taken place as long ago as 1922, when W.J. Gott was sentenced to nine months hard labour for distributing *God and Gott, Rib Ticklers,* and pamphlets with similar titles, as well as for 'annoying bystanders'. (He died a few weeks after his release from prison.) It had therefore been widely assumed that the common law of blasphemy was a dead letter whose repeal was unnecessary because it was obsolete. This assumption has now been shown to have been mistaken. No unrepealed law is ever obsolete.

The trial and conviction of Denis Lemon and Gay News Ltd, and the failure of their appeal, surprised and shocked the British public. Meetings protesting against the convictions, and demanding the abolition of the blasphemy laws, were held in London and elsewhere. In August 1977 the Committee Against Blasphemy Law was formed, while in the following year the United Order of Blasphemers, founded in 1844 and since fallen into hebetude, was re-formed with the aim of publishing and distributing works which had resulted in blasphemy prosecution. At least half a dozen political papers and several student journals republished 'The Love That Dares to Speak Its Name', the 'blasphemous' poem by James Kirkup which was the cause of all the trouble. It was also republished by the Free Speech Movement, thanks to whom thousands of copies of the poem are now in circulation, some of them bearing the signatures of more than a hundred well-known persons. On 4 July 1978, the anniversary of the by now notorious trial, copies of a petition were sent to the Home Office by individuals who had collected signatures. The petition, which had been initiated by the Committee Against Blasphemy Law, deplored the Appeal Court's decision to uphold the convictions of Denis Lemon and Gay News Ltd for blasphemous libel. It also expressed concern at the possibility of the blasphemy law being extended to cover religions other than Christianity.

One of the main reasons for the widespread nature of the concern aroused by the *Gay News* blasphemy trial is the unsatisfactory and uncertain state in which the conviction of the two defendants has left the law of blasphemy, and the fear that it will once again be used to hinder the free expression of opinion about religion. Parliament has never defined blasphemy. In the course of the last three hundred years the offence has been interpreted by various judges and juries in widely different ways. Originally, the mere denial of the truth of the Christian religion, or of any part of it (e.g. miracles, the divine authority of the Bible, the doctrine of the Trinity, the Divinity of Christ), constituted blasphemy and could be punished with fine, imprisonment, and 'infamous corporal punishment'. Later (in 1893), blasphemy was held to consist not in the denial of the truth of Christianity but in 'indecent and offensive attacks on Christianity or the Scriptures or sacred objects or persons, calculated to outrage the feelings of the general body of the community'. Finally, at the hearing of Gott's appeal, it was ruled that the law of blasphemy covers material which 'is offensive to anyone in sympathy with the Christian religion, whether he be a strong Christian, a lukewarm Christian, or merely a person sympathizing with their ideals' who 'might be provoked to a breach of the peace'. Thus between 1883 and 1922 a change in the interpretation of the law of blasphemy took place. In 1883 it was necessary to outrage the feelings of 'the general body of the community'. In 1922 all that one had to do was to offend even a single person sympathetic to Christianity.

At the *Gay News* trial there was a further change in the way the law was interpreted. Ruling against the defence argument about intention, the judge stated that in order to establish that the offence of blasphemy had been committed there was no need to prove intention to attack Christianity, or to cause a breach of the peace. Blasphemy was committed even if there was only a *tendency* to cause a breach of the peace. Despite this ruling, the prosecution produced no evidence that the publication of James Kirkup's poem had in fact had any such tendency. All they did was produce a single witness whose evidence showed that the poem had been published and that one 'sympathizer with Christianity' had been shocked and disgusted by it. *This was sufficient to secure convictions.* The current interpretation of the law of blasphemy therefore seems to be that blasphemy consists in the publishing of anything that can by proved to have shocked and outraged a single Christian or sympathizer with Christianity. There is no objective criterion of blasphemy. Anything that shocks and disgusts a Christian or sympathizer with Christianity is blasphemous. Therefore, as the Committee Against Blasphemy Law points out, 'It is impossible to know in advance what material concerning religion could be found blasphemous. The main effect of the law is to inhibit free expression about religion in a way which is elsewhere thought to be completely unacceptable.'

This is a state of affairs that gravely concerns every Buddhist in the land. It is well known that the notion of a personal God, the creator and ruler of the universe, has no place in the Buddha's teaching, and that throughout its history Buddhism has in fact rejected the notion as detrimental to the moral and spiritual development of mankind. But such a rejection is undoubtedly painful to the feelings of a great many Christians and sympathizers with Christianity: it shocks and disgusts them. Under the present interpretation of the law any Buddhist bearing public witness to the truth of this fundamental tenet of Buddhism, whether in speech or writing, therefore runs the risk of committing the crime of blasphemy and being punished accordingly. Not only that. Any Buddhist publishing those sections of the Buddhist scriptures in which the notion of an omniscient and omnipotent Supreme Being, the creator and disposer of all, is actually ridiculed by the Buddha in terms which some would regard as being 'indecent and offensive' in the extreme (e.g. *Kevaddhu Sutta, Dīgha-Nikāya No.11*) also runs the risk of committing the crime of blasphemy—even though the offending words were spoken five hundred years before Christianity was born.

It will probably be argued that, whatever the law might say, or be interpreted as saying, it is in the highest degree unlikely that in late twentieth century Britain a Buddhist would be penalized for propagating his religion. Indeed, it will probably be argued that the very idea of such a thing ever happening is absurd. But is it? The Buddhist, as one whose freedom of expression is at stake, may be forgiven for doubting whether the idea is so absurd as some people think—or would like him to think. After all, as a statement issued in December 1976 by the National Secular Society pointed out, 'For the past fifty years whenever the National Secular Society has campaigned for a repeal of the blasphemy laws, we have been assured that this is unnecessary as these laws could never be used again.' Yet they were used again. Within the year Denis Lemon and Gay News Ltd had been tried and convicted, and the worthlessness of all the assurances that had been given the National Secular Society thereby exposed. Indeed, as the Society's statement went on to say, only a few weeks before the blasphemy proceedings against Lemon and Gay News Ltd were initiated, the possibility of invoking the blasphemy laws had been raised, on separate occasions, by the Home Secretary and the Archbishop of Canterbury. Even if no direct link existed between the pronouncements of these two personages and the initiation of the blasphemy proceedings, they certainly helped to create the climate of opinion which made the trial and conviction of Denis Lemon and Gay News Ltd possible and turned 1977 into the Year of the Blasphemy Trial.

The truth of the matter is that so long as the blasphemy laws remain unrepealed they can be used, and so long as they can be used the Buddhist does not enjoy full freedom of expression: he is not free to propagate his beliefs. Even agreeing that it is unlikely, even highly unlikely, that a Buddhist who publicly rejected the notion of the existence of God in terms which Buddhists, through the ages, have been accustomed to reject it, or who criticized the moral character of Christ as defective from the Buddhist point of view, would actually be prosecuted for the offence of blasphemy, the possibility of his being so prosecuted nevertheless does, undeniably, exist, and this possibility introduces into the situation an element of uncertainty that no 'assurance' can dispel. A Damocles will derive little comfort from the argument that the sword suspended above his head by a single hair is *unlikely* to fall. In any case, we probably concede far too much in agreeing that it is unlikely that a Buddhist would be prosecuted for blasphemy in this country. Lord Willis's bill for the abolition of the blasphemy law, put forward in the House of Lords in February 1978, was withdrawn without a vote after strong opposition from their lordships 'like the baying of distant wolves'. Clearly, there are some Christians who wish to retain the blasphemy laws, and presumably those who wish to retain them would not be averse to using them. This is hardly surprising. Christians have never been remarkable for their tolerance, and after the events of 1977 and 1978 no Buddhist—no non-Christian, in fact—can feel really safe so long as the blasphemy laws remain unrepealed. The baying of wolves, however distant, is not a very reassuring sound to more pacific beasts.

That the blasphemy laws will be repealed within the next few years is at least a possibility. The Law Commission is presently reviewing various aspects of the criminal law with the aim of codification, and since this codification necessarily involves the eventual abolition of all offences at common law it will have to consider blasphemy law. If as a result of the Commission's work the offence of blasphemy is abolished, so that the susceptibilities of Christians are no longer given the special protection of the law, Buddhists will have no cause for complaint. If it is not abolished, Buddhists, in common with other non-Christians, will have to consider their position and decide what action, if any, to take. Meanwhile, we cannot do better than try to make clear what the attitude of Buddhism is towards some of the more important issues raised by the *Gay News* trial, and this is what I propose to do in the remainder of this article. In so doing I shall not be concerned with the fact that *Gay News* happens to be a newspaper for homosexuals, or that James Kirkup's poem had 'homosexual' features. The editor and publishers of *Gay News* were tried, convicted, and sentenced for blasphemous libel, and it is solely with the question of blasphemy that I shall be concerned.

The first thing that strikes us in this connection is that for Buddhism there is no such thing as blasphemy. In fact Buddhism does not even have a proper term for blasphemy.[27] This need not astonish us. According to Christian teaching, blasphemy is indignity offered to God in words, writing, or signs. Since in Buddhism there is no place for the notion of God, it follows not only that for Buddhism blasphemy does not exist but that for Buddhists the very concept of blasphemy, and therewith of an offence of blasphemy, is meaningless. St Augustine remarks that 'in blaspheming false things are spoken of God himself'.[28] According to Buddhism it is not speaking a false thing of God to assert that he does not exist, so that from the Buddhist point of view a Buddhist's denial of the existence of God not only is not but cannot be blasphemy. (What would St Augustine have thought of the 'Death of God' theology?) Buddhists are therefore unable to accept that it is possible for them to say, or write, or do, anything blasphemous, and to subject them to the operation of a Christian law of blasphemy means forcing them to recognize the offence of blasphemy and, consequently, the existence of God. It means, in effect, preventing them from being Buddhists and forcing them to be Christians.

But even though the notion of God has no place in Buddhism, might there not be some highest object of veneration occupying a position analogous to that of God, and might there not be, for Buddhists, the possibility of blasphemy in respect of that object? The highest object of veneration in Buddhism is the Three Jewels, i.e. the Buddha or spiritually enlightened human teacher, the Dharma or teaching of the way to Enlightenment, and the Sangha or Spiritual Community of disciples practising the teaching and following the way. It is to the Three Jewels that Buddhists 'go for Refuge'. The Three Jewels are the embodiments of the highest values of Buddhism and are, as such, jointly the object of the highest Buddhist aspirations. Indeed, it is commitment to the Three Jewels—to the Three Refuges—that makes anyone a Buddhist at all. Even the material symbols of the Three Jewels, in the form of sacred images, volumes of the scriptures, and 'monks', are objects of veneration. In the case of Buddhism, then, might not blasphemy consist in indignity offered to the Three Jewels? Might not Buddhists be expected to be just as shocked and outraged—just as angry and upset—when the Three Jewels are blasphemed as Christians are when God is blasphemed? For Christianity, of course, the primary blasphemy is denying the existence of God. In the case of Buddhism it would hardly be possible to regard the denial of the historical existence of the Buddha, the Dharma, and the Sangha as constituting blasphemy. In order to blaspheme the Three Jewels it would be necessary to deny the existence, in them, of the attributes which make them what they are, i.e. it would be necessary to deny that the Buddha was the Perfectly Enlightened One, that the Dharma was the way to Enlightenment, and that the Sangha was practising the Dharma and following the Way. Such 'speaking in dispraise' of the Three Jewels, as it is called, is not unknown to Buddhism. Do Buddhists, then, react to it in the same way that Christians react to blasphemy?

The answer to this question can be found at the beginning of the *Brahmajāla Sutta*, the opening sutta of the *Dīgha-Nikāya* or 'Collection of Long Discourses [of the Buddha]', and it is perhaps not without significance that this sutta—in which the Buddha catches as it were in a great net (*brahmajāla*) the sixty-two (wrong) views prevalent in his time—should stand at the very forefront of the entire Pāli Canon. The scene of the sutta is the high road between Rājagaha (Skt Rājagriha) and Nālandā (Skt Nālandā), in the then kingdom of Magadha. The Buddha is going along the high road with a great company of about five hundred bhikkhus. Behind him come Suppiya the mendicant and young Brahmadatta, his pupil. Suppiya the mendicant is speaking in many ways in dispraise of the Buddha, the Dharma, and the Sangha, while Brahmadatta, even though he is Suppiya's disciple, speaks in praise of them. The same discussion is carried on at the rest-house at which the Buddha and his bhikkhus, and Suppiya and Brahmadatta, put up for the night. In the morning the bhikkhus tell the Buddha about the unusual exchange that has been going on between master and disciple. The Buddha says:

'Bhikkhus, if outsiders should speak against me, or against the Dharma, or against the Sangha, you should not on that account either bear malice, or suffer heart-burning, or feel ill-will. If you, on that account, should be angry and hurt, that would stand in the way of your own self-conquest. If, when others speak against us, you feel angry at that, and displeased, would you then be able to judge how far that speech of theirs is well said or ill?'

'That would not be so, Sir.'

'But when outsiders speak in dispraise of me, or of the Dharma, or of the Sangha, you should unravel what is false and point it out as wrong, saying: "For this or that reason this is not the fact, that is not so, such a thing is not found among us, is not in us."

'But also, Bhikkhus, if outsiders should speak in praise of me, in praise of the Dharma, in praise of the Sangha, you should not, on that account, be filled with pleasure or gladness, or be lifted up in heart. Were you to be so that also would stand in the way of your self-conquest. When outsiders speak in praise of me, or of the Dharma, or of the Sangha, you should acknowledge what is right to be the fact, saying: "For this or that reason this is the fact, that is so, such a thing is found among us, is in us."'[29]

How great a difference there is between ancient Magadha and modern Britain! After the suffocating atmosphere of blasphemy laws and blasphemy trials, of convictions for blasphemy and punishments for blasphemy, the words of the Buddha come like a breath of clean, sweet air. This is not to say that in the course of 2,500 years of Buddhist history Buddhists were always and everywhere characterized by the spirit of sweet reasonableness that permeates this passage, but that spirit was always plainly and unmistakably present, and its influence was sufficiently powerful to ensure that the history of Buddhism was never darkened by the enormities that repeatedly disgraced the blood-stained record of Christianity.

Now why should this be so? Why should Buddhism be permeated by sweet reasonableness and Christianity by ferocious unreasonableness? The Three Jewels are as much the highest object of veneration for the one religion as God is for the other. Why, then, should Buddhism react to dispraise of the Three Jewels in such a totally different manner from that in which Christianity reacts to blasphemy against God? Why should there be calm consideration of the truth or untruth of the matter on the part of the one, but shock and outrage on the part of the other? In order to answer this question we shall need to look a little more deeply into the nature of the difference between the two religions.

A clue to the difference, or at least a starting-point for its investigation, is to be found in certain of the Buddha's words to the bhikkhus quoted above. If they should feel angry and hurt on hearing outsiders speak against the Three Jewels, he warns them, or elated on hearing them speak in their praise, that would *stand in the way of their own self-conquest*: it would render them incapable of judging the truth or untruth of what had been said. From this it is clear that Buddhism is concerned primarily with the emotional and intellectual—with the 'spiritual'—development of the individual human being, and that the Buddhist's reaction to 'speaking in dispraise' of the Three Jewels must, like his reaction to everything else, be such as to help rather than hinder this process. In other words the centre of reference for Buddhism is man, that is to say, man as a being who, if he makes the effort, is capable of raising himself from the state of unenlightened to that of enlightened—spiritually enlightened—humanity or Buddhahood.

The centre of reference of Christianity, on the other hand, is God. Or rather, it is the dignity of God. The traditional concept of blasphemy is that it is indignity offered to God in words, writing, or signs, and as the reactions of Christians to the offence make clear, Christianity is concerned primarily with maintaining the dignity of God and preserving him from indignity. But why should this be so? Why should Christianity be so concerned with maintaining the dignity of God? It would be a manifest absurdity to regard speaking in dispraise of the Three Jewels as offering indignity to the Buddha, the Dharma, and the Sangha. Why is it possible to speak of God in this way? The answer to the question is not far to seek. It is possible because God, the supreme object of veneration for Christianity, is seen as the monarch of the universe (in recent times as a constitutional rather than an absolute one, however). Besides being the Creator of the world, including man, he is its Ruler and its Judge. He possesses in and of his own self absolute power, dominion, and authority. God is king writ large—a sort of cosmic Louis XIV or Ivan the Terrible, sometimes kind, sometimes cruel, but in both his kindness and his cruelty equally despotic.

Theologians trained in the subtleties of the schools will argue that such a conception of God is a travesty of Christian belief. But is it really so? Even a cursory study of Christianity as a historical phenomenon reveals that, despite the conceptual refinements of philosophers and theologians, the religious life of Christianity has always been effectively dominated not by any such abstraction as the Ground of Being but by the grandiose image of a stupendous Power vaguely conceived as somehow personal and as accessible to the blandishments of worshippers. Even now it is this image that looms, with varying degrees of definiteness, in the murky background of a great deal of Western—European and American—life and thought. Sometimes, as in the *Gay News* blasphemy trial, we get a glimpse of it rising behind the barriers of more recent concepts much as Flaubert's Carthaginians saw towering above the roofs of their beleaguered city the monstrous brazen statue of Moloch.

It is because God is seen as a sort of cosmic Louis XIV or Ivan the Terrible that offering indignity to him is such a serious matter—such a grave and terrible offence. Offering indignity to an earthly monarch is bad enough, for it is tantamount to an assault on his authority and as such undermines the whole government of the state. Loyal subjects are therefore shocked and outraged by it and dissociate themselves from it as quickly as possible, while the incensed monarch himself is swift to punish the guilty party with a horrible death. Offering indignity to the monarch of the universe is infinitely worse. It is an attack on the divine majesty itself, and as such undermines not just the government of a single earthly state, but the whole divine government of the universe, the entire established order of things. It is a bomb planted at the foundations of existence. Good

Christians are therefore not only shocked and outraged by blasphemy but also frightened. They experience a sudden sense of insecurity, as though the ground had given way beneath their feet. Consequently, they not only dissociate themselves as quickly from blasphemy as loyal subjects from high treason (once punishable in England by hanging, drawing, and quartering), but turn with hysterical fury upon the blasphemer. Blasphemy is theological high treason. The reactions of Christians to blasphemy resemble nothing so much as the reactions of the frightened subjects of a cruel and suspicious tyrant who, in order to demonstrate their own loyalty and avert any imputation of disloyalty, are ready to fall with savage violence upon the slightest manifestation of discontent with his rule.

The penalties for blasphemy have therefore always been severe. Under the Mosaic law the punishment for blasphemy was death by stoning. This precedent was followed by Justinian and the Merovingian and Carolingian kings, who also assigned death as the punishment for the offence, as well as throughout the greater part of Christendom. In France, blasphemy was from very early times punished with particular severity. The punishment was death in various forms, burning alive, mutilation, torture, and corporal punishment. Apart from an occasional pillorying, since the end of the seventeenth century the punishment for blasphemy in England has been fine and imprisonment. As the *Gay News* trial served to remind us, this punishment is still in force.

The offence of blasphemy being held in such horror, and the penalties attached to it being so severe, one would have thought that, once the nations of the West had been brought into subjection to Christianity, blasphemy would be virtually unknown. Yet, paradoxically, this was not the case. Open and deliberate blasphemy was of course extremely rare, but a tendency to blaspheme seems to have been quite widespread even in those periods when Christianity was most dominant, lurking beneath the threshold of many a Christian consciousness and threatening to break through in moments of emotional stress. Indeed, it was when Christianity was at its most dominant that blasphemy—or the desire to commit blasphemy—seems to have been most widespread. Early Christian ascetics, medieval monks, Counter-Reformation mystics, and Puritan divines, all alike confess to being tempted to commit the terrible offence, some of them in its most extreme and most terrible—because unforgivable—form, blasphemy against the Holy Ghost. As the seventeenth-century author of *The Anatomy of Melancholy* puts it, after painting a lurid picture of the blasphemer's state of mind:

They cannot, some of them, but thinke evil; they are compelled, volentes nolentes, *to blaspheme, especially when they come to church to pray, reade, &c such fowl and prodigious suggestions come into their hearts.*

These are abominable, unspeakable offences, and most opposite to God, tentationes faedae et impiae; *yet in this cause, he or they that shall be tempted and so affected, must know, that no man living is free from such thoughts in part, or at some times; the most divine spirits have been so tempted in some sort.*[30]

No man living is free from such thoughts. These few words tell us more about Christianity, and more about its real effect on the human mind, than its sternest critics have been able to do in volumes. According to Burton 'no man living', i.e. no Christian, is wholly free from the compulsion to blaspheme. But why should this be so? Why should any man in his right senses do the very thing from which he shrinks in horror, and for doing which he knows he will be damned—especially when the offence appears to serve no useful purpose whatever? By committing a murder he might ensure his own safety. By stealing he might enrich himself. But there is no possible advantage that he might gain by offering indignity to the all-knowing and all-powerful monarch of the universe, i.e. by committing blasphemy. Why, then, does he do it?

In order to answer this question we shall have to make a distinction between rational blasphemy and irrational blasphemy. Rational blasphemy is blasphemy committed as a logical consequence of one's own beliefs, whether philosophical, religious, or scientific. Thus a Buddhist, believing that no absolute first beginning of the world can be perceived, may deny that the world was ever created and, therefore, that there exists any such being as the Creator of the world, i.e. God. Similarly a Unitarian, believing in the unipersonality of the Godhead, i.e. that the Godhead exists in the person of the Father alone, may deny the Divinity of Christ and the Divinity of the Holy Ghost. Neither the Buddhist nor the Unitarian think of themselves as committing what Christians regard as blasphemy, and their state of mind bears no resemblance to that of which Burton paints so lurid a picture. Indeed for the Buddhist at least, as we have already seen, the offence of blasphemy simply does not exist, its place being taken by the very different concept of speaking in dispraise of the Three Jewels. *Irrational blasphemy is blasphemy committed as the psychological result of the Christian's own largely unconscious resistance to, and reaction against, the very religion in which he believes.* Whereas rational blasphemy is voluntary, irrational blasphemy is involuntary or compulsive.

Rational blasphemy is the product of a contradiction between the beliefs of the non-Christian and the Christian, or of the heretical Christian and the orthodox Christian. Irrational blasphemy is the product of a conflict within the soul of the Christian believer himself. Rational blasphemy is extrinsic, irrational blasphemy intrinsic.

The main reason for the Christian's largely unconscious resistance to, and reaction against, Christianity, is to be found in the restrictive and coercive nature of Christianity itself. Christianity is theological monarchism, i.e. God is king writ large. Because God is king writ large the prescriptions of Christianity are not, like those of Buddhism, of the nature of friendly advice freely offered—offered by the Enlightened to the unenlightened—to be just as freely accepted or rejected, but behests which, since they embody the will of the Almighty, are matter not for discussion but only for obedience. In the words of St Augustine, 'God's thundering commands are to be obeyed, not questioned.'[31] These thundering commands pertain to all aspects of human life, from the most important to the most trivial. As mediated by the God-instituted and God-directed church, they oblige the Christian not only to refrain from killing, stealing, and lying, which the state would have obliged him to do anyway, but also—at different times—to hear mass once a week, confess his sins to a priest, gives up one tenth of his income to the Church, fast in Lent, abstain from meat on Fridays, not work on the Sabbath, not play on the Sabbath, and not marry his deceased wife's sister. At the present day the obligations which weigh particularly heavily on the (Roman Catholic) Christian are those pertaining to sex and marriage. Roman Catholics may not limit the size of their families by artificial means, may not engage in any form of sexual activity outside (monogamous) marriage, even within marriage may engage in coitus only in the prescribed manner and for the sake of offspring, and cannot be divorced.

But the obligation which weighs most heavily on the Christian, and which has weighed at all times—the command which thunders loudest in his ears—is the obligation not to think, i.e. not to think for himself in matters of faith and morals. As Cardinal Manning is reported to have said, 'I don't think. The Pope does my thinking for me.' Instead of thinking the Christian is obliged to believe. He is obliged to believe what the Church—or the Bible—tells him. He is even obliged to be a Christian. In 1864 Pope Pius IX censured as 'one of the principal errors of our time' the opinion that 'every man is free to embrace and profess that religion which, guided by the light of reason, he shall consider true',[32] while in 1832 Pope Gregory XVI denounced as 'insanity (*deliramentum*)' the opinion 'that liberty of conscience and of worship is the peculiar (or inalienable) right of every man'.[33] Should the Christian refuse to believe what the Church tells him to believe, or even to be a Christian at all, the Church may use force to bring him to a right way of thinking, i.e. to make him believe, the opinion that the Church 'has not the power of using force' being another of the 'principal errors of our time' censured by Pope Pius IX.[34] That the Church rarely hesitates to use force when it is in a position to do so is, of course, a matter of history.

Since God's thundering commands as mediated by the Church deprive him of his freedom of thought and conduct, and force him to believe whatever he is told to believe, the Christian experiences Christianity as an immensely powerful oppressive and coercive force that threatens to crush his nascent individuality or, at the very least, compels it to assume unnatural and distorted forms. A compulsion to commit blasphemy is his response to this situation. Blasphemy, i.e. irrational blasphemy, is the reaction of outraged human nature against a Power external to itself whose demands are incompatible with its own capacity—its own need, in fact—for free and unrestricted development, that is to say, for full actualization of its moral and spiritual potential. Not that some of the demands made by this Power might not be, in respect of their actual content, helpful to the development of the individual; but coming as they do in the shape of commands, rather than as friendly advice, their form tends to negate their content, the medium to contradict the message. Only too often does God seem to be saying to the Christian, 'Love me as I love you—or else!'

Strong as it may sometimes be, however, the Christian's compulsion to commit irrational blasphemy—his resistance to, and reaction against, Christianity—remains largely unconscious. (If it became fully conscious he might have to face up to the fact that he was no longer a Christian!) After all, with his conscious mind at least the Christian believes in God, believes in Christianity. Perhaps, like the unfortunate Cardinal Newman, he believes in God but does not trust him, but that is another matter. Moreover, in some periods of history more than in others, blasphemy cannot be committed with impunity, and the Christian will be uneasily aware that, should he venture to offer indignity to the Almighty in words, writing, or signs—or even in thought—the whole monstrous machinery of repression would at once spring into action against him. This awareness is sufficient to ensure that any tendency to blaspheme is kept largely unconscious. When the ascendency of Christianity is undisputed and the Church able to call on the secular arm to enforce its decrees, or when the mundane interests of the twin 'establishments' of Church and State coincide (from the beginning of the thirteenth century the Church assimilated the crime of high treason against God to that of high treason against temporal rulers), the compulsion to blaspheme disappears from consciousness altogether: it becomes *completely* unconscious. Thus the conflict within the soul of the Christian deepens: the more oppressive and coercive is Christianity, the greater is his compulsion to blaspheme; but the greater is his compulsion to blaspheme, the more necessary is it for him to repress the compulsion. The only way in which he can resolve the dilemma—the only way in which he can give expression to his urge to blaspheme without bringing upon himself the fearful retribution—is by projecting it on other people. As Wolff says, 'Everything unconscious is projected, i.e. it appears as property or behaviour of the object.'[35] Or as Jolan Jacobi puts it, 'Everything of which one is unconscious in one's own psyche appears in such cases projected upon the object, and as long as one does not recognize the projected content as one's own self the object is made into a scapegoat.'[36]

In France and other European countries at the beginning of the fourteenth century many Christians projected their blasphemous fantasies on the Templars, who were accused of renouncing Christ and trampling and spitting on the cross, as well as of other enormities, and who were suppressed in circumstances of extreme cruelty, hundreds of them being burned alive. Similarly, in Europe and North America in the seventeenth century the same fantasies were projected on thousands of harmless old women who were accused of trafficking with the Devil and burned as witches. Even at the present time the soul of the Christian is not free from conflict. The compulsion to blaspheme is, therefore, still projected, and scapegoats are still made. One cannot help wondering whether the *Gay News* trial itself is not a case in point and whether some of the more fanatical supporters of the prosecution of Denis Lemon and Gay News Ltd for publishing James Kirkup's 'blasphemous' poem may not in fact have been struggling to repress their own unconscious resistance to an oppressive and coercive Christianity.

Though the conflict is deepest in the soul of the Christian, it should not be thought that only Christians experience unconscious resistance to Christianity and that, therefore, only Christians experience a compulsion to blaspheme, i.e. to commit irrational blasphemy. Between the Christian and the non-Christian there nowadays stands the ex-Christian. The ex-Christian may be an atheist or an agnostic, a humanist or a rationalist, a secularist or a Marxist—or a spiritualist or a Satanist. He may even be a Buddhist, i.e. a Western Buddhist. Whatever it is he may be, it can be safely asserted that despite the completely genuine nature of his conversion to the new philosophy and the new way of life in the vast majority of cases he has *not* succeeded in abandoning the religion in which he was born and brought up as completely as he would like to do and that, to some extent, he is at heart still a Christian. The fact need not astonish us. Christianity is not just a matter of abstract ideas but also of emotional attitudes, and easy as it may be to relinquish the one it is often extremely difficult to emancipate oneself from the other. The attitudes in question have, perhaps, been sedulously instilled into one during the most impressionable and formative years of one's life, and little as one may now believe in the monarch of the universe it is sometimes difficult not to feel uneasy when one is actually disobeying his commands—however wicked and pernicious one knows those commands to be. Not without reason has an atheist been defined as a man who does not believe in God but who is afraid of him!

In order to abandon Christianity completely—in order to liberate himself from its oppressive and stultifying influence—it may be necessary for the ex-Christian not only to repudiate Christianity intellectually in the privacy of his own mental consciousness but also to give public expression in words, writing, or signs to his *emotional* rejection of Christianity and the God of Christianity, i.e. it may be necessary for him to commit blasphemy. Such blasphemy is therapeutic blasphemy. Just as the ex-Christian stands between the Christian and the non-Christian, so therapeutic blasphemy stands between the purely rational blasphemy of the non-Christian and the irrational, compulsive blasphemy of the Christian. Therapeutic blasphemy is irrational blasphemy in process of becoming rational blasphemy, just as the so-called ex-Christian is in fact a Christian trying to become a non-Christian, i.e. an imperfect atheist, or agnostic, or (Western) Buddhist, as the case may be, trying to become a perfect one. An imperfect atheist, or agnostic, or (Western) Buddhist, and so on, becomes a perfect one to the extent that he succeeds in transforming his unconscious resistance to, and reaction against, Christianity into an integral part of his conscious attitude. Therapeutic blasphemy helps him to do this.

Christianity—including the Church, especially the Roman Catholic Church—has done a great deal of harm in the world. In Europe particularly, it has done more social and psychological damage than any other system of belief known to history. Crusades, Inquisitions, wars of religion, burning of heretics and witches, and pogroms are only particularly black spots on a record almost uniformly dark. It was because

Christianity did so much harm—because its attitude was so cruelly repressive and coercive—that the largely unconscious resistance of many Christians to the religion in which they believed, and their reaction against it, was so strong—and the compulsion to blaspheme so widespread. For the last two hundred years, ever since the rise of the secular state, the power of Christianity to do public mischief has been limited, but even in the twentieth century its capacity to play havoc with the private life of the individual—its capacity to inflict severe emotional damage on those who fall into its hands, continues unabated. James Kirkup, the author of 'The Love That Dares to Speak Its Name', was one of those who suffered in this way. In the course of a statement about his reasons for writing the poem which he gave *Gay News* after the trouble started, but which could not be used at the trial (such evidence being ruled inadmissible by the judge), he gave a moving account of his experience—an experience which could, no doubt, be paralleled by many other people.

When I was a boy, I suffered the misfortune of having to attend a Primitive Methodist Chapel and Sunday School. This dreadful place, like all Christian churches ever since, filled me with gloom, boredom, despondency and sheer terror. I heard the grisly, gory details of the Crucifixion for the first time at Sunday School at the age of five. I was so overcome by revulsion and fright that I fainted with the shock of those gruesome, violent images. When I heard of the fires of Hell and the torments of the damned, my horror expressed itself in outbursts of uncontrollable giggles, my knees shook, and I wet the floor. I, who loathed meat and could not even bear the sight of a cut finger, was informed that I could be 'saved' only if I were to be washed in the Blood of the Lamb—which my poor dear parents considered a Sunday lunchtime luxury. I could never take part in Holy Communion, for the very thought of eating bits of Christ's dead flesh and drinking cups of his blood made me sick.

Now I am convinced that young people with impressionable minds should never be exposed to such brutal, sadistic and violent obscenities, whether in church, in books, in the cinema or on television. I wonder how many children were utterly disgusted by Christianity as I was through the constant repetition of these inartistic, tasteless, and crude images.[37]

Having had Christianity inflicted on him as a child in the way he has described, it is hardly surprising that, when he grew up, James Kirkup should have written a 'blasphemous' poem. In so doing he did no more than Blake and Shelley—not to mention Swinburne, Hardy, and James Thompson ('B.V.')—had done before him, and for much the same reasons. Modern literature in fact is replete with 'blasphemy', i.e. therapeutic blasphemy, as through the medium of poem, or novel, or short story, or drama, or autobiography, writer after writer strove to rid himself of the incubus of Christianity and to awaken into the light of a clearer and cleaner day. Not that—except in a few cases—the writer set out with the deliberate intention of committing blasphemy. If, as sometimes happened, he or his publisher was prosecuted for the offence, more often than not he was extremely surprised. The blasphemy was simply incidental to his own free development as a writer and as a man.

But not everybody is a writer. Not everybody is able to purge himself of the fear and guilt that were instilled into him by his Christian upbringing in ways that are not only therapeutic but creative, even if it had not been a criminal offence for him to do so. What then is the ordinary man, the man who is not a writer or an artist—the man who is not a scholar or an academic—to do? In 1883 it was ruled that 'the mere denial of the truth of Christianity is not enough to constitute the offence of blasphemy' (a ruling that has since been superseded, blasphemy being now held to be whatever shocks or disgusts a single Christian or sympathizer with Christianity), and that 'if the decencies of controversy are observed, even the fundamentals of religion may be attacked.' Thus in deciding whether the offence of blasphemy has been committed the point at issue is not the matter but the manner. But can such a distinction in fairness be made? The ordinary man, being neither a biblical scholar nor a theologian, is in most cases unable to deny the truth of Christianity not only without engaging in 'indecent and offensive attacks' but also without engaging in 'licentious and contumelious abuse applied to sacred subjects' and without speaking or writing or publishing 'profane words vilifying or ridiculing God, Jesus Christ, the Holy Ghost, the Old or New Testament or Christianity in general'. If he has to observe 'the decencies of controversy' and is prevented from expressing his rejection of Christianity in the terms which come naturally to him—in terms which are, sometimes, the only ones available to him—he is prevented from expressing his rejection of Christianity at all. He is effectively silenced.

The reason why the law should permit attacks on Christianity which observe 'the decencies of controversy', but not those which do not observe them, i.e. which are expressed in terms of abuse and ridicule, is therefore clear. It prevents the ordinary man, who after all is in the majority, from saying what he thinks. A learned article in an obscure theological journal expressing mild scholarly doubts as to the validity of Aquinas's third proof of the existence of God would not do much harm to the established order of things. But were the ordinary man ever to rise up and proclaim in his own vivid vernacular his abhorrence of God and his utter detestation of Christianity and all its ways the result might be not only a religious but also a social and political revolution. When G.W. Foote founded the *Freethinker* in 1881 he therefore made it clear that the paper was an anti-Christian organ, and therefore chiefly aggressive, and promised that he would use 'weapons of ridicule and sarcasm' as well as 'the arms of science, scholarship, and philosophy.' Ridicule and sarcasm are comprehensible to a far greater number of people than are scientific enquiry, scholarly evidence, and abstract philosophical argument, and attacks on Christianity made with the help of such weapons are likely to be far more effective than those made without them.

It is just because they are so effective that attacks on Christianity which do not observe 'the decencies of controversy', i.e. which make use of the weapons of ridicule, sarcasm, and so on, are prohibited. The point at issue is not the manner rather than the matter of the blasphemy at all. The manner *is* the matter. Ridicule, sarcasm, and the rest are not so much a different way of attacking Christianity as a different kind of attack on it altogether. In deciding whether the offence of blasphemy has been committed, therefore, the real point at issue is not, in fact, whether it has been committed in a certain manner, i.e. decently rather than indecently, but whether it has been committed effectively rather than ineffectively. Ridicule and sarcasm are comprehensible to a greater number of people, and are a different and more effective kind of attack on Christianity, because they are as much emotional as intellectual in character. If one really wants to rid oneself of the fear and guilt instilled by a Christian upbringing—if one really wants to commit therapeutic rather than irrational blasphemy and from being an ex-Christian to become a non-Christian—then a vigorous expression of one's emotional as well as of one's intellectual rejection of Christianity is necessary. It is not enough to deny in private, as an intellectual proposition, that God exists. One must publicly insult him.

This is perhaps a hard saying, and many ex-Christians who are not yet non-Christians, whether atheists, agnostics, humanists, rationalists, or even Western Buddhists, will undoubtedly shrink from the idea of offering indignity to the Power which they were brought up to revere—and fear. Some ex-Christian Western Buddhists, in fact, anxious to show their broadmindedness, not only object to anyone criticizing Christianity but even go out of their way to speak well of it. Any attempt on the part of informed Eastern Buddhists, or less psychologically-conditioned Western Buddhists, to point out the shortcomings of Christianity, or defects in the moral character of Christ, or the absurdity of many Christian doctrines, or even the most obvious differences between Buddhism and Christianity, is met not with calm consideration of the truth of the matter but with accusations of 'narrowmindedness' and 'intolerance' and the assertion that the Christianity about which the critics are talking is not the 'real' Christianity. Such 'Buddhists' are still very much Christians at heart. Though attracted towards certain aspects of Buddhism, they are still afraid of the God in whom they do not believe, and not only shrink from the idea of offering him indignity but try to ingratiate themselves with him by speaking well of Christianity. Criticism of Christianity by Buddhists upsets them because they are afraid of being identified with it and thus incurring the wrath of the Almighty and, perhaps, the displeasure of the secular powers that be. In seeking to suppress or neutralize such criticism they are, in reality, repressing tendencies within themselves which, as yet, they dare not admit into consciousness.

The individual has a right to blaspheme. He has a right to commit rational blasphemy because he has the right to freedom of speech, i.e. to the full and frank expression of his opinions, and he has a right to commit therapeutic blasphemy because he has the right to grow, i.e. to develop his human potential to the uttermost. One who was brought up under the influence of Christianity—under the oppressive and coercive influence of theological monarchism—and who as a result of that influence is tormented by irrational feelings of fear and guilt, has the right to rid himself of those feelings by openly expressing his resentment against the Power that bears the ultimate responsibility for their being instilled into him, i.e. by committing blasphemy. Christianity is not the only form of theological monarchism, of course. Judaism and Islam are also forms of theological monarchism and those who are brought up under their influence often suffer in the same way as those brought up under the influence of Christianity and have, therefore, the same right to blaspheme. At the beginning of this article we saw that the Committee Against Blasphemy Law, in deploring the Appeal Court's decision to uphold the convictions of Denis Lemon and Gay News Ltd for blasphemous libel, also expressed concern at the possibility of the blasphemy law being extended to cover religions other than Christianity. The religions which, in the persons of their official representatives, have so far shown most interest in such an extension, are Judaism and Islam. This is perhaps as one might have expected. In the light of what has just been said, however, it is clear that it would be as wrong for the law of blasphemy to be extended to cover Judaism and Islam as it would be for it to continue to cover Christianity. There is also a practical difficulty in extending the law of blasphemy. Blasphemy is not the same thing in all religions, i.e. in all religions which recognize the possibility of such an offence. For Christianity it is blasphemy to deny the Divinity of Christ. For Islam it is blasphemy to assert it. Hindus are outraged by the slaughter of cows. Muslims are no less outraged if on the festival of Bakri-Id they are not allowed to slaughter cows. Obviously it would be impossible to extend the blasphemy law in such a way as to satisfy the contradictory requirements of all those religions that recognize the possibility of blasphemy or whose followers are capable of being shocked and outraged. In the pluralistic society that now exists in Great Britain the only equitable solution is not to have a law of blasphemy at all.

What the attitude of Buddhism is towards some of the more important issues raised by the *Gay News* blasphemy trial should now be clear. It should be clear that, so far as Buddhism is concerned, there is no such thing as blasphemy, and that so long as blasphemy remains a criminal offence Buddhists, like other non-Christians, do not enjoy complete freedom of expression in religious matters and are, in effect, penalized for their beliefs. For Buddhists in Britain, whether Eastern or Western in origin, it therefore follows that: (1) The law of blasphemy should be abolished altogether. It should not be extended to cover other religions. Buddhism itself does not, in any case, require the protection of any such law. (2) There should be a complete separation of Church and State. The Church of England should be disestablished. There should be no religious instruction (as distinct from teaching about the different religions) in state-run or state-supported schools and no act of religious worship at morning assembly. The sovereign should not be required to be a member of the Anglican communion—or indeed to belong to any Christian denomination, or even to any religion, at all. Reference to the Deity should be expunged from the National Anthem. (3) Blasphemy should be recognized as healthy, and as necessary to the moral and spiritual development of the individual, especially when he has been directly subject to the oppressive and coercive influence of Christianity or any other form of theological monarchism. Far from being prosecuted, it should be encouraged. If these suggestions are acted upon, some of the harm done by Christianity will be undone, Buddhists and non-Buddhists alike will be benefited, and society at large will be happier and healthier than it was in the Year of the Blasphemy Trial.

BUDDHISM, WORLD PEACE, AND NUCLEAR WAR

GAUTAMA THE BUDDHA GAINED ENLIGHTENMENT at about the same time that Cyrus the Great captured the city of Babylon and founded the Persian Empire. Five years later he paid a visit to his home town, Kapilavastu, just inside the modern state boundary of Nepal.[38] It was fortunate that he did so. A dispute had arisen between the Śākyans of Kapilavastu and their neighbours the Koliyans of Devadaha, to whom the Buddha was related through his mother, and, as a result of this, war was about to break out between the two peoples. The original cause of the dispute was comparatively trivial. Both the Śākyans and the Koliyans were accustomed to irrigate their fields with water from the River Rohiṇī, which flowed between their respective territories, but that year it was obvious that there would not be enough water for them both. The Koliyans therefore proposed that *they* should have the water, on the grounds that *their* crops would ripen with a single watering. This proposal the Śākyans flatly rejected, saying that they would have no mind to beg food from the Koliyans later on in the year and that, in any case, their crops too would ripen with a single watering. Since neither side would give way, the dispute became very bitter and eventually blows were exchanged. To make matters worse, the Koliyans started casting aspersions on the origins of the leading Śākya families, saying that they had cohabited with their own sisters like dogs and jackals, while the Śākyans cast aspersions on the leading Koliya families, saying that they were destitute outcasts who had lived in the hollows of trees like animals. Reports of these aspersions soon reached the ears of the leading families themselves, who immediately came forth armed for battle, the Śākya warriors shouting

'We will show the strength of those who have cohabited with their sisters!' and the Koliya warriors shouting 'We will show the strength of those who live in the hollows of trees!'.

Thus it was that, one fine morning, the Buddha came to know that war was about to break out between his paternal and maternal relations. Realizing that unless he intervened they would destroy each other, he at once went to the place where the two armies were gathered. As soon as they saw him his kinsmen on both sides threw away their weapons and respectfully saluted him. When the Buddha asked them what the quarrel was all about, however, they were unable to tell him. Eventually, after cross-examining various people, the Buddha succeeded in establishing that the cause of the quarrel was water. Having established this, he asked 'How much is water worth?' 'Very little, Reverend Sir.' 'How much are warriors worth?' 'Warriors are beyond price, Reverend Sir.' Then said the Buddha 'It is not fitting that because of a little water you should destroy warriors who are beyond price,' and they were silent.

Some features of this 'Rohiṇī incident' are only too sickeningly familiar to us today. They are, in fact, characteristic of disputes and wars from the Stone Age down to modern times. There is the same clash of vital interests between different groups of people, the same unwillingness to compromise, the same dreadful escalation from harsh words to isolated acts of violence, and from isolated acts of violence to preparations for full-scale war. There is the same fatal spirit of belligerence, the same readiness, on the part of large numbers of people, to fight without really knowing what they are fighting for. There is even, we note, the same irrelevant mutual vilification, suggestive of antipathies that have long lurked beneath the surface and now have an opportunity of breaking out. But there is also—and this is more encouraging—the same solitary voice of sanity and compassion that, if only we listen carefully enough, we can hear even today. There is the same appeal to reason, the same reminder of what is truly most valuable, that has been heard if not from the Stone Age than at least from the Axial Age, and heard, perhaps, with increasing frequency—regardless of whether men paid attention to it or not.

But although there are similarities between the Rohiṇī incident and the situation in which we find ourselves today there are differences too. The quarrel between the Śākyans and the Koliyans involved only the inhabitants of two small city states living side by side at the foot of the Himalayas. The quarrel between the superpowers of the twentieth century involves hundreds of millions of people occupying continents separated by vast oceans and it affects, directly or indirectly, the whole world. The Śākyans and the Koliyans were armed, like the heroes of Ancient Greece, with swords and spears and bows-and-arrows, and they fought either on foot or from horse-drawn chariots. The superpowers are armed with a variety of nuclear weapons, i.e. they are armed with a variety of weapons capable of destroying life on a scale not only unprecedented in history but not even imaginable before the present century. The Śākyans and Koliyans could actually see each other across the waters of the River Rohiṇī. They spoke the same language, even as they worshipped the same gods, and it was possible for one man to make himself heard by the warriors on both sides. Now it is possible for hundreds of millions of people to quarrel without actually seeing one another, and even to prepare to destroy one another without knowing, humanly speaking, who it is they are preparing to destroy. As for their all speaking the same language, they speak it neither literally nor metaphorically, even as they certainly do not worship the same gods, and despite our marvellously improved facilities of communication it is not really possible for one man to make himself heard by them all. Indeed, those same marvellously improved facilities of communication are used, only too often, either for the exchange of insults or for the reiteration of positions known to be unacceptable to the other side. Thus facilities of communication are used for purposes of non-communication.

Highly significant as these differences are, there is one difference between the Rohiṇī incident and the situation in which we find ourselves today that is more significant, perhaps, than any of them. Had war actually broken out between the Śākyans and the Koliyans there would have been the possibility of one side winning. No such possibility exists in the case of nuclear war between the superpowers. Even limited nuclear war would be so destructive of human life, and do so much damage to civilization and to the earth itself, that neither side could be victorious in any humanly meaningful sense of the term. Limited nuclear war must therefore be regarded as an absolutely unacceptable option. Full-scale nuclear war is even more unacceptable, if that is possible. Full-scale nuclear war is a prospect so frightful that no one with the slightest imagination can even contemplate it without an effort of will. All the deepest instincts of humanity recoil from it in utter horror. Full-scale nuclear war means nuclear holocaust, with hundreds of cities reduced to rubble, hundreds of millions of people burned or blasted out of existence, and millions more doomed to an agonizing death from the short- or long-term effects of nuclear radiation. Full-scale nuclear war means fire-storms and 'black rain'. It means the destruction of the ecosphere. It means the death of the earth. It means the suicide of humanity.

Nuclear wars are fought with nuclear weapons. If even limited nuclear war is unacceptable it follows that nuclear weapons are unacceptable too. Nuclear weapons must therefore be abolished. They would still have to be abolished even if there was at present no intention, on the part of the superpowers and others who have produced them, ever actually to make use of their dreadful destructive capacity. So long as nuclear weapons exist in the world there will always be the risk of accidental nuclear attack due to mechanical failure or human error—not to mention sudden insanity in one or other of the seats of power—and so long as there is the risk of accidental nuclear attack there will be the risk of full-scale nuclear war. Thus we are obliged to regard the very existence of nuclear weapons as being tantamount, in the long term at least, to the actual use of those weapons. Control of nuclear weapons is therefore not enough. There is no way of ensuring that nuclear weapons are not used, and that a nuclear holocaust does not take place, other than by making sure that nuclear weapons no longer exist. So long as the superpowers and the small powers have their stockpiles of nuclear weapons prevention of nuclear war is no more than a pleasant dream. Indeed, it is a dangerous dream, since it tends to make us oblivious to the very real threat to humanity that the mere existence of such stockpiles represents. There is no one in the world, perhaps, who does not want peace (what peace really is I shall try to explain later on), but if one wants peace it is important to realize that even in the very limited sense of absence of nuclear conflict peace is impossible without the total abolition of nuclear weapons. Working for peace therefore involves, to a great extent, working for the abolition of nuclear weapons, and working for the abolition of nuclear weapons involves working for peace.

Peace of course means world peace. Even if the Rohiṇī incident had led to war, and Śākyans and Koliyans had been killed by the thousand, hostilities would no doubt have remained confined to that particular stretch of the Terai. For thousands of years it was possible for some parts of the world to suffer all the horrors of what we now term 'conventional war' while others remained profoundly at peace. It is highly unlikely that anyone in Magadha knew that Cyrus the Great had captured Babylon until many years after the event, and equally unlikely that anyone in the Persian Empire knew that King Ajātaśatru had, shortly after the demise of the Buddha, defeated the Vṛiji confederacy, until long after that unscrupulous monarch had achieved his purpose. Even during the First and

Second World Wars there were countries that were not affected, to any serious extent, by the events that were convulsing the rest of the globe. On the contrary, in some cases they even profited from them. But peace is no longer divisible in this kind of way. Peace has become a seamless garment, and the world has either to wear the whole garment or go naked to destruction. There can no longer be any question of a scrap of peace covering one part of the world's nakedness and not another.

This makes it impossible for us to think in merely geo-political terms. We have also to think in geo-ethical, geo-humanitarian, or geo-philanthropic terms. Since peace is indivisible, so that the stark choice before us is either world peace or no peace, one world or no world, we shall be able to achieve peace only if we realize that humanity too is indivisible, and if we consistently act on that realization. In other words, we shall be able to achieve peace only by regarding ourselves as citizens of the world, and learning to think not in terms of what is good for this or that nation-state, this or that political system, this or that ideology, but simply and solely in terms of what is good for the world, or for humanity, as a whole. There can be no peace—no world peace—so long as the governments and peoples of sovereign nation-states insist on regarding their separate, sometimes mutually exclusive, interests as paramount and to be pursued at all costs. Nationalism is in fact the curse of modern history. It is nationalism that was responsible for the rise of sovereign nation-states, and it is sovereign nation-states that produced nuclear weapons in the first place, that produce and possess them now, and that have the power to unleash their destructive capacity upon mankind. Peace and nationalism are therefore incompatible. Nationalism is not, of course, the same thing as patriotism. Nationalism is an exaggerated, passionate, and fanatical devotion to one's national community at the expense of all other national communities and even at the expense of all other interests and loyalties. It is a pseudo-religion, an idolatrous cult that demands bloody sacrifices. Patriotism, on the other hand, is simply love of one's country, in the sense of an attachment to, and a desire to care for and protect, the place where one was born and grew up, and it does not exclude smaller or larger interests and loyalties, or honest pride in such things as one's own history and culture. Thus patriotism, unlike nationalism, is not incompatible with peace, even though peace goes beyond patriotism which, in the famous words of Edith Cavell, is 'not enough'.[39] This does not mean that in order to achieve peace we have to stop loving our own village or city, our own province, our own country, or our own continent, but rather that we have to love them because they are all parts of the world and because we love the world. It means that we have to identify ourselves with humanity, rather than with any particular section of it, and love humanity as ourselves. We have to feel for the different national communities, and the different ethnic and linguistic groups, the same kind of love that we feel for the different limbs of our own bodies.

Of this kind of love the Buddha, as he stands between the opposing Śākya and Koliya forces, is the supreme exemplar. The Buddha identified himself with both the Śākyans and the Koliyans, and because he identified himself with them both he could love them both. After all, even apart from the fact that he had attained Enlightenment and thus identified himself with all living things (not in any abstract, metaphysical sense, but in the sense of experiencing the joys and sorrows of others as his own), he was related by blood to both parties in the dispute. Through his father he was related to the Śākyans, and through his mother to the Koliyans. Among the warriors on both sides he had uncles, cousins, and nephews, besides old friends and childhood companions. Thus the Buddha's position was similar to our own. We too stand between opposing forces, though the forces with which we have to deal are as much superior to those of the Śākyans and Koliyans as the Buddha's sanity and compassion are superior to ours. Moreover, in our case we do not stand unambiguously between these forces but only too often identify ourselves with one or the other of them and are perceived so to identify ourselves. If peace is to be achieved, however, we have to identify ourselves with both parties, just as the Buddha identified himself with both the Śākyans and the Koliyans. Though we may not be related to them by blood in the way that the Buddha was related to his embattled paternal and maternal relatives, nevertheless we are related to them, inasmuch as we all belong to the same organic species, *homo sapiens*, and it should not be necessary for us to attain Enlightenment in order to realize this fact. If we identify ourselves with both parties and with humanity in this manner, then we shall be able to stand cleanly and unambiguously between the 'fell incensed points' of the mighty opposites of our day. We shall be able to speak as the Buddha spoke, because we shall love as the Buddha loved. We shall be a voice of sanity and compassion in the world. We shall be able to appeal to reason. We shall be able to remind humanity, in its own name, what things are of greater value and what of less. We may even be able to remind it what is the most valuable thing of all.

But between the Rohiṇī incident and the situation in which we find ourselves today there are, as I have pointed out, both similarities and differences. Some of those differences are very great, even if only in terms of scale. Though the implications of the incident are of universal significance, and although that significance has already emerged to a limited degree, it will have to be explored much more deeply if we are to appreciate the full extent of its applicability to the issue of world peace and nuclear war. In exploring the significance of the Rohiṇī incident in this way we shall naturally have to go beyond the immediate context of the incident itself. We shall even have to go beyond the issue of world peace and nuclear war, though not beyond Buddhism, and at least touch upon closely related issues of even greater consequence to every individual human being and, in fact, to mankind as a whole. We shall have to touch upon issues on account of which the issue of world peace and nuclear war itself is of such overwhelming importance. In other words, we shall have to touch upon questions of ultimate significance for every 'rational animal' or 'thinking reed'.

Now what I have already said on the subject of Buddhism, world peace, and nuclear war, as well as what I am going to say, all rests on a single assumption. Some people would regard it as a very big assumption indeed, but I nevertheless hope it is an assumption you share with me, since otherwise it will be difficult for us to explore together the significance of the Rohiṇī incident in the way that I have proposed. Indeed, it might even be useless for us to do so. The assumption to which I refer is the assumption that nuclear war, particularly full-scale nuclear war and nuclear holocaust, is not inevitable. It is the assumption that nuclear weapons can be abolished and world peace, in the sense of the absence of nuclear conflict, achieved. If that was not my assumption I would not be wasting my time and yours by talking to you this evening. Admittedly the risk of nuclear war is very great. Admittedly world peace is very difficult to achieve. But as we contemplate the possibility—perhaps the increasing possibility—of nuclear holocaust we should not allow the sheer horror of the prospect to reduce us to inaction, like frightened rabbits mesmerized into immobility by the headlights of an approaching car. Neither should we allow ourselves to be seduced by the united siren voices of fanaticism, fundamentalism, and fatalism as they seek to assure us that nuclear holocaust is in fact the prophesied Armageddon and that instead of trying to avert it we should welcome it as the righteous judgement of an angry God on sinful humanity. Whatever other religions may believe, Buddhism, like secular humanism, believes that ills created by man—and many not created by man—can be remedied by man. This does not mean that it underestimates the difficulties involved, least of all those which stand in the way of the achievement of world peace through the abolition of nuclear weapons, and it certainly does not mean that it subscribes to the shallow optimism of which some forms of secular humanism have been guilty.

But it is time we returned to the figure of the Buddha, as he stands between the opposing Śākya and Koliya forces, and began our deeper exploration of the significance of that sublime incident as it applies to the situation in which we find ourselves today. One of the things that strikes us as we look at the pro-peace, anti-nuclear movement is that it is not a strong and unified body of opinion speaking with one voice about what has to be achieved and the means to its achievement. It is not a movement at all, so much as a motley collection of forces eddying more or less confusedly about matters of growing popular concern. Some of these forces even seem to be moving in contrary directions, as we can see in the case of the great debate as to whether nuclear disarmament should be unilateral or multilateral. All such differences are, of course, differences about means rather than ends. What the solitary figure, and solitary voice, of the Buddha serves to remind us of is the fact that if we are to speak of the opposing forces of our own day with any effect we have to speak to them as one man. We have to speak with one voice: we all have to say the same thing. At present our energies are divided to far too great an extent. Time that should be spent impressing upon the authorities that what we desire above all things is the total abolition of nuclear weapons is spent arguing with one another about the exact way in which they should be abolished—thus letting the authorities off the hook. The authorities in question are, of course, the governments of the various sovereign nation-states which possess, or are about to possess, nuclear weapons, including the government of this country. The way in which nuclear weapons are abolished is a matter of secondary importance, and one that can be finally settled only at international level, when the governments of nuclear and non-nuclear powers alike meet together and, in response to the irresistible pressure of world opinion, apply such wisdom as they collectively possess to the question of how best to lift the shadow of nuclear weapons and nuclear war from mankind. Until then we must simply keep up the pressure, firstly on our own government, and secondly on the governments of other countries to whatever extent we can. Such pressure should be massive, unanimous, and unmistakable, and we should keep it up until we see governments in general, and the

governments of the nuclear powers in particular, making the total abolition of nuclear weapons their top priority. We should keep it up until we
see the nuclear stockpiles dwindling. We should keep it up until the
abomination of nuclear weapons disappears from the face of the earth,
and mankind can breathe freely once again.

There are a number of ways in which we can bring pressure on a
government to take steps towards the abolition of nuclear weapons, but
which ones we adopt will depend on the kind of government with which
we are dealing, as well as on the political and cultural history of the
country concerned, and even on the psychological make-up of its people.
Where parliamentary democracy prevails, and governments are elected
by popular vote, it will be possible to bring pressure to bear simply by
refusing to vote for any party, or any candidate, not unambiguously
committed to working for the total abolition of nuclear weapons. Pressure can also be brought to bear by the persistent lobbying of members
of parliament, by the presentation of petitions, by public meetings,
marches, and demonstrations, by fasts and solemn vigils—even by 'love-
ins' and 'be-ins'. By these and similar means the government should be
left in no doubt as to what the wishes of the electorate really are. If it
remains unresponsive to those wishes, or not sufficiently responsive—
and the situation is one of extreme urgency, where every day is precious—
then more serious measures should be taken and pressure brought to bear
on the government by means of mass civil disobedience along Gandhian
lines.

About one thing, however, we must be quite clear. In whatever way
pressure is brought on a government to make the abolition of nuclear
weapons its top priority, that pressure must be brought non-violently.
Violence of any kind would be totally out of place on a march, or at a
demonstration, or in connection with any other such expression of public
opinion, the purpose of which was, ultimately, the achievement of world
peace. The dove is not a bird of prey, and should what purported to be a
dove be seen with bleeding flesh in its beak and claws one would rightly
suspect that it was not a dove at all but belonged to some more ferocious
species. Besides adopting only such means of bringing pressure on the
government as are compatible with strict non-violence, we should also
avoid wasting time and energy on empty gestures that have no other
purpose than to give expression to purely personal feelings of resentment
and frustration—feelings which have, more often than not, no real connection with the issue with which we are supposedly concerned. Similarly, we should resist any temptation to use pro-peace, anti-nuclear

activities for the furtherance of any sectional interests, however important to us personally those interests may be, and regardless of whether they are of a social, a party political, or an ideological nature. There must be no attempt to hijack the peace express. The abolition of nuclear weapons is of such transcendent importance for the future of humanity that, whether the pressure we are able to bring on governments is great or small, we cannot allow it to be weakened by any doubts as to the true nature of the interests on behalf of which it is being exerted. To weaken it in this way would be in the highest degree irresponsible, and a betrayal of the trust of mankind.

Keeping up the pressure on our own and other governments until nuclear weapons are abolished is not the only thing that must be done, though it is probably the most crucial. Indeed, it is not only on governments that pressure must be brought to bear. We also need to bring it to bear on our fellow world citizens, and in particular on other members of our own national community. Here too pressure can be brought to bear in a number or ways, mainly by disseminating information about the danger of full-scale nuclear war and by helping people to develop a more positive attitude towards other national communities—especially if they too happen to possess nuclear weapons. Information about the danger of nuclear war, and about what the consequences of nuclear war would be for civilization, for the human race, and for life on this planet, should be disseminated as widely as possible and by whatever means. Such information is now readily available. It can be disseminated by means of the written or spoken word, as well as audio-visually. More specifically, we can write books and articles, make speeches, show films, hand out leaflets, put up posters, and buttonhole friends, acquaintances, and perfect strangers in pubs and at parties, on buses and trains, at our places of work, and even in the street. Those of us who have access to press, radio, and television are particularly well placed to disseminate information and have a special responsibility to do so. People can be helped to develop a more positive attitude towards other national communities by being encouraged to learn more about them. Knowledge will lead to understanding, understanding to sympathy, and sympathy to love. To be more specific here too, we can encourage people to study the history and culture of other countries, to read translations of their literature, and to learn their language. We can also encourage them to visit those countries for the purpose of business or pleasure, or for the sake of cultural exchange, and to develop personal friendships with as many of their nationals as circumstances permit. Above all, perhaps, we can teach people to practise the *mettā bhāvana*, or 'development of (universal) friendliness', a traditional Buddhist method of developing an increasingly positive attitude towards all other living beings, including those persons with whom ordinarily we do not get on very well, or whom we may dislike or even hate. It is one of the fundamental postulates of Buddhism that the individual is responsible for his own mental and emotional states. This means that he can change those states—provided he really wants to do so and provided he knows the right way to go about it. If people were to take up the practice of the *mettā bhāvana* in sufficiently large numbers it could result in the development of a more positive attitude towards other national communities not only on the part of private citizens but on the part of governments too, and this would undoubtedly contribute to the reduction of international tension and thereby to the eventual abolition of nuclear weapons. Those of us who are Buddhists should, perhaps, give serious consideration to the possibility of our teaching the *mettā bhāvana* on a nation-wide scale.

In bringing pressure to bear on governments and on our fellow world citizens we should not, of course, forget to bring pressure to bear on our own selves. That we bring it to bear on our own selves is presupposed by the fact that we bring it to bear on others, since we can hardly expect others to disseminate information about the danger of nuclear weapons or to develop a more positive attitude towards other national communities unless we ourselves are prepared to do likewise. Those who take any sort of initiative, or give any sort of lead, should in fact be prepared to do more than they ask others to do. It is not enough simply to take the initiative, or give a lead. One must also set an example (setting an example indeed is the best way of taking the initiative, or of giving a lead), and in the present instance the example that is set has to be a very lofty one. It has to be an example of impartiality and detachment, an example of love for humanity as a whole, an example of genuine devotion to the achievement of world peace by non-violent means. It has to be an example of a sanity and compassion which, though it may fall very far short of the sanity and compassion of Enlightenment, is yet more nearly commensurate to the strength of the opposing forces between which we stand, and with which we have to deal, than is at present the case.

This brings us back to the figure of the Buddha, and to another turning in our deeper exploration of the significance of the Rohiṇī incident in relation to the situation in which we find ourselves today. Besides the fact that it does not speak with one voice, what strikes us about the pro-peace, anti-nuclear movement is that its many different voices do not always speak the same language. When the Buddha asked the Śākya and Koliya warriors to tell him what the quarrel was all about they could understand the meaning of his question, and were eventually able to give him a reply. He in his turn could understand their reply, and when he went on to ask them how much water was worth and how much warriors were worth they knew exactly what he was talking about and could reply according- ly. Similarly, they knew exactly what he was talking about when he told them it was not fitting that because of a little water they should destroy warriors who were beyond price. There was no problem of communica- tion, as we call it nowadays. The Śākyans and the Koliyans, and the Buddha himself, all spoke the same language, both literally and meta- phorically. When the Buddha wanted to know what the quarrel was all about neither the Śākya nor the Koliya warriors denied that they were quarrelling. Neither protested that *they* had simply staged a peaceful demonstration on which the warriors on the other side had proceeded to launch a vicious and entirely unprovoked attack. In the same way, neither the Śākya nor the Koliya warriors attempted to argue that 'water' could mean 'earth' or that in the case of the warriors on the other side 'beyond price' really meant 'worthless', or that there was in any case no question of destroying warriors but only of *eliminating* them. Thus the Rohiṇī incident could be dealt with much more easily than the situation in which we find ourselves today, when the superpowers, unlike the Śākyans and Koliyans, do not speak the same language either literally or metaphori- cally and when, therefore, there is a problem of communication. In extreme cases, one superpower will even insist that the other superpower is saying no to a proposal when that superpower, no less emphatically, insists that it is saying yes. Such mutual miscomprehension would be laughable if it were not so tragic, and it is tragic because miscomprehen- sion as chronic as this between superpowers armed with nuclear weapons could well cost us our lives.

Since they do not speak the same 'language' it is difficult for us to speak to the opposing forces of our day in the way that the Buddha spoke to the Śākyans and Koliyans at the time of the Rohiṇī incident. It is even difficult for all those who are involved in the pro-peace, anti-nuclear movement to speak with one another, since what for one is 'pro-peace' and 'anti-nuclear' for another may be 'anti-peace' and 'pro-nuclear', so that there is no agreement even about basic terms and, therefore, no real unity and of course no really united voice. Thus there is a serious problem of communication, not only between the superpowers, and between the sovereign nation-states both large and small, nuclear and non-nuclear, but also within the peace movement itself, as well as between the super-powers and other sovereign nation-states, on the one hand, and the peace movement on the other. There is also, of course, a problem of communication between the different races and religions of mankind, and sometimes this problem adds to, and complicates, that of communication between the superpowers. So chronic, indeed, has this problem of communication between the superpowers become that one is now faced by an actual 'failure' of communication (in the sense in which one speaks of a failure of electricity) between large and important sections of the human race, and unless this 'failure' can be overcome and communication restored—unless humanity, especially the superpowers, can learn to speak a genuinely common 'language'—world peace will be very difficult to achieve and nuclear war very difficult to avoid.

We shall be able to overcome this failure of communication, however, only if we can understand on what it is really based. There is a lot that could be said on this topic, as well as on the topic of communication in general, but let us go straight to the heart of the matter without wasting time either on the commonplaces of the encounter group or the subtleties of the communications theory seminar. The failure of communication which is so striking a feature of our times is based, ultimately, on a breakdown of the notion of objective truth, that is to say, on a breakdown of the notion that truth is truth regardless of our subjective feelings about it and regardless of the way in which it affects our personal interests. That people do not, in practice, exhibit total loyalty to the notion of objective truth, even though they may uphold it in theory, is of course well known and widely accepted. Indeed, in the ordinary transactions of life due allowance is generally made for this fact. We no more expect the used car dealer or the estate agent to dwell as much on the less favourable features of the car, or the house, he is trying to sell us than we expect him to tell us a deliberate, downright lie. But even if people do not, in practice, exhibit total loyalty to the notion of objective truth, it is important that such loyalty as they do display to it is not allowed to fall below a certain point, since otherwise the transactions of ordinary life will become impossible. Unfortunately, it often does fall below that point. Loyalty to the notion of objective truth becomes *selective*. Actual lies may not be told, but those facts which are not in accordance with the feelings and interests of this or that individual or group are increasingly ignored, mis-represented, distorted, and suppressed. In extreme cases such facts are not allowed ever to have existed at all. From the stage where loyalty to the notion of objective truth becomes selective—that is to say, becomes that which is in accordance with certain personal or sectional interests—it is not a very big step to the stage where that which is in accordance with those interests becomes the truth. At this stage, therefore, there is a breakdown of the notion of objective truth. 'Truth' is whatever happens to be in accordance with the interests of a particular class, sovereign nation-state, or ideology. Since there are many classes, sovereign nation-states, and ideologies, and therefore many different, even conflicting, interests, there will be not one truth but many truths. Thus there is not only a breakdown of the notion of objective truth but also a substitution of the notion of objective truth by the notion of subjective truth. Subjective truth in effect becomes, for a particular group, objective truth, and since there can be only one objective truth the objective truth of all other groups—including what might be termed objectively objective truth—necessarily becomes untruth. Under these circumstances communication is impossible. Words no longer have the same meaning for everybody, and what one group regards as facts another regards as non-facts. There is a 'failure' of communication. Indeed, those whose views and attitudes are not in accordance with the interests of a particular group are treated as non-individuals in the same way that facts that are not in accordance with these same interests are regarded as non-facts. Such an individual is not so much wrong as, in theory, non-existent, and since he is non-existent in theory it is only natural that he should very quickly become non-existent in practice too. Thus we arrive at a state of affairs such as is characteristic of the nightmare totalitarian world of George Orwell's *1984*, where the three slogans of the Party are 'War is Peace,' 'Freedom is Slavery,' and 'Ignorance is Strength,' where Newspeak is fast replacing Oldspeak, where history is being continually rewritten, and where a word from Big Brother can turn a person into an unperson overnight.

Fortunately, the 1984 which has actually come to pass is not wholly that of Orwell's grim foreboding. The nightmare has not yet come true to more than a limited extent. Nevertheless, the situation in which we find ourselves today is sufficiently alarming, and one of its most dangerous features is that we are faced by a failure of communication between large and important sections of the human race, particularly between the superpowers. As I have tried to show, this failure is based, ultimately, on a breakdown of the notion of objective truth, so that if communication is to be restored, and if the superpowers are to learn to speak the same 'language', the notion of objective truth will have to be reinstated in its former central position in human affairs. Only if the notion of objective truth is reinstated in this way shall we be able to speak to the opposing forces of our day as the Buddha spoke to the Śākyans and Koliyans, because only then will it be possible for us really to communicate with them. Only then will it be possible to ascertain the facts of the situation. Only then will it be possible for the voice of sanity and compassion to make itself heard at last. Only then will it be possible to appeal to reason. Only then will it be possible to come to an agreement as to what things are of greater value and what of less. Only then will it be possible to achieve peace and avoid nuclear war by the total abolition of nuclear weapons. Until the notion of objective truth has been reinstated in its rightful position all our attempts to communicate, whether with one another or with the superpowers, are doomed to end in frustration. Though people may visit foreign countries by the score, and develop personal friendships with the nationals of those countries by the thousand, in the absence of a common reverence for the notion of objective truth all this will be of little avail. The reinstatement of the notion of objective truth to its rightful position therefore ranks as one of our most urgent tasks. To work for the reinstatement of the notion of objective truth is, in the long run, to work for the achievement of world peace, for it is one of the most important conditions upon which the achievement of world peace depends.

But even if world peace, in the limited sense of the abolition of nuclear weapons, is actually achieved, and the shadow of nuclear war lifted from mankind, this will certainly not mean that we have solved all our problems. If I have so far spoken of the achievement of world peace and the abolition of nuclear weapons as though the two things were practically synonymous this was only because the avoidance of nuclear war is our most immediate and pressing concern. Though there can be no world peace without the abolition of nuclear weapons, abolition of nuclear weapons is far from being synonymous with world peace in the full sense of the term. Nuclear weapons are not the only weapons in the arsenals of the sovereign nation-states. There are many others, some of them hardly less horrible than nuclear weapons themselves, and even if nuclear war ceases to be a possibility these could still do irreparable damage to civilization and inflict untold suffering on mankind. If peace in the full sense of the term is to be achieved we shall therefore have to work not only for the abolition of nuclear weapons but also for the abolition of conventional weapons too. We do not want to abolish nuclear weapons only to find ourselves in the same kind of situation that we are in today, minus nuclear weapons. Neither do we want to abolish them only to find ourselves in the same kind of situation that we were in yesterday, or even the day before yesterday. Though it will undoubtedly be an unspeakable blessing to mankind, and an infinite relief, the abolition of nuclear weapons is by no means enough. Even the abolition of both nuclear and non-nuclear weapons is by no means enough. Peace in the full sense of the term will be achieved only when disputes between sovereign nation-states, as well as between smaller groups and between individuals, are settled entirely by non-violent means.

In order to achieve peace—world peace—in this fuller sense we shall have to deepen our realization of the indivisibility of humanity, and act on that realization with even greater consistency. We shall have to regard ourselves as citizens of the world in a more concrete sense than before, and rid ourselves of even the faintest vestige of nationalism. We shall have to identify ourselves more closely with all living things, and love them with a more ardent and selfless love. We shall have to be a louder and clearer voice of sanity and compassion in the world. We shall also have to bring to bear on the governments and peoples of the world, and on ourselves, the same kind of pressure that was required for the abolition of nuclear weapons but to an even greater extent. Above all, we shall have to intensify our commitment to the great ethical and spiritual principle of non-violence, both in respect to relations between individuals and in respect to relations between groups. Ever since the dawn of history—perhaps from the very beginning of the present cosmic cycle itself—two great principles have been at work in the world: the principle of violence and the principle of non-violence or, as we may also call it, the principle of love—though love in the sense of *agape* rather than in the sense of *eros*. The principle of violence finds expression in force and fraud, as well as in such things as oppression, exploitation, intimidation, and blackmail. The principle of non-violence finds expression in friendliness and openness, as well as in such things as gentleness and helpfulness, and the giving of encouragement, sympathy, and appreciation. The principle of violence is reactive, and ultimately destructive; the principle of non-violence is creative. The principle of violence is a principle of Darkness, the principle of non-violence a principle of Light. Whereas to live in accordance with the principle of violence is to be either an animal or a devil or a combination of the two, to live in accordance with the principle of non-violence is to be a human being in the full sense of the term, or even an angel. So far, of course, men have lived in accordance with the principle of violence rather than in accordance with the principle of non-violence. They could do this because it was possible for them to live in accordance with the principle of violence without destroying themselves completely. But now this is no longer the case. Owing to the emergence of superpowers armed with nuclear weapons it is now virtually impossible for us to live in accordance with the principle of violence without, sooner or later, annihilating ourselves. We are therefore faced with the necessity of either learning to live in accordance with the principle of non-violence or not living at all. Thus the possibility of nuclear holocaust has not only enabled us to realize the true nature of violence, by showing us what the consequences of violence on the biggest conceivable scale would be, but it has also given us a much deeper appreciation of the real value of non-violence.

It is because of this deeper appreciation of the real value of non-violence that we are able to realize what peace in the full sense of the term really means, as well as how the problem of its achievement is to be solved. Peace—world peace—is something we can hardly imagine today. We can hardly imagine a state of affairs in which disputes between groups and between individuals are settled entirely by non-violent means because all men alike are committed to the principle of non-violence and live in accordance with its precepts. Such a world, in which the principle of Light had overcome the principle of Darkness to so great an extent, would be a world that surpassed More's Utopia, Bacon's New Atlantis, Campanella's City of the Sun, and Morris's Nowhere as much as these dreams of an ideal world surpassed the real worlds of their respective days. Such a world would be a heaven on earth. It would be a world of the gods. But even the gods have their problems. Even if we achieved world peace in the full sense of the term we still would not have solved all our problems by any means. One problem that the gods have to face is the problem of leisure, or the problem of what to do with their time, and even though we have less leisure than the gods this is the kind of problem that faces us too. Indeed, it faces us in the still more acute form of what are we to do with our lives. It would be a thousand pities if, having achieved world peace in the full sense of the term, we were to make no better use of our time, or of our lives, than many of us do at present. In Tennyson's 'The Lotos-Eaters' the gods—the gods of Homeric Greece—are imagined as lying beside their nectar and looking over lands wasted by plague, famine, earthquake, and war, and on a human race subject to the painful necessity of wringing a laborious subsistence from the cultivation of the soil. It would be a thousand pities if, when we had solved the problem of world peace, the gods were to look down on a world that in many respects resembled theirs only to see us playing bingo or watching third-rate television programmes. Idealists—or cynics—

might even be tempted to wonder whether it was really worth while delivering humanity from the horrors of nuclear war only that it might fall victim to trivial interests and worthless pursuits. Thus even if we succeed in solving the problem of peace in the full sense of the term we shall still be faced—as we are now faced—with the even greater problem of what to do with our lives.

But even if that problem too had been solved, and we were living in a manner that was truly worthy of a human being, there would still be one problem that we had not solved. It would not be strange that we had not solved it, for it is a problem that the gods themselves, despite their nectar, are unable to solve. Indeed, it is a problem that no form of sentient conditioned existence is able to solve—so long as it remains merely conditioned. As we know from Tibetan Buddhist scroll-paintings of the Wheel of Life, there are six main forms of conditioned existence, or six main classes of sentient beings: gods, anti-gods, men, animals, hungry ghosts, and beings in states of torment. These six classes of sentient beings occupy the six principal 'worlds' or 'spheres', and these worlds are depicted as occupying the six (or five) segments into which the third—and widest—circle of the Wheel of Life is divided. The first (and inner-most) circle is depicted as being occupied by a cock, a snake, and a pig, symbolizing greed, aversion, and delusion, the three unskilful mental states that keep the Wheel of Life turning; the second circle is divided into two segments, one representing the Path of Light, the other the Path of Darkness; while the fourth and outermost circle is divided into twelve segments representing the twelve 'links' that make up the entire process in accordance with which one passes from one form of sentient condi-tioned existence to another. All four circles, and thus the Wheel of Life in its entirety, are supported from behind by a dreadful monster, whose four sets of claws are seen curving round the edge of the Wheel, while his scaly reptilian tail protrudes below and his bared fangs project over the top of the Wheel beneath fiercely glaring eyeballs and locks crowned with skulls. This dreadful monster is the demon of Impermanence, the demon of Death, who holds in his inexorable grasp not only the six worlds but the whole of conditioned existence, from the electron spinning about its nucleus to the extragalactic nebula receding from us at an unimaginable rate. He holds in his grasp the highest as well as the lowest heavens, the least evolved as well as the most highly evolved forms of earthly life, from the amoeba to *homo sapiens*. Even if we succeed in abolishing nuclear weapons, even if we achieve world peace in the full sense of the term, even if we live in a way that is meaningful and purposeful, we shall still have to face the problem of death. Whether we live in a hell or in a heaven on earth, we shall still see the demon of Impermanence, the demon of Death, glaring down at us over the edge of the Wheel.

More than that. The demon of Death glares at us not only individually but collectively. He glares not only at you and at me but at the whole world, the whole earth. Whether or not nuclear war is averted, we shall still have to die, each one of us; the human race will still have to go the way of the dinosaurs; civilization will still have to collapse, the earth itself will still have to come to an end, even if after thousands of millions of years. Indeed, the very solar system to which the earth belongs will come to an end, as will the galaxy of which that solar system forms part. All conditioned things are impermanent. Whatever comes into existence must one day cease to exist. Thus the solution of the problem of world peace and nuclear war does not really solve anything at all. We still have to face the problem of death. Even though the Buddha was able to prevent the Śākyans and Koliyans from destroying each other on that morning twenty-five centuries ago, he could not save them from death itself. In the case of the Śākyans, he could not even save them from an untimely death at the hands of their enemies. So thoroughly had his paternal relations been converted to the principle of non-violence that when, some years later, they were attacked by the King of Kosala, they decided to offer no resistance and were massacred to a man—thus giving us, for the first time in history, an example of personal—as distinct from political—pacifism.[40] It was not fitting, they declared, that the relations of the Enlightened One should commit the sin of taking life.

Not only could the Buddha not save the Śākyans and Koliyans from death, he could not save himself from death. Truth to tell, he did not wish to save himself from death or even to prolong his earthly existence to the extent that, according to tradition, he could have prolonged it had he been requested to do so. Forty years after the Rohiṇī incident, therefore, when the Śākyans themselves were dead and when the ashes of his two chief disciples, Śāriputra and Maudgalyāyana, lay beneath their memorial mounds, the Buddha came to the little wattle-and-daub township of Kuśinagara and lay down between the two sal trees in the sal grove of the Mallas to die or, in traditional Buddhist phrase, to enter into *parinirvāṇa*, a state as much beyond non-existence as it is beyond what we call existence. And having lain down between the twin sal trees, with his head to the north and his feet to the south, he did, at the age of eighty, die. No miracle intervened to save him. Having traversed all eight *dhyānas* or 'meditations' his consciousness came down to the first *dhyāna*;

having come down to the first *dhyāna* it traversed the first four *dhyānas* a second time and then, as it passed from the fourth *dhyāna* and entered *parinirvāṇa*, the Buddha died. His body was cremated, and the ashes placed beneath a memorial mound. The Buddha had to die, as we all have to die, and there was no resurrection, whether on the third day or any other day. In connection with the sublime scene in the sal grove the notion of a bodily resurrection indeed appears, if I may say so, a little cheap, as indicating an inability to accept the fact of death, or a clumsy attempt to negate the fact of death on its own level instead of transcending it. The Buddha had to die, as we all have to die, because he had been born, and because even for him there could be no exception to the rule that, birth having taken place, death must inevitably follow. Even his Enlightenment could not save him, any more than our knowledge, or virtue, or riches, or friends and relations, can save us. When the messengers of death come, willing or unwilling, ready or unready, Enlightened or un-Enlightened, we have to go.

Only too often we try to ignore this fact. We refuse to face the problem of death, as though we hoped that by our not looking at the monster with the fiercely glaring eyeballs we could ensure his not looking at us. We may even try to convince ourselves, and others, that it is morbid to think about death. The truth of the matter is that it is morbid *not* to think about death. Not only do we in fact know that we must die, but it is the one thing about ourselves that we really do know. However unsure we may be about other things, we can at least be quite sure of this. Not to think about death is therefore to deprive ourselves of the most certain knowledge that it is possible for us to have. It is to deprive ourselves of the one thing on which we can rely absolutely. Moreover, not to think about death is to deprive ourselves of the possibility of knowing what we really and truly are. Indeed, it is to deprive ourselves of our very humanity. All conditioned things are impermanent. All sentient beings are subject to death. Man is the only being (in the sense of the only form of terrestrial life) who is not only subject to death but also aware that he is subject to death. Man is the only being for whom death is a problem. Indeed, man may be defined as the being for whom death is a problem. For him to ignore the face of death, or to refuse actually to face the problem of death, is therefore to be untrue to his own nature. It is not to be a human being in the real sense of the term.

The Buddha certainly did not refuse to face the problem of death. He faced it, in fact, quite early in life. According to what became the standard traditional account, he faced it when, as a young Śākya warrior of the ruling class, he drove out from the luxurious mansion in which he lived with his wife and infant son and saw, for the first time in his life, an old man, a sick man, and a corpse. On seeing them he realized that although young, healthy, and very much alive, he too was subject to old age, disease, and death. He also realized that being himself subject to birth, old age, disease and death, sorrow and corruption, he sought what was subject to birth, old age, disease, death, sorrow, and corruption, and thus lived an unethical and unspiritual life. In other words the Buddha, or Buddha-to-be, became aware of the fact of death. He faced the problem of death. But there was another sight that he saw for the first time, and that was a yellow-robed wandering 'monk' who had gone forth from home into the homeless life. On seeing him the Buddha-to-be realized something else about himself. He realized that although he was subject to birth, old age, disease, death, and corruption, and sought what was of like nature, he could change; he could seek, instead, what was *not* subject to birth, old age, disease, death, and corruption, and thus lead an ethical and spiritual life. He could seek nirvāṇa. He could seek the Unconditioned. In other words, he became aware of the possibility of there being a solution to the problem of death and that the finding of that solution was somehow connected with the homeless life. Accordingly he left home, sat at the feet of various teachers, none of whom could satisfy him for long, practised extreme self-mortification, realized the futility of self-mortification, adopted a middle way, refused a half share of a kingdom, and eventually, at the age of thirty-five, sat down under a peepul tree at what afterwards became known as Buddha Gayā. While meditating he realized that death arises in dependence on birth, and that birth, i.e. rebirth, arises in dependence on craving, i.e. craving for continued existence on this or that plane of conditioned being. He realized that when craving ceases birth ceases, and that when birth ceases death ceases. With the cessation of craving one attains nirvāṇa, or the Unconditioned. One attains a state of irreversible spiritual creativity in which there is no birth and no death because in passing beyond the 'cyclical' and entering upon the 'spiral' order of existence one has transcended all such pairs of opposites. Paradoxically, though the Buddha had solved the problem of death he still had to die beneath the twin sal trees forty-five years later. But it did not really matter that he had to die. Because he had eradicated craving and the other unskilful mental states that make for birth, i.e. for rebirth, he had solved the problem of birth, and because he had solved the problem of birth he had solved the problem of death in the sense that he would not have to die again.

Thus the Buddha could face the problem of death when he saw his first corpse, and because he could face it—because he could look at the monster with fiercely glaring eyeballs without shrinking—he could also find the solution to the problem of death. In our case it usually takes much more than the sight of a single corpse to make us realize that we too are subject to death. It takes much more than the sight of a single corpse to convince us that death is a problem. In our case we are able to ignore any number of corpses, especially if we only read about them in the newspapers or see them on television. Even if we do become vaguely aware of the problem of death we usually hope, no less vaguely, that we can somehow solve it without having to solve the problem of birth, just as we usually hope, with the same vagueness, that we can somehow achieve peace without having to give up violence. In other words, we usually become aware of the problem of death only to the extent of hoping—or perhaps praying—for the impossible. So far as the problem of death, at least, is concerned, it is a true saying that 'What men usually ask of God when they pray is that two and two should not make four.' But now all that has changed. We have begun to realize that we cannot have peace without abolishing war. We have begun to realize that we cannot have birth without also having death. We have, in short, woken up to the problem of death. In fact, we have woken up to it to a greater extent than ever before in history. The reason for this is not far to seek. The reason is that we, the human race, are now faced by the possibility of full-scale nuclear war. We are faced by the fact that each one of us may at any time meet with a premature, painful, and horrible death, and that the whole human race may be destroyed. It is the realization of this frightful fact that has had, upon some of us at least, the same kind of effect that the sight of his first corpse had upon the Buddha. It has made us aware of the problem of death. It has made us aware that the fundamental problem is not the abolition of nuclear weapons, or even the achievement of world peace in the full sense of the term. The fundamental problem is not living in a way that is worthy of a human being in a purely material sense. For a human being worthy of the name, the fundamental problem is the problem of death, and the real significance of the possibility of nuclear holocaust that now confronts us is that it sharpens our awareness of this problem to a greater extent than has ever before been the case. The possibility of nuclear holocaust thus represents not only the greatest threat that humanity has ever faced but also the greatest opportunity. Formerly it was possible for some men to dwell in peace while others were at war. It was possible for some men to live in accordance with the principle of non-violence while others lived in accordance with the principle of violence. It was possible for some men to face the problem of death while others ignored it. Now this is no longer the case. The possibility of nuclear holocaust means that we must all dwell in peace, all learn to live in accordance with the principle of non-violence, all become more aware of the fundamental problem of death. It means that we must all rise to our full stature as human beings—or perish.

What, then, are we to do? Once again we look at the figure of the Buddha, not only as he stands between the Śākyans and the Koliyans but as he stands beside—and above—the Wheel of Life. In some Tibetan Buddhist scroll-paintings the Buddha is depicted in the top right-hand corner, well outside the Wheel, with one arm raised, and pointing in an upward direction. He is pointing out the Way—the Way to nirvāṇa, the state where there is no death because there is no birth. What we have to do is to realize not only the significance of the Rohiṇī incident, and the meaning of the Buddha's exchange with the Śākyans and Koliyans, but also the significance of that solitary wordless gesture. We have to solve both the problem of world peace and nuclear war *and* the problem of death. The very enormity of the problem of world peace and nuclear war indeed serves to make us—if we have any imagination at all—more aware than ever of the problem of death, and unless we can solve the problem of death even the solving of the problem of world peace and nuclear war would, despite the unexampled magnitude of such an achievement, be only the most magnificent of our failures. We must therefore not only abolish nuclear weapons, achieve peace in the full sense of the term, and learn to live in accordance with the principle of non-violence, as well as deepen our realization of the indivisibility of humanity and restore communication by the reinstatement of the notion of the objectivity of truth, but we must also eradicate craving, transcend both birth and death, and attain nirvāṇa, or the Unconditioned.

The situation in which we find ourselves today is dangerous in the extreme, perhaps more dangerous for humanity than at any other period in history, and time is running out. Whether we shall be able to achieve world peace and avert nuclear war we do not know. We can but do our best in a situation which, to a great extent, is not of our own personal making. But whether we succeed in achieving world peace and averting nuclear war or not we shall still have to die, still have to face the problem of death. If we solve the problem of death it will not, in the most fundamental sense, matter whether we solve the problem of world peace and nuclear war or not—though, paradoxically, if we do succeed in solving the problem of death then we shall, in all probability, succeed in solving the problem of world peace and nuclear war too. In any case, if we solve the problem of death, the problem of birth, the problem of craving, then we shall be able to live in the world as the Buddha and his disciples lived. We shall be able to join them in chanting those celebrated verses of the *Dhammapada*, the first three of which the Buddha, according to tradition, recited to the Śākyans and Koliyans by way of admonition immediately after he had prevented them from destroying each other:

> *Happy indeed we live, friendly amid the hateful. Among men who hate we dwell free from hate.*
> *Happy indeed we live, healthy among the sick. Among men who are sick (with craving) we dwell free from sickness.*
> *Happy indeed we live, content amid the greedy. Among men who are greedy we dwell free from greed.*
> *Happy indeed we live, we for whom there is no attachment. Feeders on rapture shall we be, like the Gods of Brilliant Light.*
> *Victory begets hatred, (for) the defeated experiences suffering. The tranquil one experiences happiness, giving up (both) victory and defeat.*[41]

If we can chant these verses from the very depths of our hearts then we shall be living in accordance with the teachings of Buddhism, and working together for what we all most ardently desire: the achievement of world peace and the avoidance of nuclear war.

THE BODHISATTVA PRINCIPLE
KEY TO THE EVOLUTION OF CONSCIOUSNESS, INDIVIDUAL AND COLLECTIVE—
A BUDDHIST VIEW

WE ARE LIVING IN THE MIDST of a great debate. It is a debate which, in one form
or another, has been going on ever since simple consciousness evolved
into reflexive consciousness or, in other words, ever since man became
man. All civilizations have been involved in this debate, all cultures, and
all religions. Some of the greatest triumphs of the human spirit are the
product of this debate, and some of its most terrible disasters. Among the
speakers in this debate, so to speak, on the one side or the other, have
been names so well known to history that it is unnecessary for me to
mention them. In the course of the last century, and particularly in the
course of the last decade, this great debate has been growing in intensity,
and involving an increasing number of concerned and thoughtful people
in every quarter of the globe. On the outcome of this debate depends,
perhaps, the future of humanity, for the debate is in fact nothing less than
a debate between the forces of life and the forces of death, between
creation and destruction, power and love, chaos and order, and the
motion that is being debated, so to speak, is the motion 'Man is/is not a
spiritual being with a spiritual destiny.'

The debate to which I refer does not take place in any one session, or
at any one time, nor are the same participants always present. It takes
place in a number of subsidiary sessions, as it were, in a number of
different places, and one group of participants is constantly being
replaced by another. Nor is that all. There are debates, and conferences,
on the great debate itself, and it is in one of these that we ourselves are
involved here today. For the last six years the Wrekin Trust has sponsored
a series of major conferences concerned, in its own words, 'with different

aspects of the emerging relationship between the mystical and the scientific experience of the nature of reality', and of this series the present conference is the sixth. We meet, as previous conferences have met, in the ancient and historic, indeed legendary, city of Winchester, with which some of our authorities identify Camelot, the capital of the illustrious King Arthur, and the seat of that goodly fellowship of the Round Table through which the once and future king strove to stem the tide of barbarism then flooding Britain. In later, perhaps more historic times, Winchester was the capital of the kingdom of Wessex, and the seat of the noble Alfred, who in a time of darkness was not only the ruler but the educator of his people, and after whom the building in which we are now meeting is most appropriately named.

Both Arthur and Alfred made contributions to the great debate of which I have spoken. We know on which side of the question they stood, whether they were for or against the motion, and their contribution was none the less effective for being expressed in deeds as well as in words. Today our task is infinitely more difficult than theirs. The forces of death have assumed forms incomparably more noxious than they ever knew, so that the forces of life are obliged to assume forms correspondingly more healthful and benign. If we are not to become the hapless victims of destructiveness without limit, power without restraint, and chaos without end, we shall need a richer and more abundant creativity, a purer and more ardent love, and a more harmonious and stable order, than the world has ever known before. This is not all that we shall need. The terms in which the debate is being conducted are today more complex than ever before. Many cultures are involved, many scientific disciplines, and many spiritual traditions. Many languages too are involved, both in the literal and in the metaphorical sense. We shall therefore need a greater open-mindedness than ever before, as well as a greater mental agility, and greater powers of sympathy and understanding.

So far this series of conferences has conducted its contribution to the great debate, or at least to the debate about the debate, mainly in terms of Western (i.e. occidental) culture. The overall title of the series, indeed, is 'Mystics and Scientists', and both the word 'mysticism' and the word 'science', together with their respective derivatives, are terms of Western cultural provenance. Moreover, the theme of last year's conference was 'The Evolution of Consciousness', while this year our theme is, of course, 'Reality, Consciousness, and Order'. All these are, again, terms belonging to Western culture, and in using them we are therefore speaking a particular language, both literally and metaphorically, and the fact that we are doing so determines, at least to an extent, the nature of our contribution to the debate as well as the conception we have of the debate itself.

That these conferences should speak the language of Western culture, and that their discussions should take place within a framework of Western cultural and spiritual values, is of course natural. The conferences themselves are held in the West, and they are attended (I think) by Westerners, whether by birth or by adoption. More important still, it is in the West that the great debate of which I have spoken has reached its highest pitch of intensity, generating shock waves that have travelled to the remotest parts of the world. Scientism, the Industrial Revolution, Capitalism, Parliamentary Democracy, Marxist Communism, and Secular Humanism, are all movements the effects of which are now felt, directly or indirectly, throughout the whole 'global village', and all are movements of modern (i.e. post-medieval) Western origin. It was only to be expected, however, that sooner or later these conferences would begin to speak, or at least begin to understand, the language of some of the great non-Western cultures. It was only to be expected that they would eventually widen the framework within which their discussions took place, as I am sure the sponsors of these conferences would wish them to widen it. Even in King Arthur's day, a paynim was once admitted to membership of the Round Table. It was only to be expected that, sooner or later, Buddhism would enter into the discussions, even as it plunged, centuries ago, into the thick of the great debate itself. It was only to be expected that a Buddhist View should be heard in this hall.

In seeking to give expression to that View I am confronted by a serious difficulty. Like its predecessors, this conference brings together Mystics and Scientists, those working in the sciences with those following spiritual disciplines, and as I have already pointed out both the word 'mysticism' and the word 'science', together with their respective derivatives, are words of Western cultural provenance. As a follower of Buddhism, which historically speaking is an Eastern (i.e. oriental) cultural and spiritual tradition, with a highly developed and indeed sophisticated 'language' of its own, I therefore find myself wondering which of these terms is the more applicable to me and in what capacity I am here. A Scientist I certainly am not, for I am not one of those working in the sciences. Does this then mean I am a Mystic, as presumably it must mean if the terms 'science' and 'mysticism' are not just contraries but contradictories? Although I have followed Buddhist spiritual disciplines for many years, I have no more thought of myself as a Mystic than I have thought of Buddhism itself as 'a form of Eastern mysticism'. To me, as a Buddhist, terms such as 'mystic' and 'mysticism' are in fact quite strange, even alien, not to say repugnant, and in speaking and writing about Buddhism I prefer to avoid them. Notwithstanding the title of a well known book by Dr D.T. Suzuki[42]—a writer remarkable for fluency rather than precision of expression—they do not really correspond to anything with which I am familiar within the field of Buddhism.

Such being the case it is obvious that I am here in neither of the two capacities in which I imagine the rest of you to be present. I belong neither with the mystical sheep nor with the scientific goats (perhaps I should say scientific wolves) but to a rather different breed that some of you may not have encountered before. In speaking to you on the 'Bodhisattva Principle: Key to the Evolution of Consciousness, Individual and Collective', and thus giving expression to a Buddhist View, I therefore speak neither as a Mystic nor as a Scientist, but simply as a Buddhist, leaving it to you to determine the extent to which my View as a Buddhist coincides with your View as a Scientist or a Mystic, a worker in the sciences or a follower of a spiritual discipline. In speaking as a Buddhist I speak as one who, having immersed himself in Buddhism for more than forty years, both in the East and the West, finds in Buddhism the Reality that works through Consciousness to achieve Order. To use Buddhism's own language, I speak as one who finds in Buddhism the Buddha who, together with the Bodhisattvas, works through the Dharma to create the Sangha—to create Sukhāvatī.

Yet though I speak as a Buddhist it is your language I shall be speaking today, the language of Western culture, not the language of Buddhism. Indeed, the fact that I speak to you as a Buddhist, and speak about Buddhism, means that I have started speaking your language already, for the terms 'Buddhist' and 'Buddhism' are not found in what I am obliged to refer to as Buddhism, both terms being quite recent Western coinages. It might even be said that I started speaking your language from the moment I agreed to address this conference not just on the subject of the Bodhisattva Principle, but on the subject of the Bodhisattva Principle as the Key to the Evolution of Consciousness, Individual and Collective, for the terms 'Evolution', 'Consciousness', and 'Individual', are terms having no exact equivalents in any of the canonical languages of Buddhism. Since to speak about Buddhism in any 'language' other than its own is, inevitably, to distort it, and even to misrepresent it completely, I shall be able really to speak to you about Buddhism—really to communicate a Buddhist View—only with the help of a certain amount of indulgence on your part. Though in a literal sense I am speaking to you in my own language, in a metaphorical sense I am speaking to you in a language that is not really my own, and am therefore at a disadvantage. Since I am meeting you half way by speaking as a 'Buddhist', and speaking about 'Buddhism', I hope you will meet me half way by concentrating your attention on the spirit rather than on the letter of my address. Without sympathy no human communication is possible, least of all when one is seeking to translate one's View, or one's Vision, into terms other than those in which it was originally conceived and expressed. With this by way of preamble, let me begin by making a few general observations on Buddhism.

The historical and the spiritual importance of Buddhism is, of course, beyond dispute. It is the major cultural and spiritual tradition of Asia, and what we most readily think of when mention is made of the Wisdom of the East. The image of the Buddha, seated in meditation beneath the Tree of Enlightenment, is one of the best known of all the religious symbols of mankind. Together with Christianity and Islam, which are younger than Buddhism by five and eleven centuries respectively, Buddhism is one of the three great 'universal' religions of the world, that is to say, it is not an ethnic religion, like Confucianism or Shinto, but a religion whose message is in principle addressed to every human being *qua* human being, irrespective of caste, race, sex, social position, nationality, or culture. For centuries together Buddhism was, in fact, the religion of between one quarter and one third of the human race. As distinct from both Christianity and Islam, however, Buddhism is not a theistic but a non-theistic religion. In Buddhism there is no personal God, the creator and ruler of the universe. There is no divine revelation, in the sense of a communication of God's will to mankind either through the life and sacrificial death of his incarnate son or through the inspired utterance of his chosen messenger. There is no sacred book in the sense of an inerrant and authoritative record of that communication. There is no prayer in the sense of petition to, or communion with, a Heavenly Father. Such being the case, some people have doubted whether Buddhism is a religion at all. To them religion is essentially theistic, and a non-theistic religion therefore a contradiction in terms. Perhaps in the last analysis the question is simply one of definition. In any case, one nowadays hears talk, in some quarters, of non-theistic Christianity, of religionless Christianity, and even of Christian Buddhism, whatever that might mean.

Since Buddhism is certainly non-theistic, and possibly not a religion, some people, again, have not only doubted whether it was a religion but have even wondered whether it was not a form of Science. Thus one occasionally hears talk of something called Scientific Buddhism. Buddhism is supposed to be 'scientific', or even a 'scientific religion'. This misunderstanding is sufficiently serious, even though not sufficiently widespread, to warrant correction. Buddhism is certainly not scientific in the sense that anticipations of modern scientific thought, and even of actual scientific discoveries, are to be found in ancient Buddhist texts, thereby somehow 'proving' the truth of Buddhism, as Scientific Buddhism at its most naïve has been known to assert. Such an assertion is little more than a clumsy attempt to appropriate, on behalf of Buddhism, some of the immense prestige of modern Science, and betrays a lack of confidence in Buddhism as a spiritual tradition. Buddhism is 'scientific' only in the very limited and indeed metaphorical sense of being imbued with the scientific spirit, i.e. with that spirit of open-minded inquiry that in the modern West is associated with Science rather than with religion, as well as in the sense of being empirical rather than dogmatic in its approach to the problems of existence—which in the case of Buddhism means strictly human or, more correctly, strictly sentient existence. Buddhism is *non*-scientific to the extent that it recognizes the 'existence' of a transcendental Reality with regard to which Modern Science, in the person of its official representatives, is at best agnostic. (There are, of course, signs that the monolithic materialist unity of Science is beginning to crack, as this conference itself bears witness.) This transcendental Reality can actually be experienced by man, a human being who experiences it in the highest degree being known as a Buddha, or Enlightened One. Buddhism also differs from science in making use not only of the intellect but also of the emotions. Indeed, according to Buddhism the problems of existence can be solved, and transcendental Reality be experienced, only when reason and emotion unite and there comes into existence a higher spiritual faculty variously known as Vision, Insight, and Imagination. In other words, transcendental Reality is to be experienced by the *whole man*, functioning with the utmost intensity at the height of his unified being.

Risking an oversimplification, one might say Science represents the extreme of objectivity and reason, whereas Mysticism represents the extreme of subjectivity and emotion—in this context, emotion purified by spiritual discipline.[43] Science seeks to reduce the subject to the object, Mysticism to absorb the object in the subject. Buddhism, following here as elsewhere a Middle Way, represents a dissolution of the subject–object duality itself in a blissful, non-dual Awareness wherein that which, without, is beyond the object, coincides with that which, within, is beyond the subject, or, in other words, wherein that which is most exterior coincides with that which is most interior. When expressed in terms of objectivity, this blissful, non-dual Awareness appears as Wisdom; when expressed in terms of subjectivity, it manifests as Compassion—Wisdom and Compassion being the twin 'attributes' of Buddhahood or Enlightenment.

Besides the one represented by 'Scientific Buddhism', there are other misunderstandings of Buddhism. As I discovered on my return to England in 1964, after spending twenty years uninterruptedly in the East, mainly in India, such misunderstandings are extremely persistent and very difficult to account for. Though Buddhism has been known in the West for well over a hundred years, the blurred and shifting 'image' of Buddhism that flickers on the screen of public consciousness is hardly a positive one. More often than not Buddhism appears as cold, bleak, inhuman, and anti-social. It is seen as a system of rigid asceticism which, by means of a great mass of prohibitions and restrictions, seeks to bring about the extinction of all human desires and the achievement of a state of passionless calm indistinguishable from death. For some people the mere mention of its name immediately brings to mind high walls surmounted by rows of spikes, darkened rooms, and joyless lives. 'Are you allowed to go out of the monastery?' 'Are you allowed to speak to other people?' 'Who sent you to England?' These were some of the questions which, on my return to England, I was asked by editors of women's magazines and members of the general public. When I explained that I could go out of the monastery whenever I wished, and speak to whoever I thought fit, and that I had come to England entirely on my own initiative, my questioners were clearly surprised. (I should mention that in those days I was shaven-headed, and wore my yellow robes constantly, not just for ceremonial purposes as I do now.) At the same time, Buddhism is also seen as strange, exotic, colourful, weird, and mysterious. Indeed, in recent years the image of Buddhism as a system of rigid asceticism has been partly overlaid—perhaps in the United States more than in Britain—by more fascinating images of absurdity (= 'Zen') and erotic abandon (= 'Tantra')—thus adding to the confusion. But rather than spend any more time correcting misunderstandings, or telling you what Buddhism is not, let me try to tell you, in the clearest and most general terms, what Buddhism *is*. Let me try to draw for you a picture of Buddhism that will obliterate, once and for all, the old misleading images.

This will give us a means of approach to the Bodhisattva Ideal, and enable us to see why it is the key to the Evolution of Consciousness.

Speaking in the clearest and most general terms, then, Buddhism is a Path or Way. It is a Path leading from the impermanent to the permanent, from sorrow to happiness, from the darkness of ignorance to the light of perfect wisdom. This is the Path for which the Buddha himself, in the days before his Enlightenment, is represented as searching. For the sake of this Path he went forth from home into homelessness. For the sake of this Path he sat at the foot of the Bodhi Tree. This is the Path he discovered at the time of his Supreme Enlightenment, this is the Path which, after initial hesitation, he made known to mankind. In his own words, as recorded in the *Dhammapada*,

> *Walking this Path you shall make an end of suffering.*
> *This is the Path made known by me when I had learnt to remove all darts.*

This Path it was that, for the forty-five years of his teaching life, in one formulation or another made up the principal content of the Buddha's message. The formulations were indeed very numerous. Perhaps the most basic was that of the Path as consisting of the three great stages of right conduct (*śīla*), meditation (*samādhi*), and wisdom (*prajñā*).

> *Great becomes the fruit, great the advantages of meditation, when it is set round with (i.e. supported by) upright conduct.*
> *Great becomes the fruit, great the advantage of wisdom, when it is set round with meditation.*[44]

Such was the gist of the 'comprehensive religious talk' which the Buddha delivered in eleven out of the fourteen places he visited in the course of the last six months of his life. No less important, and even better known, is the formulation of the Path as Eightfold, that is to say, as consisting in the gradual extension of Perfect Vision—the vision of the transcendental—successively to one's emotional attitude, one's communication with other people, one's actions, one's means of livelihood, one's energy, one's recollection, and one's overall state of being and consciousness. Much rarer is a formulation which in fact occurs only once in the Pāli Canon. This is the formulation of the Path in terms of the Seven Stages of Purification—ethical, emotional, intellectual, and so on. Together with right conduct, meditation, and wisdom, this formulation provides the double framework of Buddhaghosha's great exegetical work the

Visuddhimagga or 'Path of Purity', the standard work of Theravāda Buddhism, i.e. of the Pāli-Buddhism of Sri Lanka, Burma, Thailand, Cambodia, and Laos.

In the Mahāyāna scriptures many other formulations are found. Some of these are extremely comprehensive in scope, so that with them the Path begins to take on a more universal character. Among these more comprehensive formulations the most important, both historically and spiritually, is that of the Path of the Ten Perfections, the Ten Perfections being Generosity, Right Conduct, Patience and Forbearance, Vigour, Meditation, Wisdom, Skilful Means (= Compassion), Salvific Vow, Strength or Power, and Knowledge or Transcendental Awareness. This Path of the Ten Perfections is, of course, the Path of the Bodhisattva, 'he whose nature or essence is Bodhi' (interpretations vary), the great spiritual hero who instead of aiming at the inferior goal of individual Enlightenment, i.e. Enlightenment for oneself alone, out of compassion seeks to attain the universal Enlightenment of a Buddha, so as to be able to deliver all sentient beings from suffering. For the accomplishment of this sublime purpose he practises the Ten Perfections not for one lifetime only but for an unthinkable number of lifetimes, being reborn in many different worlds, and on many different planes of existence. In this way he traverses the ten great 'levels' (*bhūmis*) of spiritual progress—another formulation—from that called 'the Joyful' right up to 'the Cloud of Dharma', at which stage he becomes a Buddha. Thus he fulfils the Bodhisattva Ideal, as it is called—an ideal which the Mahāyāna regards the historical Buddha as himself exemplifying. Yet another formulation of the Path found in the Mahāyāna scriptures is that of the eleven 'abodes' (*vihāras*), which are, also, stages of spiritual progress traversed by the Bodhisattva, and which coincide to some extent with the ten 'levels'. Perhaps the most comprehensive of all formulations of the Path is that of the Nyingmapa School of Tibetan Buddhism, according to which the total Path consists of nine 'ways' (*yānas*) which between them cover all the three major *yānas*, i.e. the Hīnayāna, the Mahāyāna, the Vajrayāna, conceived not only as stages in the historical development of Indian Buddhism but as stages in the spiritual evolution of the individual Buddhist.

The number and importance of these abstract formulations of the Path should not blind us to the fact that the Path also finds vivid concrete embodiment in actual human lives, whether as depicted in the scriptures or as recorded by profane history. The Path in truth *is* the pilgrim, and the pilgrim the Path, so that 'Thou canst not travel on the Path before thou hast become the Path itself.' Travelling on a path implies a journey, and it is of a journey that both the scriptures and history often speak. Thus in the *Gaṇḍavyūha* or 'Flower-Array' *Sūtra* the youth Sudhana, in order to achieve what the text calls 'the highest knowledge of Enlightenment,' goes on a journey that takes him to various parts of India and in the course of which he visits more that fifty spiritual teachers. Similarly, in the *Prajñāpāramitā* or 'Perfection of Wisdom' *Sūtra* (the version in 8,000 lines), the Bodhisattva Sadāprarudita or 'Ever-Weeping', advised by a divine voice, goes east in search of the perfection of wisdom, encountering many adventures on the way until, in the city of Gandhavatī, he meets with the Bodhisattva Dharmodgata and hears his demonstration of the Dharma. On a more mythic level, in the *Saddharma-puṇḍarīka* or 'White Lotus of the True Dharma' *Sūtra* the journey is a *return* journey not unlike that of the king's son in the Gnostic 'Hymn of the Pearl'. In more strictly geographical terms there is Yuan Chwang's famous pilgrimage from China to the West, i.e. to India—and Monkey's. There is also Basho's 'Journey to the Far North.'

Though the promised picture of Buddhism has now been drawn, and though the rough outline of the Path has been filled in with details of abstract formulations and concrete embodiments in actual human—and animal—lives, this is by no means enough for our purpose. If we are really to understand what Buddhism is we must understand what the Path is *in principle*, i.e. must understand what it is that makes the Path the Path. In order to understand this we shall have to go back, so to speak, to the fundamental principles of what, in the absence of any more suitable term, we are obliged to call Buddhist philosophy. This will bring us close to the very essence of Buddhism and to the heart of this address.

Philosophy takes for its object all time and all existence. It is the science which, as metaphysics, investigates the most general facts and principles of reality (the dictionary definition). The fundamental principles of Buddhist philosophy, from which all its other principles derive, are therefore principles that embody its understanding of the nature òf existence in the most general sense—though in the case of Buddhism this understanding is the product not of systematic reflection on sense experience but of direct spiritual vision. According to Buddhism the nature of existence is best described in terms of change, or becoming. This does not mean that existence changes, in the sense of being subject to change but distinct from it, but that existence itself *is* change, *is* becoming. One of the fundamental principles of Buddhism, therefore, is that which finds embodiment in the well known equation 'Existence (or Reality) = Change (or Becoming).' This change or becoming is not fortuitous, but takes place in a certain fixed manner, in accordance with a certain definite law. (Not that the law really exists apart from the changing physical and mental phenomena it is said to govern. The law simply describes the way in which physical and mental phenomena behave in accordance with their inherent nature.) The general formula for this law, a formula which according to the Pāli scriptures goes back to the Buddha himself, is that 'This being, that becomes; from the arising of this, that arises. This not being, that does not become; from the ceasing of this, that ceases.' The law is thus a law of conditionality or, in more specifically Buddhist language, it is a law of dependent origination or conditioned co-production, as the term *pratītya-samutpāda* is variously translated. Just as existence is change, so change is conditionality. The Vision that Buddhism sees—the Vision that the Buddha saw on the night of his Enlightenment—is a vision of existence in terms of an infinitely complex, constantly shifting network of physical and mental phenomena, all arising in dependence on certain conditions and ceasing when those conditions cease.

Universal though it is in scope, however, the law of conditionality is not uniform in operation—not all of one same kind, so to speak. Within the infinitely complex, constantly shifting network of physical and mental happenings—within the totality of existence—it is possible to distinguish two distinct trends or types of conditionality. In the one case there arises, in dependence on the immediately preceding factor in a 'dependently originating' series, a factor which is the opposite of the preceding one, as when good arises in dependence on evil (or vice versa), happiness in dependence on suffering, death in dependence on birth. In the other case there arises, in dependence on the preceding factor, a factor which far from being the opposite of the preceding one, and thus negating it, is what may be termed its positive counterpart, so that it actually augments it, as when joy arises in dependence on happiness, rapture in dependence on joy, bliss in dependence on rapture. One trend or type of conditionality consists in a rotary movement between pairs of factors which are opposites, and the order of conditionality is therefore said to be cyclical in character. The other consists in a cumulative movement between factors which are counterparts or complements, and the order of conditionality is therefore said to be progressive. The first trend or type or order of conditionality Buddhism sees as a wheel endlessly turning round—a wheel of birth and death. The second it sees as a spiral constantly ascending—a spiral of spiritual development. We are now in a position to understand what the Path is in principle, and therefore what Buddhism really is. *The Path is in principle identical with the progressive order of conditionality.* The Path is essentially an ascending series of mental factors or mental states.

That the Path is in principle just this, that it is just this that makes the Path the Path, might have been obvious, to a limited extent, even in the case of the specific formulations of the Path already mentioned, such as the Noble Eightfold Path and the Path of the Ten Perfections. In the case of certain other formulations, almost equally well known and scarcely less important, it is more obvious still. Indeed, it could hardly be more obvious. It is crystal clear. The Seven Factors of Enlightenment, for example, are a series of mental states and spiritual experiences consisting of recollection or awareness, investigation of mental events, energy or vigour, rapture, 'tension-release', meditative absorption, and tranquillity or equanimity, each succeeding factor arising in dependence on the factor immediately preceding it and carrying that factor, so to speak, to a higher power of itself. Here the upward, cumulative movement of the progressive order of conditionality is particularly noticeable. It is no less noticeable in the second half of what is undoubtedly the most comprehensive formulation of the whole process of dependent origination or conditioned co-production to be found in the entire extent of the Pāli canonical literature, a formulation which includes both the cyclical and the progressive orders of conditionality in one gigantic synthesis. This most comprehensive and therefore philosophically most significant formulation is a twenty-fourfold one, consisting of twelve factors or 'links' (*nidānas*) successively arising in accordance with one trend or type of conditionality and twelve factors or 'links' successively arising in accordance with the other. Placed end to end, so to speak, the two sets of factors or two halves of the formulation, one 'cyclical' and the other 'progressive' in character, form a single continuous series. The factors or 'links' that make up the first half, which does not concern us here, are traditionally regarded as illustrating the process of human birth, death, and rebirth. The factors or 'links' that make up the second half exemplify the Path. Here the series of mental and spiritual experiences consists of faith (in the sense of a positive emotional response to spiritual ideals), tranquillity, satisfaction and delight, rapture, 'tension-release', bliss, concentration, knowledge and vision of things as they are, disentanglement, dispassion, freedom or liberation, and knowledge of the destruction of the defilements. In this formulation, as in that of the Seven Factors of Enlightenment, the upward, cumulative movement of the series is unmistakable, and the fact that the Path is in principle identical with the progressive order of conditionality therefore clearly established. Even without a proper understanding of such terms as 'tension-release' and disentanglement, the meaning of which is far from evident at first sight, the nature of the Path as essentially an ascending series of mental factors or mental states can be strongly felt.

If we look closely at the series of mental and spiritual experiences that makes up the second half of the twenty-fourfold formulation of the principle of conditionality, the series beginning with faith and ending with the knowledge of the destruction of the defilements, we shall see that this in turn consists of two halves, or two sets of factors or 'links' placed end to end. One set consists of seven factors, i.e. faith, tranquillity, satisfaction and delight, rapture, 'tension-release', bliss, and concentration. The other set consists of five factors, i.e. knowledge and vision of things as they are, disentanglement, dispassion, freedom or liberation, and knowledge of the destruction of the defilements. Between the two sets of factors there is a world of difference. The difference consists in the fact that while both sets are progressive, in the case of the set consisting of five factors the forward, cumulative movement characteristic of the progressive order of conditionality is irreversible, whereas in the case of the set consisting of seven factors that movement can actually be reversed. From this it follows that the point of transition from one set of factors to the other, i.e. the point at which in dependence on concentration there arises knowledge and vision of things as they are, is of crucial importance in the spiritual life. One who reaches this point, the point of no return as it is called, cannot fall away from the Path: he can only go forward. Such a person becomes what in the Hīnayāna form of Buddhism is known as a Stream Entrant or, in the slightly differing context of Mahāyāna, as an Irreversible Bodhisattva.

The fact that the series of mental and spiritual experiences beginning with faith and ending with knowledge of the destruction of the defilements consists of two different sets of factors or 'links', one reversibly and the other irreversibly progressive, means that it is possible to distinguish, within the totality of existence, not two trends or types of conditionality but three. Conditionality can operate by way of a rotatory movement, by way of a movement that is both cumulative and dispersive, and by way of a movement that is only cumulative. In other words, there is a trend or type of conditionality that is cyclical, a trend or type that is both progressive and regressive, and a trend or a type that is irreversibly progressive. Moreover, inasmuch as existence itself is conditionality, and conditionality existence, the fact that there are three kinds of conditionality means that there are also three kinds of existence. Substituting a static for the dynamic model, one could say that there is a stratification of existence, so to speak, into three different planes, each plane being governed by one or another of the three trends or types of conditionality. Using popular rather than traditional Buddhist terms for these planes one could speak of them as the worldly plane, the spiritual plane, and the transcendental plane. The worldly plane is governed by the cyclical trend or type of conditionality, the spiritual plane by the trend or type of conditionality that is both progressive and regressive, and the transcendental plane by the trend or type that is irreversibly progressive. In traditional Buddhist terms, the three planes (or realms) are those of sensuous desire, of archetypal form and of no-form, and the transcendental or nirvanic plane. The first plane is inhabited by the inferior gods, human beings, anti-gods, hungry ghosts, and hell beings; the second by the superior gods, and the third by Stream Entrants and the rest of the Holy Persons, by irreversible Bodhisattvas, Bodhisattvas of the *dharma-kāya*, and by Buddhas. The worldly plane, or plane of sensuous desire, is represented by the figure of Māra, the Evil One; the plane of archetypal form and of no-form by the figure of Brahmā, the lord of a thousand worlds, and the transcendental or nirvanic plane by the figure of the Stream Entrant or the irreversible Bodhisattva. Spiritual life and spiritual development consists, according to Buddhist tradition, in the gradual ascent through all three planes or realms, from that of sensuous desire to that of archetypal form and of no form, and from that of archetypal form and of no form to the transcendental or nirvanic plane or realm, so that one's life is successively governed by the cyclical, both progressive and regressive, and by the irreversibly progressive, trends or types of conditionality. Subjectively, the spiritual life consists in an ascent through mental factors and mental states, i.e. consists in the actual development of such factors or states. Objectively, it consists in an ascent through worlds or realms or planes. In the latter case, despite the spatial nature of the model, we should not think of the three planes as being in reality spatially separated. The three do in fact interpenetrate.

At this point we might venture on a generalization that traditional Buddhism does not actually make, or at least does not make in quite the same way. Inasmuch as existence consists of three planes or three realms, and inasmuch as these three planes or three realms are all governed by the law of conditionality, it could be said that each plane or realm comes into existence in dependence on the one immediately preceding, i.e. the plane of archetypal form and of no form in dependence on the plane of sensuous desire, and the transcendental or nirvanic plane in dependence on the plane of archetypal form and of no form. That Buddhism sees this movement from one trend or type of conditionality to another as taking place within the life of the individual has already been pointed out. The generalization consists in extending the process from the life of the individual to the life of the universe, so to speak, or from the sphere of psychology—in the broadest sense—to the sphere of cosmology. In modern Western terms, the generalization consists in seeing a parallel, or even a partial coincidence, between the process of spiritual development as depicted in traditional Buddhist teaching and the course of human evolution as described by modern science.

For Buddhism the idea of there being a parallel, or even a partial coincidence, between these two processes, is not a wholly fantastic one, as we can see by briefly referring to what modern scholarship regards as the historical origins of the Bodhisattva Ideal. In the great autobiographical discourses of the Pāli Canon the Buddha often describes experiences as belonging to the period before his Enlightenment, and whenever he does this it is as a Bodhisattva, in the sense of a seeker after *bodhi* or Enlightenment, that he invariably refers to himself. Thus the term 'Bodhisattva' originally referred to the historical Buddha in his pre-Enlightenment days. But of course the Buddha or Buddha-to-be had lived even before being born as the son of Suddhodhana and Māyādevī, and had been a seeker after *bodhi* or Enlightenment even then…. Gradually the use of the term Bodhisattva was extended and came to refer to the Buddha in these previous existences of his, existences in which he had practised the Ten Perfections, and his life as a Bodhisattva came to be regarded, for historical and doctrinal reasons into which I cannot enter now, as representing the ultimate spiritual ideal for all Buddhists. Details of these previous existences are given in a class of works known as Jātakas or Birth Stories. Jātakas are of two kinds, canonical and non-canonical, the latter being by far the more numerous. In the canonical Jātakas the Buddha-to-be is invariably depicted as a famous sage or teacher of ancient times, or as a righteous king. That is to say, he is depicted as *taking the lead*, whether in the sphere of ethical and religious life or in the sphere of political activity. In the non-canonical Jātakas he is depicted in a number of different ways, for instance as a caravan leader, a master mariner, a family priest, a tree spirit, a god, an ascetic, an elephant trainer, a thief, and a gambler. He is even depicted as an animal. In whatever way he is depicted, here too he is always the most outstanding member of his group or class, and besides practising the Ten Perfections displays, in human and non-human existences alike, exceptional qualities of responsibility, initiative, and enterprise. Here too the Buddha-to-be is always depicted as *taking the lead*.

Thus although there was 'no Darwinian rise from lower to higher forms' in the repeated births of Gautama Buddha there was certainly not 'a mere jumble of metamorphoses', as an eminent Victorian orientalist believed.[45] A parallel, even a partial coincidence, between the process of spiritual development and the course of human evolution, can indeed be seen. In the case of the canonical Jātakas there is an ascent, Darwinian or otherwise, from lower to higher, and this process is continuous with that of the Buddha's search for Enlightenment. In the case of the non-canonical Jātakas, though there is no question of 'a mere jumble of metamorphoses' this does not mean that they are arranged in such a way that the stories of the Buddha's previous existences form one continuous, progressive series analogous to the biological series of organic forms, or even that they could be arranged so as to form one.[46] What it really means is that, despite their immense variety, all the non-canonical Jātakas follow the same pattern and exemplify the same principle. A Jātaka is a Birth *Story*. In every story there is a hero. This hero is always the most outstanding member of his circle, and always takes the lead. Moreover this hero is none other than the Bodhisattva, i.e. the Buddha himself in a previous existence, and a Bodhisattva by definition is one who seeks after *bodhi* or Enlightenment and practises the Ten Perfections. Thus the hero, or the being who represents the growing point of evolution within each group or class of beings, is at the same time the being who follows the Path. The course of human—and animal—evolution and the process of spiritual development are parts of one and the same upward movement of life and consciousness. We are therefore justified in speaking in terms of a Bodhisattva principle at work in every form of existence, from the lowest to the most lofty. As I have commented elsewhere, 'the urge to Enlightenment in immanent in all forms and spheres of life, from the humblest to the highest, and manifests whenever a kind and intelligent action is performed.'[47]

This upward movement of life and consciousness, of which the course of evolution and the process of spiritual development both form part, is one that on planet Earth alone has continued for hundreds of millions of years. From the human point of view the most important point in the entire vast and complex movement is that at which sense consciousness evolved into reflexive consciousness or, in Buddhist terms, at which in dependence on sense consciousness reflexive consciousness arose. At that point man became man, i.e. an animal who in some respects resembled a man was succeeded by a man who in some respects resembled an animal. Reflexive consciousness means individuality. Individuality means spiritual development. (When I speak of individuality I am not, of course, speaking of individualism, a very different thing. I am speaking of the possibility of taking responsibility for one's own life.) Spiritual development means the development of consciousness, that is to say, it is essentially an ascent through mental factors and mental states. Evolution from amoeba up to man-like animal is sometimes spoken of as the Lower Evolution. Similarly, evolution from animal-like man up to Buddha or Enlightened man is sometimes spoken of as the Higher Evolution. The Lower Evolution is a collective process, the Higher Evolution is an individual process. The one takes place unconsciously rather than consciously, and its course is erratic and uncertain; the other takes place consciously rather than unconsciously, and its course is more direct and definite. While one is measured in aeons, the other can be telescoped within a single human lifetime. Since the Bodhisattva principle, as I have called it, is at work in every form of existence, Lower Evolution and Higher Evolution are in reality continuous. The Buddha-to-be is identical with the human or animal hero of the Jātakas, and the human or animal hero of the Jātakas is identical with the Buddha-to-be. Striking what may well sound like an unfashionable Hegelian note, we might even say that in the Higher Evolution the Lower Evolution attains self-consciousness, and that this self-consciousness is the Bodhisattva and the Bodhisattva this self-consciousness.

Though Lower Evolution and Higher Evolution are continuous this does not mean that there are no qualitative differences between them. Some of these differences have been indicated. The most important difference is that whereas the Lower Evolution is unconscious rather than conscious the Higher Evolution is conscious rather than unconscious. As I have already said, spiritual development means the development of consciousness, or an ascent through mental factors and mental states. In other words, whereas Lower Evolution is a development in respect of material form, Higher Evolution is a development in respect of mental and spiritual attitude. Lower Evolution takes place on the plane of sensuous desire, Higher Evolution on the plane of archetypal form and of no form and, eventually, on the transcendental or nirvanic plane. It was therefore only to be expected that those formulations of the Path in which the Path was most clearly seen as being in principle identical with the progressive order of conditionality should be the very formulations in which the Path most clearly consisted of a series of mental and spiritual experiences. It was only to be expected that Buddhism, as a Path or Way, should be concerned with the development of consciousness, and that in the course of its long history it should have devised a number of methods that were helpful in this connection. These methods are of two kinds, direct and indirect. The direct or subjective method, in which the level of consciousness is raised by working directly on the mind itself, is what is known in the West as meditation. As is well known, Buddhism is particularly rich in this field, some methods of meditation being the common property of all Buddhist traditions, while others are peculiar to one tradition only, or to a group of traditions.

Particular instances are intelligible only in the light of general principles. Buddhism sees in the figure of the Bodhisattva the highest embodiment of that urge to Enlightenment which is immanent in all forms and spheres of life. That urge becomes conscious, so to speak, in the process of the Higher Evolution, which in turn finds its fullest and clearest expression in the Path, particularly in that part of it which consists of the development or evolution of consciousness. Except in the light of the Bodhisattva, who embodies the common principle of them all in its clearest and most concentrated form, expressions such as Higher Evolution, Path, and development of consciousness remain unintelligible, or at best only partially intelligible. In the Bodhisattva, Buddhism finds its highest expression and its ultimate meaning. The Bodhisattva is indeed the meaning of human life, even the meaning of existence. Hence it is not surprising that the Bodhisattva principle should be regarded as the key to the evolution of consciousness, in fact the key to every manifestation of the progressive order of conditionality. By 'key' is not meant a scientific explanation of the evolution of consciousness, or of anything else, but a concept, or an image, in the light of which the whole process can not only be rendered intelligible but brought within a wider, more 'cosmic' context.

In terms of Western thought, the Bodhisattva principle is the principle of perpetual self-transcendence. Self-transcendence is the ultimate nature of Higher Evolution and Lower Evolution alike. Self-transcendence is the ultimate nature of existence. Above all, it is the true meaning of everything that goes by the name of religion, spiritual life, development of consciousness, and so on. Further than this it is perhaps not possible for me to go, at least not on the present occasion. Let me therefore conclude this Buddhist View with a few remarks on the subject of consciousness, individual and collective.

Individual consciousness, which is broadly equivalent to reflexive consciousness, is the consciousness appropriate to the truly human, i.e. consciously evolving, individual. Such an individual is characterized by awareness, emotional positivity, responsibility, intelligence, creativity, spontaneity, imagination, and insight, and his consciousness is of the corresponding type. Collective consciousness, in this context, is not group consciousness, i.e. is not the consciousness common to a number of living beings who have not yet attained to individuality—even though the Bodhisattva principle is as much the key to the development of collective consciousness in this sense as it is to the development of individual consciousness or, indeed, to the development of collective consciousness in the sense in which I am using the term in this context. For collective consciousness in this latter sense there is really no suitable term in the English language, or indeed in any other European language, unless the Russian *sobornost* comes near it to some extent, which is why I generally enclose the two words within single inverted commas. Collective consciousness, in the present context, is a special kind of consciousness common to, in a sense even shared by, a number of truly human individuals who follow the same spiritual disciplines and have the same spiritual ideals, or who are engaged in the same creative activities. Collective consciousness in this sense is as much above individual consciousness, taken separately, as group consciousness is below it. The Bodhisattva principle is the key to collective consciousness in this higher sense in that the Bodhisattva, even though appearing as an objectively existing personality, in reality transcends the distinction between subject and object, self and others.

'Collective consciousness' is the consciousness appropriate to what we in the Western Buddhist Order have come to speak of as the Spiritual Community—giving this term a special meaning which it does not possess in ordinary English usage. By the Spiritual Community—the Order—we mean a group, as we have necessarily and misleadingly to call it, of truly human individuals who have Enlightenment, the Path, and the Spiritual Community itself as their ideals or who, in traditional Buddhist language, go for Refuge to the Buddha, the Dharma, and the Sangha. Of this Spiritual Community the Bodhisattva is the spirit, even as the Spiritual Community is the expression, at least to some extent, of the Bodhisattva principle in the world. It is the Bodhisattva who, from the Beyond which is within as well as from the Beyond which is without, leads the Spiritual Community, on the Path, to Enlightenment. The Bodhisattva always has led, and always will lead. We see him in the

Jātakas as the hero, the being who represents the growing point of evolution within each group or class of beings. We see him always taking the lead. In some of the great Mahāyāna sūtras we see him establishing what is known as the Pure Land, or ideal environment for the pursuit of the spiritual life. We see him as Avalokiteśvara, Lord of Compassion, whose eleven faces look down upon the sufferings of sentient beings in the eleven directions of space, and whose thousand arms are outstretched to help. We see him as Mañjuśrī, Lord of Wisdom and Eloquence, who with his right hand whirls above his head the flaming sword of knowledge, that cuts asunder the bonds of ignorance, while with his left he presses the book of the Perfection of Wisdom to his heart. We see him as Vajrapāṇi, Lord of Might, whose blazing thunderbolt cuts through the obstructions of the cyclic order of conditionality and opens up the way for the progressive order. We see him—we see *her*—as Tārā, Lady of Salvation, who delivers from all dangers, temporal and spiritual. We see, in fact, the Glorious Company of Bodhisattvas, who are the Spiritual Community in the highest sense, of which our earthly Spiritual Community is a pale and indistinct reflex. We see him—we see *them*—as embodiments of the Bodhisattva principle, key to the evolution of consciousness, individual and collective.

In giving expression here to this Buddhist View, I have had to speak, for the most part, the language of Western culture. Whenever I slipped, as I am sure I slipped more than once, into a more characteristically Buddhist idiom, I may well have ceased to be comprehensible—assuming, of course, that I was comprehensible in the first place. I have also had to speak, as a Buddhist, to an audience consisting of Mystics and Scientists, of those following spiritual disciplines and of those working in the sciences. In so doing it has been necessary for me to leave many threads hanging loose, to present the conclusions without the reasoning that has led to those conclusions, and to make use of concepts for which there is, perhaps, no emotional equivalent in your own experience, as there is in the spiritual experience of Buddhists. Nonetheless I hope I have been able to communicate to you something, at least, of the spirit of Buddhism. If this conference is to make any contribution to the great debate in the midst of which we are now living, and if we ourselves are to make any contribution to this conference, we must be able to communicate with one another, and, as I reminded you at the beginning of this address, without sympathy no human communication is possible. When the tide of barbarism was flooding Britain Arthur founded the Round Table. In a time of darkness Alfred translated *The Consolation of Philosophy*. Today our Round Table must include all who are in any way concerned with Reality, Consciousness, and Order, and we must translate our own special holistic vision more and more into the terms of a common language intelligible to all. Only in this way, perhaps, will the ultimate triumph of the forces of life, of love, and of order, be assured. Only in this way will the truth that man is a spiritual being with a spiritual destiny be finally vindicated.

THE GLORY OF THE LITERARY WORLD
REFLECTIONS ON THE BUDDHIST CANONICAL LITERATURE

IT HAS BEEN SAID THAT THE RENAISSANCE that would be brought about by the discovery, in the nineteenth century, of the treasures of oriental literature, would be incomparably more glorious than that which had been ushered in during the fifteenth and sixteenth centuries by the recovery of the classics of Greece and Rome. Whether that prediction will be fulfilled it is difficult for us, in the middle of the penultimate decade of the twentieth century, to be sure, but we can at least be sure that there is a possibility of its being fulfilled. The treasures of oriental literature have indeed been discovered, that is, discovered by the peoples of the West, and have proved to be even richer than was originally supposed. Not only have they been discovered, but many of them have been made more generally available by being translated into the major occidental languages, especially English. Thus today, less than two hundred years after the discovery of those same treasures, we find that hundreds of thousands —perhaps millions—of people in Europe and the Americas are able to read, in their own tongue, some of the greatest works of Sanskrit, Pāli, Chinese, Japanese, Tibetan, and Persian literature. What people read cannot but affect them, and what affects hundreds of thousands—perhaps millions—of people cannot but affect the civilization and culture to which they belong, at least in course of time. We may therefore say that the second, more glorious renaissance that, it was predicted, would be brought about by the discovery of the treasures of oriental literature, has in a sense already begun, even though it has begun on a very small scale, and to a very limited extent, and though we cannot be sure whether the process will ever be completed.

There are, of course, differences between the two renaissances. The first was ushered in by the recovery of the classics of Greece and Rome, whereas the second hopefully is being brought about by the discovery of the classics of India, China, Japan, Tibet, and Persia. Moreover, in the case of the first renaissance the Greek and Roman classics were in most instances recovered from the hands of a people (i.e. the Byzantine Greeks) whose religion—and culture too, to a great extent—was quite different from that of the authors of those classics, whereas in the case of the second renaissance the treasures of oriental literature have in almost all instances been discovered among people whose spiritual outlook was broadly identical with that of the ancient poets and sages by whom that literature had been produced. This latter circumstance has meant that the discovery of the treasures of oriental literature has been associated with the discovery of those who were, so to speak, the natural heirs to those treasures and who were therefore in a position to help us appreciate their value and significance. When the Italian humanists recovered the Dialogues of Plato, for example, they did not recover any living Platonists along with them; but when British orientalists discovered the *Bhagavad Gītā* they at the same time discovered many learned and pious Hindus who had studied and practised its teachings. In other words, whereas the humanists recovered books the orientalists discovered both books and men, that is, men who were the living representatives of the tradition to which the books belonged. Another difference between the two renaissances is that the actual number of Sanskrit, Pāli, Chinese, Japanese, Tibetan, and Persian classics discovered in the course of the last two hundred years far exceeds the number of Greek and Roman classics recovered during the fourteenth, fifteenth, and sixteenth centuries.

In view of all these differences it is obvious that if the second renaissance succeeds in coming to maturity it will be not only more glorious but more thoroughgoing and more far-reaching in its effects than the first. Indeed, it will be more glorious precisely because it is more thoroughgoing and more far-reaching in its effects. However, it is not with the vast subject of the two renaissances that I propose to deal on the present occasion. I do not even propose to deal with one of them separately. My purpose is much more modest. All I propose to do is to offer a few more or less random remarks on one particular aspect of the renaissance that has been brought about by the discovery of the treasures of oriental literature—a renaissance in the midst of whose very tentative beginnings we are all, to some extent, now living.

As I have already indicated, the treasures of oriental literature are to be found in Sanskrit, Pāli, Chinese, Japanese, Tibetan, and Persian. These are the six principal languages involved. If we look at the corresponding literatures, however, we shall see that, taken in their respective totalities, Sanskrit, Pāli, Chinese, Japanese, and Tibetan literature all have much more in common with each other than any of them has with Persian literature. These five literatures thus form a kind of natural group. If we look again, we shall see that what the five literatures have in common is the fact that they are all, to a greater or lesser extent, Buddhist literatures. Indeed, in a number of cases a work that is a classic of Buddhist literature in one language is also a classic of Buddhist literature in another language, into which it has been translated. This is particularly the case with Sanskrit Buddhist literature, on the one hand, and Chinese and Tibetan Buddhist literature on the other. In England we are not unfamiliar with the phenomenon, the Authorized Version of the Book of Job and Fitzgerald's translation of the *Rubáiyát of Omar Khayyám*, for example, being as much classics of English literature as the original works are classics of Hebrew and of Persian literature.

The most important part of that part of Sanskrit, Pāli, Chinese, Japanese, and Tibetan literature which is also Buddhist literature is what is traditionally known as the Tripiṭaka or 'Three Collections' (literally 'baskets') of the Buddha's teachings, that is, the Sūtra Piṭaka or Collection of Discourses, the Vinaya Piṭaka or Collection of Monastic Discipline, and the Abhidharma Piṭaka or Collection of Further Doctrine. In Tibet and its cultural dependencies the Tibetan version of the Tripiṭaka is known as the Kangyur or '[Translated] Word of the Buddha'. This designation draws attention to the fact that the contents of the Tripiṭaka are traditionally regarded as *Buddhavacana*, the word or utterance of the Enlightened One. Buddhist literature, whether in Sanskrit, Pāli, Chinese, Japanese, or Tibetan, thus falls into two great divisions, one consisting of works composed by the Buddha's disciples, immediate or remote, the other consisting of works purporting to embody the *Buddhavacana*, either in its original form or in translation. It is this latter group of works that comprises what I have termed Buddhist canonical literature, by 'canonical' meaning that the literature in question is traditionally regarded as *Buddhavacana*. Besides being the most important part of Buddhist literature, this Buddhist canonical literature is probably the most valuable of all the many treasures of oriental literature that have so far been discovered. Such being the case it is to be expected that it will make an especially significant contribution to the second, more glorious renaissance that the discovery of those treasures hopefully is bringing about, and it is on the subject of Buddhist canonical literature that I therefore propose to offer a few remarks on this occasion.

In offering these remarks on this particular aspect of the second renaissance, as I have called it, I shall not be trying to give you a résumé of *The Eternal Legacy,* useful as that might be. I shall not even be trying to determine the exact nature of the contribution that Buddhist canonical literature is likely to make to the second renaissance. Instead, I shall be seeking to share with you a few reflections on Buddhist canonical literature as literature.

Before I can do this, however, it will be necessary for me to deal with a possible objection. We know that the Buddha himself wrote nothing. We know that he taught orally, and that before being written down around the beginning of the Common Era his teachings were preserved entirely by oral means. But the word literature means 'writing'. If the canonical literature consists of works purporting to embody the *Buddhavacana,* therefore, is it not a contradiction in terms to speak of Buddhist canonical literature? The objection is more apparent than real. Both the *Iliad* and the *Odyssey* are universally regarded as works of classical Greek literature: indeed, they are regarded as its greatest works; but there is no doubt that both epics existed as oral compositions for centuries before they were committed to writing in the sixth century BCE. From this it is obvious that literature, which a modern dictionary defines as 'written material such as poetry, novels, essays, etc.' and as 'the body of written work of a particular culture or people', includes both material that was written down at the time of composition and material that was written down subsequently, after it had been preserved by oral means for a longer or a shorter period. No contradiction in terms is therefore involved in speaking of Buddhist canonical literature.

What, then, do I mean when I speak of sharing with you a few reflections on Buddhist canonical literature as literature? What sort of difference of attitude does such an emphasis imply? In any case, what is literature, in the real as distinct from the merely formal sense of the term, and in what other way or ways could one approach Buddhist canonical literature if one does not approach it as literature? In discussing these questions I shall, in fact, be doing what I proposed to do and sharing with you my reflections on Buddhist canonical literature as literature, so that when the discussion is complete I shall have little more to say on the subject, at least for the present.

Let me begin with a few definitions, that is, definitions of literature, since it is on the question of the real nature of literature that the whole discussion hinges. These definitions will enable us to see to what extent we are justified in approaching Buddhist canonical literature as literature. According to Carlyle, literature is 'the thought of thinking Souls'. There is no doubt that the great being who was so deeply moved by the sight of an old man, a sick man, a corpse, and a wandering ascetic that he left home in quest of Supreme Enlightenment was a 'thinking Soul' in the fullest sense of the term, and no doubt that the Buddhist canonical literature—the *Buddhavacana*—contains what we may well describe as the Buddha's thought—especially if, with D.H. Lawrence, we understand by thought not just the manipulation of abstract ideas but 'a man in his wholeness wholly attending'. The next definition does not bear quite so directly on the present discussion, but it is of considerable general interest. 'Literature, taken in all its bearings', says William Godwin, the author of *Political Justice*, 'forms the grand line of demarcation between the human and the animal kingdoms.' One is reminded here of the fact that in Tibetan representations of the Wheel of Life the blue Buddha is depicted showing the inhabitants of the animal world a book. The book stands for literature. It is the possession of literature, rather than the possession of language, that distinguishes man from the animals, for even though it may be argued that animals can, in fact, speak (as distinct from making inarticulate noises), it can hardly be argued that they can write books. Moreover, if it is literature that forms the line of demarcation between man and animals that line will be formed most definitively by that literature which, in the terms of the previous definition, is the thought of the most deeply thinking Soul. This would appear to suggest that inasmuch as the Buddha is traditionally regarded as the deepest thinking Soul known to history Buddhist canonical literature is not only literature but literature *par excellence*.

Though in certain respects very illuminating, both these definitions—Carlyle's and Godwin's—are at the same time rather narrow. A much more comprehensive definition is provided by the classical scholar J.W. Mackail, who writes 'Language put to its best purpose, used at its utmost power and with the greatest skill, and recorded that it may not pass away, evaporate, and be forgotten, is what we call, for want of a better word, literature.' This definition must be examined clause by clause. To begin with, literature is 'language put to its best purpose'. But what is the best purpose to which language can be put? From a Buddhist point of view the answer to this question is to be found in the exhortation with which the Buddha sent his first sixty disciples out into the world. 'Go ye now, monks,' he is reported as saying, 'and wander for the gain of the many, for the happiness of the many, out of compassion for the world, for the good, for the gain, and for the welfare of gods and men.... Preach the Dhamma ...; proclaim a consummate, perfect, and pure life of holiness. There are beings whose mental eyes are covered by scarcely any dust, but if the Dhamma is not preached to them, they cannot attain salvation.'[48] In other words, the monks are to preach—are to make use of language— in order that beings endowed with awareness may be enabled to live the holy life (*brahmacariya*) and attain salvation, and they are to do this out of compassion. Thus the best purpose to which language can be put is to communicate salvific truth (*dhamma*). Buddhist canonical literature contains this salvific truth. Hence Buddhist canonical literature is literature in the most real sense of the term.

Next, literature is 'language used at its utmost power and with the greatest skill'. There is no doubt that in communicating the salvific truth the Buddha stretched the language that was available to him to the utmost limits of its capacity. There are, indeed, those who maintain that Middle Indic was in fact insufficient for his purposes, much as the English language 'sunk under' Milton. Thus Buddhist canonical literature is literature in this sense too. Finally, literature is 'language recorded that it may not pass away, evaporate, and be forgotten'. That Buddhist canonical literature is literature in this sense is obvious. After being preserved entirely by oral means for nearly half a millennium, the salvific truth communicated by the Buddha was committed to writing for the benefit of future generations. In the case of the Pāli Tipiṭaka—the Theravāda version of the *Buddhavacana*—this took place in Sri Lanka towards the end of the first century BCE. 'The text of the three *Piṭakas* and the *aṭṭhakathā* thereon did the most wise bhikkhus hand down in former times orally,' says the *Mahāvaṁsa* or 'Great Chronicle' of Sri Lanka, 'but since they saw that the people were falling away (from religion) the bhikkhus came together, and in order that the true doctrine [*saddhamma*] might endure, they wrote them down in books.'[49] Whether by oral or literary means, the preservation of the *Buddhavacana* has indeed been ever regarded as the special responsibility of the Monastic Order.

This more comprehensive definition not only gives us a better understanding of the real nature of literature, not only helps us to see to what extent we are justified in approaching Buddhist canonical literature as literature; it also suggests that Buddhist canonical literature is, in fact, literature 'writ large', in the sense that by approaching Buddhist canonical literature as literature we in fact endow the concept of literature with a fuller and richer content than it possessed before. It is therefore interesting to note that Mackail concludes by saying of language 'put to the best purpose' and so on that it is 'what we call, for want of a better word, literature.' For want of a better word! It is almost as though he felt that the phenomenon he had so carefully defined so far transcended what was ordinarily understood by the term literature that a more appropriate word was really needed. Might one suggest that that more appropriate word would be one that was reminiscent of the term *Buddhavacana* or, if that was considered as representing too high an ideal for the phenomenon in question, one that was reminiscent of what the poet-monk Vangīsa, in verses addressed to the Buddha, spoke of as 'deathless speech (*amatā vācā*)'—that deathless speech which is, at the same time 'truth (*sacca*)'?[50]

Nowadays we are not accustomed to thinking of literature in this kind of way. We are not even accustomed to thinking of poetry in this kind of way. Though once defined as 'the record of the best and happiest moments of the best and happiest minds', poetry seems to have become, in the hands of some recent practitioners of the art, the record of the worst and most depressing moments of the worst and most deeply disturbed minds. In other words literature—including poetry—nowadays tends to be 'clinical': it is a record of symptoms—of symptoms of disease. So much is this the case that we often find it difficult to think of literature, and indeed the arts in general, in any other way. We find it difficult to think of literature in terms of Mackail's definition, especially when this is commented on from a Buddhist point of view, and still more difficult to understand what is meant by that fuller and richer content with which, it is claimed, the concept of literature becomes endowed when we approach Buddhist canonical literature as literature. Let me therefore read you a section from Lu Chi's rhyme-prose Essay on Literature. I had intended to read this a little later on, when the definitions of literature had all been dealt with, but perhaps I had better read it now and deal with the two remaining definitions afterwards. Lu Chi was a Chinese writer who lived from 261 to 303CE. His essay is in eleven sections, and I am going to read the fourth section, entitled 'The Joy of Writing'. Since writing here means nothing less than the creation of literature, what Lu Chi has to say about the joy of writing will at the same time show us in what kind of way he thinks of literature.

Writing is in itself a joy,
Yet saints and sages have long since held it in awe.
For it is Being, created by tasking the Great Void,
And 'tis sound rung out of Profound Silence.
In a sheet of paper is contained the Infinite,
And, evolved from an inch-sized heart, an endless panorama.
The words, as they expand, become all-evocative,
The thought, still further pursued, will run the deeper,
Till flowers in full blossom exhale all-pervading fragrance,
And tender boughs, their saps running, grow to a whole jungle of splendour.
Bright winds spread luminous wings, quick breezes soar from the earth,
And, nimbus-like amidst all these, rises the glory of the literary world.[51]

Writing is 'Being, created by tasking the Great Void'. It is hardly necessary for me to tell you that nowadays we do not usually think of writing in this kind of way, and perhaps not everybody did even in fourth and fifth century China. Lu Chi's conception of the writer, especially the poet, and of the use of literature, is on a level with his conception of writing. The first section of his essay, entitled 'The Motive', opens with the ringing declaration:

Erect in the Central Realm the poet views the expanse of the whole universe,
And in tomes of ancient wisdom his spirit rejoices and finds nurture.[52]

'The poet views the expanse of the whole universe.' This is surely reminiscent of Plato's famous definition of the philosopher as 'the spectator of all time and all existence', though it will be noticed that the poet's spirit rejoices and finds nurture in 'tomes of ancient wisdom'. Thus the poet is not simply an untutored child of nature. He is also deeply versed in traditional philosophy. As for Lu Chi's conception of the use of literature, this is the subject of the concluding section of his essay. I was going to read only the first two lines, but it is so important and so evocative that I think I had better read it all:

The use of literature
Lies in its conveyance of every truth.
It expands the horizon to make space infinite,
And serves as a bridge that spans a myriad years.
It maps all roads and paths for posterity,
And mirrors the images of worthy ancients,

> *That the tottering Edifices of the sage kings of antiquity may be reared*
> *again,*
> *And their admonishing voices, wind-borne since of yore, may resume full*
> *expression.*
> *No regions are too remote but it pervades,*
> *No truth too subtle to be woven into its vast web.*
> *Like mist and rain, it permeates and nourishes,*
> *And manifests all the powers of transformation in which gods and spirits*
> *share.*
> *Virtue it makes endure and radiate on brass and stone,*
> *And resound in an eternal stream of melodies ever renewed on pipes and*
> *strings.*[53]

No doubt there is much that could be said on the conception of literature that emerges from these quotations from Lu Chi's remarkable essay, but any commentary must be reserved for some future occasion. For the present I am concerned with the section entitled 'The Joy of Writing', and the two other passages I have read, only to the extent that they give us a general idea of what is actually meant by the concept of literature having a 'fuller and richer' content. In Lu Chi's own words, I am concerned with them only to the extent that they give us a glimpse of 'the glory of the literary world'. Let me, then, now proceed straight to the two remaining definitions.

The first of these will not detain us long, since it has much in common with Mackail's definition, though expressed with a succinctness that makes it particularly memorable. 'Great literature', says Ezra Pound, 'is simply language charged with meaning to the utmost possible degree.' Here the distinction between oral and recorded literature seems to be ignored—perhaps because Pound considered it unimportant. Unlike Carlyle, Godwin, and Mackail he does, however, distinguish (at least by implication) between what is great literature and what is not great literature, the latter presumably being language that is charged with meaning only to a moderate degree.

Our last definition of literature is concerned with the relation between the spoken and the written word. According to Robert Louis Stevenson 'Literature in many of its branches is no more than the shadow of good talk.' The operative word here is 'shadow'. Good and even great as literature may be, in many of its branches it is to good talk as the shadow to the substance. What makes the written record of an oral communication so much more 'shadowy', in some instances, than the oral communication itself, is the fact that in oral communication the language of words is supplemented by the language of gestures, of facial expression, of intonation, and in short by the total impact of the personality of the speaker on his auditor. This is certainly the case with the Buddhist canonical literature, which indeed is no more than the shadow of the Buddha's 'good talk'. ('Good talk' could, in fact, be regarded as the English equivalent of *dhamma-kathā*, usually translated as 'pious talk'.) What the Buddha communicated by virtue of the impact of his Enlightened personality on the unenlightened personalities of his disciples far outweighed what he was able to communicate to them simply by means of words. The Buddhist canonical literature, however, contains only the words. In reading that literature, therefore, we should never forget that although the Buddha stretched Middle Indic to the utmost limits of its capacity he was still far from being able to communicate his 'Vision of Truth' in its fullness by purely verbal means. Buddhist canonical literature thus partakes of the same limitations as all literature, including even poetry. Though much is conveyed, there is much that is not—indeed cannot be—conveyed by words. Speaking of his experience not of truth but of beauty, Marlowe's Tamburlaine gives magnificent expression to this fact in lines that I have already quoted in *The Eternal Legacy* and which I make no apology for quoting again.

> *If all the pens that ever poets held*
> *Had fed the feeling of their masters' thoughts,*
> *And every sweetness that inspired their hearts,*
> *Their minds, and muses on admired themes;*
> *If all the heavenly quintessence they still*
> *From their immortal flowers of poesy,*
> *Wherein, as in a mirror, we perceive*
> *The highest reaches of a human wit;*
> *If these had made one poem's period,*
> *And all combin'd in beauty's worthiness,*
> *Yet should there hover in their restless heads*
> *One thought, one grace, one wonder, at the least,*
> *Which into words no virtue can digest.*[54]

It is because language—and therefore literature—is unable to communicate experience in its fullness that the Buddha declared in the *Laṅkāvatara Sūtra* that from the night of his Supreme Enlightenment to the night of his Final Passing Away he had not uttered a single word.[55] He had not uttered a single word because he had been unable to give full expression to his profound inner experience—in a sense, had not been able to give expression to it at all. Words alone, therefore, cannot reveal the secret of the Buddha's teaching. In order truly to understand that teaching we have to rely not merely on words but on the spirit (*artha*) as opposed to the letter (*vyañjana*) of the Dharma. As some of you will know, this is one of the four reliances (*pratisaraṇa*) of the *Vimalakīrti-nirdeśa* and other texts. However, I digress. It is time we got back into the main track of the discussion.

The real nature of literature having transpired from the definitions provided by Carlyle, Godwin, Mackail, Pound, and Stevenson, particularly as commented on from a Buddhist point of view, it is clear that we are fully justified in approaching Buddhist canonical literature as literature. Indeed, it is clear that in approaching Buddhist canonical literature in this way we in fact endow the concept of literature with a fuller and richer meaning than it possessed before, at least in recent times. What, then, does it actually mean, in practical terms, to approach Buddhist canonical literature as literature? Let me take as my point of departure a similar kind of approach to the canonical literature of another religion, as encountered by me in my own early life.

In 1940 I was in Torquay. It was the time when, as a result of reading *Isis Unveiled*, I had realized I was not a Christian. One day, in the window of a bookshop in the main street, I saw a new publication on sale. The publication in question was *The Bible Designed to be Read as Literature*. It was a large, thick volume, and since it lay there open I could see that it was printed like an ordinary book, the text not being divided into the usual numbered verses. At that time the idea that the Bible could be read as literature was comparatively new, at least to the wider reading public. It was certainly new to me. From school and church I had imbibed the idea that the Bible was essentially a repository of texts. Texts lay side by side in the Bible like bullets in a bandolier, and these bullets could be fired off at anyone with whom one happened to be having an argument, whether about religion or about anything else. To quote a text—or texts—from the Bible settled the matter. This kind of attitude still prevails, of course, among fundamentalist Christians of all denominations. Reading the Bible as literature meant, so far as I remember, reading it in much the same way as one would read the works of Shakespeare, and the layout of the volume that I saw in the window of my Torquay bookshop was intended to facilitate this process. It was intended to encourage one to think of the Bible as a book rather than as a collection of bullets, and to approach it accordingly. Thus *The Bible Designed to be Read as Literature* was the Bible designed to be read for enjoyment. It was the Bible designed to be read as a whole—or rather as a series of wholes—rather than as chopped up into bits in the form of numbered 'verses'. It was the Bible designed to be read, in the case of some of its books, as poetry rather than as prose. It was the Bible designed to be read for its own sake rather than for the sake of some ulterior purpose. To the fundamentalist, reading the Bible in this way was irreverent, even blasphemous. How could one possibly read the Bible as one read the works of Shakespeare? The Bible was the Word of God. How could one possibly compare profane literature, however great, with literature that had been inspired, even dictated, by the Holy Spirit?

At this point I had intended to read you the section on 'The Joy of Writing' from Lu Chi's *Essay on Literature*, which shows that the difference between so-called profane literature, on the one hand, and canonical literature or 'scripture', on the other, is far less than the Christian fundamentalist, at least, supposes. Since I have read that section already, as well as other passages from the same work, let me pass from *The Bible Designed to be Read as Literature* to the question of what it actually means, in practical terms, to approach Buddhist canonical literature as literature, without further delay, taking 'The Joy of Writing' as having been read at this point.

In Buddhism there is, of course, no such thing as fundamentalism in the full-blown Christian sense. Buddhists have never chopped up the Buddhist canonical literature into bits and used the bits as bullets in the way Christians have done. Nevertheless, it has to be admitted that in some Buddhist circles there exists a sort of quasi-fundamentalism that could, if it were allowed to develop, be as much of a hindrance to our approaching Buddhist canonical literature as literature as Christian fundamentalism is to the appreciation of *The Bible Designed to be Read as Literature*. This quasi-fundamentalism takes the form of appealing to the authority of the canonical literature in support of a particular belief or practice but only in a general way, i.e. without actually citing any individual text or texts. An appeal of this sort is usually couched in such language as 'the Buddha says', or 'according to the Tipiṭaka', or 'it is stated in all the Sūtras and Tantras'. This quasi-fundamentalism is strengthened by the fact that in many parts of the Buddhist world the beautifully written and richly bound volumes of the canonical literature are often ceremonially worshipped rather than read—even in the case of those very bhikkhus and lamas who appeal to their authority in this manner. This is not to say that there is anything wrong in making the volumes of the Buddhist canonical literature an object of ceremonial worship. Such is far from being the case. But ceremonial worship of the volumes of the Buddhist canonical literature is no substitute for the actual reading of that literature. Unless we read the canonical literature we cannot understand and practise the Buddha's teaching and—what is of particular relevance to the present discussion—unless we read the canonical literature there can be no question of our approaching it as literature.

Even the quasi-fundamentalism that exists in some Buddhist circles is not easy to eradicate, however. Indeed, it may be said that despite the fact that in Buddhism there is no such thing as fundamentalism in the full-blown Christian sense, the possibility of fundamentalism exists wherever a canonical literature exists, irrespective of whether that literature is regarded as the Word of God or as the written record of the utterance of a supremely Enlightened human teacher. Such being the case, it should be possible for us to apply the same general principles that were responsible for the appearance of the large, thick volume of *The Bible Designed to be Read as Literature* in the window of that Torquay bookshop forty-five years ago to the Buddhist canonical literature. More than that. It should be possible for us to utilize my explanation of what *The Bible Designed to be Read as Literature* was, in fact, designed to be read for, in such a way as to enable us to understand what it actually means, in practical terms, to approach Buddhist canonical literature as literature. Thus, to approach Buddhist canonical literature as literature means, in the first place, reading the canonical literature for enjoyment. This does not mean reading it for the sake of amusement, or simply to while away the time. Reading the canonical literature for enjoyment means reading it because, in so doing, we find ourselves immersed in an emotionally positive state of being such as—outside meditation—we hardly ever experience. Reading the canonical literature for enjoyment means reading it without any sense of compulsion. We do not *have* to read it. Whether as represented by the *Dhammapada* or the *White Lotus Sūtra*, the *Middle Length Sayings* or the *Perfection of Wisdom 'in Eight Thousand Lines'*, the Buddhist canonical literature is not a sort of prescribed text on which we are going to be examined at the end of the year and rewarded or punished in accordance with how well—or how badly—we have done. Reading the canonical literature for enjoyment means reading it because we want to read it. It means reading it because we have an affinity for it, and are drawn to it naturally and spontaneously. Having said this, however, I must add that

I always find it a little strange when someone who professes to be a committed Buddhist does not read at least some parts of the canonical literature for enjoyment, especially if he or she enjoys reading other kinds of literature.

To approach the Buddhist canonical literature as literature also means reading it as a whole. This does not mean reading the whole of that literature (it is in any case fifty times more extensive than the Bible) but rather reading this or that item of canonical literature as a whole. Reading the *Sutta-nipāta*, or the *Vimalakīrti-nirdeśa*, for example, in this manner, means reading it not piecemeal, not concentrating on the parts at the expense of the whole, but reading it in such a way as to allow oneself to experience its total impact. Only if we read it in this kind of way will we be able to grasp the fundamental significance of the work or, if one likes, its gestalt. This is particularly the case, perhaps, where the work in question possesses a definite artistic unity and where it has been cast in poetic form. In the latter case, to approach the Buddhist canonical litera-ture as literature means, of course, reading it as poetry. It was one of the special features of *The Bible Designed to be Read as Literature* that it printed the poetical books of the Old Testament as poetry, which gave them a rather Whitmanesque appearance, instead of chopping them up into numbered bits as though they were prose. (Not that even prose should really be treated in this way.) In the case of Buddhist canonical literature there is no danger of works, or parts of works, that are in poetic form being chopped up into numbered bits—at least, not when they are printed in the original. The danger is that when they are translated into a modern language they will be translated not into poetry but into prose and read accordingly. I shall be returning to this point later on.

Finally, and perhaps most importantly, to approach the Buddhist canonical literature as literature means to read it for its own sake rather than for the sake of some ulterior purpose. The ulterior purposes for the sake of which it is possible to read the canonical literature are very numerous. I shall mention only a few of them, leaving you to think of the rest for yourselves. Buddhist canonical literature can be read simply for the sake of the languages in which it has come down to us, that is, it can be read with a view to furthering our knowledge of linguistics. Similarly, it can be read for the sake of the light it sheds (particularly in the case of the Āgamas/Nikāyas and the Vinaya-Piṭaka) on the political, social, economic, and religious condition of India at the time of the Buddha and his immediate disciples. Buddhist canonical literature can also be read for the sake of its contribution to comparative religion and mythology and to the intellectual history of mankind. It can even be read for the purpose of refuting Buddhism, as when a Christian missionary reads it before going off to work in a Buddhist country. With the possible exception of the last, there is nothing actually wrong in reading the Buddhist canonical literature for the sake of any of these purposes. But the fact remains that they are all ulterior purposes—ulterior, that is, to the purpose that the Buddhist canonical literature itself exists to subserve and for the sake of which, therefore, it should really be read.

The purpose that the Buddhist canonical literature exists to subserve is the happiness and welfare—the highest happiness and highest welfare—of all sentient beings, and we read that literature for its own sake when we read it with this in mind. The Buddhist canonical literature is, after all, the *Buddhavacana*, the word or utterance of the Enlightened One. It is a communication from the heart and mind of an Enlightened human being to the hearts and minds of those who are as yet unenlightened. It is a communication from the Buddha to ourselves. Reading the canonical literature for its own sake therefore means reading it in order to listen to what the Buddha has to say to us—which means listening seriously. Indeed, we cannot really listen in any other kind of way. Some of you know that I have more than once said of the poets—especially the great poets—that far from merely indulging in flowery language they in fact mean exactly what they say, and that they are trying to communicate to us something which they think worth communicating. How much more so is this the case with the Buddha, and how much more seriously, therefore, ought we to listen to the words of the *Buddhavacana*! How much more seriously ought we to read the Buddhist canonical literature!

This, then, is what it actually means, in practical terms, to approach the Buddhist canonical literature as literature. It means reading the Buddhist canonical literature for enjoyment, reading it as a whole, reading it—wherever appropriate—as poetry rather than as prose, and reading it for its own sake rather than for the sake of some ulterior purpose. But before bringing these reflections of mine to a close I would like to make it clear that when I speak of approaching Buddhist canonical literature as literature I do not mean to imply that that literature is all equally literature, or all literature in the same sense of the term. A distinction made by De Quincey will be useful here. According to De Quincey, there are two kinds of literature. 'There is first the literature of knowledge, and secondly, the literature of power. The function of the former is—to teach; the function of the second is—to move; the first is a rudder, the second an oar or a sail. The first speaks to the mere discursive understanding; the second speaks ultimately, it may happen, to the higher understanding of reason.' In another place De Quincey goes so far as to suggest that the literature of knowledge is not really literature at all. 'All that is literature seeks to communicate power: all that is not literature seeks to communicate knowledge.' In the last analysis the difference between the two kinds of literature, or two kinds of communication, would seem to be one of degree rather than one of kind. Literature is not all equally literature, nor all literature in the same sense of the term, in that some works of literature communicate more power—and therefore move us more—than do others. In the case of the Bible, the Book of Job moves us more than the Book of Leviticus, even though the Book of Leviticus contains a great deal more information about the ancient Jewish sacrificial system. Thus the Book of Job belongs to the literature of power. It is literature proper. It is 'great literature'.

Applying this to the Buddhist canonical literature, we may say that the *Mahā-parinibbāna Sutta* moves us more than does the *Dhātu-kathā* (I am taking extreme examples to make the distinction clear), the *Vimalakīrti-nirdeśa* more than the *Suvikrāntivikrāmī-paripricchā*, and the 'Confession' chapter of the *Suvarna-prabhāsha Sūtra* more than the 'Śūnyatā' chapter of the same work. Thus the *Mahā-parinibbāna Sutta*, the *Vimalakīrti-nirdeśa*, and the 'Confession' chapter of the *Suvarna-prabhāsha Sūtra* all belong to the literature of power, while the *Dhātu-kathā*, the *Suvikrāntivikrāmī-paripricchā*, and the 'Śūnyatā' chapter of the *Suvarna-prabhāsha Sūtra* all belong to the literature of knowledge. Since it is the literature of power that constitutes literature in the real sense, or great literature, reading the Buddhist canonical literature as literature therefore means reading such works as the *Mahā-parinibbāna Sutta* rather than such works as the *Dhātu-kathā*. Indeed, we might even go so far as to say that just as literature is not all equally literature so canonical literature is not all equally canonical literature, and that it is the more truly canonical the more deeply it moves us. This is not to say that, from the Buddhist point of view, there is a real distinction between teaching, which according to De Quincey is the function of the literature of knowledge, and moving, which according to De Quincey is the function of the literature of power. From the point of view of Buddhism, the Buddha teaches by moving, because his 'teaching' is addressed not to what De Quincey calls 'the mere discursive under-standing' or what we might call the alienated intellect, but rather to what De Quincey calls 'the higher understanding of reason' or what we might call the heart, in the sense of the deepest part of our being, or the spiritual intuition, or the whole man. Reading the Buddhist canonical literature as literature therefore means reading it as the literature of power and allowing ourselves to be moved by that power to the fullest possible extent.

One last point. I have said that when works, or parts of works, of Buddhist canonical literature that are in poetry are translated into a modern language there is the danger that they will be translated into prose and read accordingly. The danger consists in the fact that poetry is the literature of power *par excellence*, which is the reason why poetry is capable of moving us to a far greater extent than prose, so that when poetry is translated into prose it loses much of its original power and, therefore, much of its capacity to move. In reading works of Buddhist canonical literature in translation we should be careful to read them, wherever possible, in translations which do justice to their poetic quality. Otherwise we shall be unable to read them as literature in the fullest sense and thus will not be moved by them to the extent that we might have been.

If we are able, however, to read poetry as poetry, if we are able to understand the real nature of literature, if we are able to see to what extent we are justified in approaching Buddhist canonical literature as literature, and able to see what it actually means, in practical terms, to approach it in this way, if we allow ourselves to feel the power of works like the *Mahā-parinibbāna Sutta* and the *Vimalakīrti-nirdeśa*, then we shall obtain at least a glimpse of the glory of the literary world, and gain a better understanding of the real nature of Buddhist canonical literature.

A Note on *The Burial of Count Orgaz*

In the autumn of 1990 I spent two weeks visiting Madrid and its environs and some of the most ancient and historic cities of southern Spain. There were mainly two reasons for my embarking on this little tour. I wanted to see the great mosque of Córdoba and other monuments of the Moorish civilization of Spain; and I wanted to see the paintings of El Greco—especially his *Burial of Count Orgaz*.

My acquaintance with El Greco had begun early, when I was still very much in my teens. It was an acquaintance at second hand, so to speak, for with the National Gallery virtually closed 'for the duration' my knowledge of the master's *oeuvre* was perforce confined to monochrome reproductions in art books and literary descriptions by such writers as Aldous Huxley and Sacheverell Sitwell. Perhaps the closest I got to El Greco at this time, in purely visual terms, was when I saw, in the window of a bookshop in Torquay, a folio art book that was open at a full page colour plate of one of his paintings—a painting in which two richly clad ecclesiastics supported, between them, the body of a man in black armour, while behind was a row of white-ruffed faces and above Christ, the Virgin Mary, and all the host of heaven. It was the famous *Burial*. But though I was acquainted with El Greco only at second hand, and even then only to a very limited extent, there must have been something about the man and his work that fascinated me greatly, for the novel I wrote in my eighteenth year contained descriptions of his paintings, and of those of no other artist. A year later I found myself in the East, where I remained for twenty years and where I had no opportunity of furthering my acquaintance with El Greco, even at second hand. After my return to the

West in 1964 I saw such of his works as were in the National Gallery and the Metropolitan, notably the 'Agony in the Garden' and the 'Storm over Toledo', thus at last making the master's acquaintance at first hand. The bulk of El Greco's production, however, was still in Spain, especially in Toledo, and to Spain I would have to go if I wanted really to extend my acquaintance with the artist. During the late eighties I in fact visited Spain several times, but it was only in the autumn of 1990 that I could devote two weeks to the monuments of Moorish civilization and the paintings of El Greco.

In the Prado I saw the *Baptism* and the *Resurrection*, and some thirty other paintings by El Greco, and in the Escorial I saw the 'St Maurice and the Theban Legion', rejected by Philip II but described by Sacheverell Sitwell in 1950 as the artist's masterpiece. Thus by the time I reached Toledo I had seen quite a lot of El Greco's work, but this only made me eager to see more—especially *The Burial of Count Orgaz*. Having checked in at the hotel we immediately made our way, my companion and I, to the church of Santo Tomé, only a few hundred yards up the cobbled street. By a happy accident, we arrived just after opening time and there were only a couple of dozen people in the small, uncluttered chapel that housed the famous painting. Before long we found places on one of the benches in front of the altar, above which the *Burial* was displayed, and so were able to sit contemplating it for as long as we wished. That evening, and in the course of the following day, I saw in the Cathedral, in the Hospital de Santa Cruz, and in the museum of the 'Casa del Greco', three or four dozen more paintings by the Cretan-born master (including copies and alternative versions), but these I shall not particularize. I shall stay with *The Burial of Count Orgaz*. Not that I shall attempt to describe the painting or even give a general account of it. I shall stay with it only to the extent of making a single point.

A few weeks after my tour, when I was back in England, I happened to dip into James A. Michener's best-selling *Iberia* (1968), and in particular into the chapter on Toledo. Originally he had not intended saying anything about *The Burial of Count Orgaz*, the author tells us, it having been so well and so repeatedly described that there seemed little he might add; but happening to revisit Santo Tomé one afternoon with a party of English tourists (apparently he was actually writing the book at the time) he decided simply to look at 'the magisterial painting' as if he had never seen it before. The result, as one might have expected, is that he has quite a lot to say about it after all.

'Like most universal masterpieces,' he declares, with American forthrightness, 'this one has many fine passages and others that are frankly bad.' Michener does not ignore the fine passages. Slowly studying the canvas as he sits before it in his Renaissance chair, he in fact finds hidden beauties which had escaped him on previous visits (the naked figures throwing rocks, in the right-hand panel of St Stephen's cloak, if painted on a full scale canvas of their own would have anticipated Cézanne's 'Bathers' by three hundred years), and having described them he gives us some useful information about the Conde de Orgaz, about the origin of the painting, and about the painting itself. Michener's most trenchant comments, however, relate to the 'bad' passages in 'this monumental work' of El Greco's. 'There are three glaring defects,' he assures us. 'The picture breaks into two unrelated halves, an upper and a lower; the yellow-robed angel that is supposed to unite them is one of the sorriest of figures El Greco ever drew and fails completely in his mission (in Spain all angels must be male); and the clouds of little bodiless angels consisting only of head and wings are ridiculous and, unlike the similar putti of Raphael and other Italians who used the convention with charm, accomplishing nothing. The unresolved breaking into two halves is caused by that much-vaunted line of heads which is one of the glories of the work but which in its excellence creates a problem that El Greco could not surmount. The faulty angel is poorly designed, poorly placed, and poorly executed, which is curious, since El Greco used the same device with success in other paintings.... What I object to most, however, is that the putti are badly painted, and as one looks at the canvas with a fresh eye unimpeded by what others have seen, they merely add to the general clutter of a work that was poorly organized to begin with.'[56]

I have nothing to say in defence of the putti (not that they necessarily need defending), and nothing to say about the drawing of the yellow-robed angel, though I shall have something to say about the failure of his supposed mission of uniting the upper and lower halves of the painting. The point I want to make relates to what Michener considers the poor organization of the work, in particular his allegation that the line of heads breaks the picture into two unrelated halves, an upper and a lower, and this creates a problem that El Greco could not surmount.

But is *The Burial of Count Orgaz* in fact broken into two halves? This view, it seems to me, attributes far too much 'weight' to the part played in the organization of the painting to the line of heads. It also fails to do justice to the fact that the painting is held together as much by colour as by design. The greys on the friar's habit on the left and the whites of the priest's surplice on the right, in the lower half of the painting, connect with the diagonal grey-and-white of the two cloud forms which, in the upper half, converge to support the figures of the Virgin Mary and St John the Baptist and, at their apex, the white-robed figure of Christ. Moreover the golds of St Stephen's dalmatic and St Augustine's cope, as the two saints bend to lower the dead Count into his grave, in the lower half, are echoed by the golds of the angel's robe and the robes of St Peter and other saints, in the upper half. The painting could in fact be described as a symphony in grey-and-white and gold, on a ground of black, varied here and there—in the upper half especially, with notes of purple and red. In terms of abstract design the painting is held together by the fact that the figures of Christ, the Virgin Mary, St John the Baptist, and the angel, in the upper half of the painting, form a mandorla, and that this mandorla has a common axis with the sphere formed by the figures of St Stephen and St Augustine directly underneath, in the lower half of the painting. Moreover, the point at which the 'much-vaunted line of heads' bisects this axis is midway between the bottom of the mandorla and the top of the sphere, while the convergent cloud forms of the upper half protract themselves beyond their apex and pass behind the figures of the Virgin and St John to describe a St Andrew's cross. The geometric centre of the mandorla and the apex of the convergent clouds or the centre of the St Andrew's cross are thus coincident. Far from being badly organized, as Michener claims, *The Burial of Count Orgaz* is extremely well organized, with both colour and design contributing to the welding of the various figures and forms of the painting into one uniform pattern. The work is in fact no less rigorously schematic than are the icons of El Greco's native Crete.

Nor is that all. The halves into which the *Burial* is 'broken' are held together not just by means of colour and design; they are also held together by what may be described as the painting's underlying philosophy. Looking at the line of heads, one notices a number of things about them. Including the heads of the two friars and the two priests, there are altogether twenty-five of them, not all of which are fully visible. Some of the heads are portraits of contemporaries, as Michener tells us; one of them may even depict El Greco himself. One also notices that the head of the grey-robed friar on the left, just within the border of the painting, and the head of the white-surpliced priest on the right, are on a slightly higher level than the line of heads in between (not counting the four rather 'shadowy' heads in the background), which they seem to enclose in a sort of parenthesis. Midway between the friar's head and the priest's, however, there is a head that is on a slightly higher level again than theirs. This head is on the same axis as the mandorla, in the upper half of the painting, and the sphere, in the lower, and occupies the space between the bottom of the one and the top of the other. Mandorla and sphere are thus joined together by a second, much smaller, mandorla. In other words, the painting is untied not just by colour and design but, in particular, by means of the middle head in that same 'much-vaunted line' which, according to Michener, breaks it into two unrelated halves. What does this mean? Why does the head occupy the position in the line—and in the painting—that it does? In order to answer these questions we shall have to study the head itself more closely.

It is the head of a young man. The Ancient Greeks would probably have styled him 'a beardless youth', with all that that implied, for in marked contrast to the bearded and moustached worthies on either side of him, some of whom are grizzled and balding, he has only an incipient moustache. The young man is handsome, even beautiful. His ruff-surrounded face, which is fully visible, is perhaps a shade less beautiful than that of the even younger-looking St Stephen who, in contrast to the wrinkled, white-bearded St Augustine, appears in the very bloom of youth. But then St Stephen has come down from heaven in order to help bury Count Orgaz: like the Virgin Mary and the other saints he belongs wholly to heaven. The unknown young man, on the other hand, belongs to the earth. Or rather, he belongs partly to earth and partly to heaven, which is perhaps what gives him his pensive, almost melancholy expression. He belongs partly to earth and partly to heaven on account of his beauty, for there is a beauty that is of the earth, earthly, and a beauty that is of heaven, heavenly, the former being the latter's reflection. Because he belongs partly to earth and partly to heaven he belongs to both earth and heaven, and because he belongs to both he is the means by which they are joined together. He is the means by which they are joined together and he is beautiful. Thus the two halves of the *Burial* are held together by colour and design *and* by the painting's underlying philosophy. They are held together by its underlying philosophy because, in that philosophy, it is beauty that holds together the two halves of the universe—beauty that holds together heaven and earth.

Beauty is the object of love, for as Diotima tells Socrates in Plato's *Symposium*, Love is a lover of Wisdom because Wisdom is beautiful and 'Love is love of beauty.'[57] Like beauty itself, love is of two kinds, the earthly and the heavenly. Earthly love is the love of earthly things, while heavenly love is the love of the things of heaven. The soul ascends from earth to heaven as it learns to love the things of heaven more than the things of earth, and it loves the things of heaven more than the things of earth as it perceives the greater beauty of the things of heaven, earthly beauty being but the faint, distorted reflection of heavenly beauty in the mirror of sense. The classic description of the soul's ascent to heaven—to the goal of the mysteries of love—is that found in the *Symposium*. As Diotima explains to Socrates:

The man who would pursue the right way to this goal must begin, when he is young, by applying himself to the contemplation of physical beauty, and, if he is properly directed by his guide, he will first fall in love with one particular beautiful person and beget noble sentiments in partnership with him. Later he will observe that physical beauty in any person is closely akin to physical beauty in any other, and that, if he is to make beauty of outward form the object of his quest, it is great folly not to acknowledge that the beauty exhibited in all bodies is one and the same; when he has reached this conclusion he will become a lover of all physical beauty, and will relax the intensity of his passion for one particular person, because he will realize that such a passion is beneath him and of small account. The next stage is for him to reckon beauty of soul more valuable than beauty of body; the result will be that, when he encounters a virtuous soul in a body which has little of the bloom of beauty, he will be content to love and cherish it and to bring forth such notions as may serve to make young people better; in this way he will be compelled to contemplate beauty as it exists in activities and institutions, and to recognize that here too all beauty is akin, so that he will be led to consider physical beauty taken as a whole a poor thing in comparison. From morals he must be directed to the sciences and contemplate their beauty also, so that, having his eyes fixed upon beauty in the widest sense, he may no longer be the slave of a base and mean-spirited devotion to an individual example of beauty, whether the object of his love be a boy or a man or an activity, but, by gazing upon the vast ocean of beauty to which his attention is now turned, may bring forth in the abundance of his love of wisdom many beautiful and magnificent sentiments and ideas, until at last, strengthened and increased in stature by this experience, he catches sight of one unique science whose object is the beauty of which I am about to speak....

The man who has been guided thus far in the mysteries of love, and who has directed his thoughts towards examples of beauty in due and orderly succession, will suddenly have revealed to him as he approaches the end of his initiation a beauty whose nature is marvellous indeed, the final goal,

Socrates, of all his previous efforts. This beauty is first of all eternal; it neither comes into being nor passes away, neither waxes nor wanes; next, it is not beautiful in part and ugly in part, nor beautiful at one time and ugly at another, nor beautiful in this relation and ugly in that, nor beautiful here and ugly there, as varying according to its beholders; nor again will this beauty appear to him like the beauty of a face or hands or anything else corporeal, or like the beauty of a thought or a science, or like beauty which has its seat in something other than itself, be it a living thing or the earth or the sky or anything else whatever; he will see it as absolute, existing alone with itself, unique, eternal, and all other beautiful things as partaking of it, yet in such a manner that, while they come into being and pass away, it neither undergoes any increase or diminution nor suffers any change.

When a man, starting from this sensible world and making his way upward by a right use of his feeling of love for boys, begins to catch sight of that beauty, he is very near his goal. This is the right way of approaching or being initiated into the mysteries of love, to begin with examples of beauty in this world, and using them as steps to ascend continually with that absolute beauty as one's aim, from one instance of physical beauty to two and from two to all, then from physical beauty to moral beauty, and from moral beauty to the beauty of knowledge, until from knowledge of various kinds one arrives at the supreme knowledge whose sole object is that absolute beauty, and knows at last what absolute beauty is.[58]

Thus the underlying philosophy of *The Burial of Count Orgaz* is broadly Platonic, even though the painting's subject-matter is a fourteenth century local legend and though its images are drawn from Catholic Christian mythology. (It could also be said to be basically Buddhistic, the soul's ascent from a lower to a higher beauty being exemplified by the well known episode in which the Buddha transports the monk Nanda, who had been troubled by thoughts of his beautiful ex-girlfriend, to the Heaven of the Thirty-Three and shows him five hundred nymphs. In comparison with the nymphs, Nanda declares, his ex-girlfriend is like a scalded she-monkey with her nose and ears lopped off, the nymphs being infinitely more lovely and beautiful and alluring.) That the underlying philosophy of the *Burial* is broadly Platonic does not necessarily mean that El Greco has read Plato. In any case he would have had to read him either in the original Classical Greek or in Latin, complete Greek editions having been published in Venice (1513) and Paris (1578) and Latin versions in Florence (1496) and Paris (1578). Not that El Greco needed to read Plato in order to be influenced by him. Since the Renaissance Platonism had been in the air, like a delicate perfume, and though it was Florence and not Venice that was, or had been, the great centre of Platonic studies, it is not unlikely that during his sojourn in the city of the Doges El Greco should have breathed in some particles of the Platonic essence. Moreover, as his art itself suggests and as stories that have come down to us about him testify, El Greco was something of a visionary, a man who saw more clearly in the darkness than in the light and who found in the words of a modern writer on Spain, 'no use for the splendid Spanish sun'.[59] Like many poets and artists both before and after his time, he was a Platonist by nature. To him it was self-evident that there existed a higher, spiritual world and that the right contemplation of human beauty was a means of access to that world.

Which brings us back to the head of the unknown young man. Though it is entirely feasible that El Greco, Platonist by nature that he was, should have evolved the underlying philosophy of his great painting from the depths of his own experience, certain features in his treatment of the young man's head suggest that this was not the case and that he had, in fact, read Plato, even read the *Symposium*, or at least been privy to the latter's ideas on love and beauty. It is not just that the head joins together the two halves of the painting, or that the young man is beautiful. El Greco seems to want to emphasize these facts. While the tip of the rear half of St Augustine's mitre points upwards to the young man's chin, almost touching his ruff, the twin folds of the angel's robe, pointing downwards, form a right-angle just above his head; the saint's mitre is gold and white, the angel's robe gold (or yellow). The young man's head is thus at the point of intersection between a black and white horizontal and a gold and white vertical; it also occupies a position, vertically, exactly midway between the dead Count's heart and the naked white infant on to which the angel is holding and which is, presumably, the Count's recently departed soul.

But what of the gold-robed angel himself? Does he fail completely in his mission of uniting the two halves of the picture, as Michener asserts, and is he 'one of the sorriest of figures El Greco ever drew'? Is he 'poorly designed, poorly placed, and poorly executed'? How well or how badly he is drawn compared with El Greco's other figures I cannot say, nor can I say if he is poorly designed or poorly executed. What I can say, in the light of my previous observations on the painting, is that the angel neither succeeds nor fails in his mission of uniting the upper and lower halves of the picture. He neither succeeds nor fails because it is not his mission to unite them. The two halves of the painting are united by the head of the young man. It is the young man, not the angel, who is the intermediary between heaven and earth, and he is the intermediary between them because he is beautiful and because, in the underlying philosophy of the *Burial*, it is with the right contemplation of *human* beauty that the soul commences its ascent from earth to heaven. The figure of the angel is therefore not poorly placed at all. Since not he but the young man is the intermediary he is rightly placed, not between heaven and earth, as the young man is, but in heaven, where he forms a mandorla with Christ, the Virgin Mary, and St John the Baptist, and El Greco makes use of the folds of his gold robe to emphasize the fact that it is the young man's head that unites the two halves of the painting. When Michener looked at the *Burial* he should have noticed this. He indeed thinks it 'curious' that 'since El Greco used the same device with success in other paintings' the angel should be 'poorly designed, poorly placed, and poorly executed'. What he ought to have asked himself was whether the artist was, in fact, using the same device in the *Burial* as in other paintings, that is, using the figure of the angel to unite the upper and lower halves of the picture. Had he asked himself this question he might have perceived that the two halves were united by the head of the young man, and perceiving this he might have gone on to ask himself why El Greco should have given the mission of uniting them to the young man's head rather than to the figure of the angel. Proceeding in this way he might even have realized that at least one of the 'glaring defects' that he attributed to *The Burial of Count Orgaz* existed only in his mind and that actually the artist had solved the problem created by the 'unresolved' breaking of the picture into two unrelated halves by the line of heads.

But we have not quite finished with the angel. Though it is not his mission to unite the two halves of the picture—to join together heaven and earth—he does have a function. His function is to be the midwife, so to speak, of the deceased Count's soul, which seems to be ascending to the judgement seat of Christ up a narrow passage between the two diagonal cloud forms—a passage that has reminded at least one commentator of the human birth canal. The Virgin Mary looks down in compassion, while St John the Baptist and the other saints, as well as sundry angels and blessed spirits, intercede for it with Christ. All this is in full accordance with Catholic Christian teaching. But the Count's soul—the naked white infant (actually it may not be naked but wearing a ghostly white integument) is vertically aligned with the head of the beautiful young man and with the Count's heart, the young man's head being situated exactly midway between the Count's heart and his soul. What does this mean?

The answer to the question is to be found in the *Symposium*. Earlier in their conversation, before her great speech on the ascent from the contemplation of physical beauty to the knowledge of absolute beauty, Diotima tells Socrates that the function of love is to procreate in what is beautiful, and that such procreation can be either physical or spiritual. Procreation, she says, is the nearest thing to perpetuity and immortality that a mortal being can attain. 'Those whose creative instinct is physical have recourse to women, and show their love in this way, believing that by begetting children they can secure for themselves an immortal and blessed memory hereafter for ever; but there are some whose creative desire is of the soul, and who conceive spiritually, not physically, the progeny which it is the nature of the soul to conceive and bring forth.' Diotima continues:

> If you ask what that progeny is, it is wisdom and virtue in general; of this all poets and such craftsmen as have found out some new thing may be said to be begetters; but far the greatest and fairest branch of wisdom is that which is concerned with the due ordering of states and families, whose name is moderation and justice. When by divine inspiration a man finds himself from his youth up spiritually pregnant with these qualities, as soon as he comes of due age he desires to bring forth and to be delivered, and goes in search of a beautiful environment for his children; for he can never bring forth in ugliness. In his pregnant condition physical beauty is more pleasing to him than ugliness, and if in a beautiful body he finds also a beautiful and noble and gracious soul, he welcomes the combination warmly, and finds much to say to such a one about virtue and the qualities and actions which mark a good man, and takes his education in hand. By intimate association with beauty embodied in his friend, and by keeping him always before his mind, he succeeds in bringing to birth the children of which he has been long in labour, and once they are born he shares their upbringing with his friend; the partnership between them will be far closer and the bond of affection far stronger than between ordinary parents, because the children that they share surpass human children by being immortal as well as more beautiful. Everyone would prefer children such as these to children after the flesh.[60]

Does it not appear, in the light of this passage, that the naked white infant might be not just the soul of Count Orgaz but the spiritual child that he has brought to birth by intimate association with beauty embodied in his friend and that his friend is none other than the beautiful young man whose head occupies a position exactly midway between the Count's heart and his soul? Should this be the case, it could also be that the little page standing in the foreground of the picture, to the extreme left, who is believed to be a portrait of El Greco's son, represents physical procreation, just as the naked white infant represents spiritual procreation. The page holds in his left hand a torch, symbolizing mortality, the flame of the torch being echoed by the flames of the torches at either end of the row of heads, as well as by the vertical arms of the red Maltese crosses(?) on the cloaks of two of the gentlemen in the middle of the row, one behind St Augustine and the other between St Augustine and St Stephen. With the forefinger of his left hand the page points to the centre of the white rose embroidered on the sleeve of St Stephen's dalmatic. What *this* means I cannot say, unless the rose is the snow-white rose of celestial love described by Dante in Canto XXX of the *Paradiso*, in which case the page's gesture would indicate that earthly beauty, rightly contemplated, points to heavenly beauty, physical love to spiritual love.

Finally, could it not be that the head of the beautiful young man is a portrait of someone personally known to El Greco, and that the *Burial* itself is a child brought forth by the artist 'by intimate association with beauty embodied in his friend and by keeping him always before his mind'? This is only a speculation, but it is a speculation fully in accordance with the underlying philosophy of the painting. What is certain is that, universal masterpiece or no universal masterpiece, *The Burial of Count Orgaz* does *not* break into two unrelated halves and is *not* poorly organized, its two halves being held together not only by colour and design but by the painting's broadly Platonic underlying philosophy. When he looked at the canvas Michener looked not so much with a fresh eye as with a raw eye. For my own part, I would like to pay a second visit to Toledo and see *The Burial of Count Orgaz* again. Perhaps I, too, would find hidden beauties that had escaped me on my previous visit. In which case there might be another Note.

CRITICISM EAST AND WEST

WHEN KEITH SAGAR INVITED ME TO TAKE PART in this weekend school I hesitated a long time before accepting. *Criticism in Crisis* was indeed an exciting topic, but I was conscious that I knew very little about the present state of literary criticism and was therefore hardly in a position to make a positive contribution to the proceedings. However, Keith Sagar seemed not to share these misgivings, or rather, was inclined to dismiss them as irrelevant. He was sure I didn't know any less about the present state of literary criticism than he did, he cheerfully assured me, and in any case the school would be hearing enough about *that* from the first two speakers. What was wanted from me, as the speaker 'with a perspective from outside our culture altogether', was much more on what criticism ought to be doing.

My role was therefore clear. I was to be present among you as a belated avatar of that once well known figure, the Outsider, and it was as an 'outsider' that I was to contribute to the weekend's proceedings. But before trying to do this perhaps I had better explain in what sense, exactly, I am an 'outsider'. Firstly I am an 'outsider' in that my life work has lain not in the field of English, whether university or non-university, but almost entirely in the field of Buddhism, with only occasional excursions into other areas. In pursuit of my Buddhist studies I in fact spent twenty years uninterruptedly in the East, mainly in India, returning to England for good only in 1967. Secondly I am an 'outsider' in that I have never held a permanent academic post, though I have to confess that I was once a lecturer at an American university. There were, of course, mitigating circumstances, and in any case I was only a visiting lecturer, and not in the department of English but only in the department of Philosophy, besides which I stayed there for no more than a single semester.

But though a genuine avatar of the Outsider I am not so much of an 'outsider' as not to be aware, however vaguely, that there is something wrong in the field of English and particularly, perhaps, in the field that deep-browed Leavis once ruled—or tried to rule—as his demesne. Only a few weeks ago, leafing through a collection of essays on poetry by that cantankerous and opinionated bard Robert Graves I happened to light upon the following anecdote. It comes at the end of the fourth of Graves's Clark Lectures, which were of course sponsored by Trinity College, Cambridge. 'Before closing,' Graves says, 'I must tell you about a girl who is reading English here under Professor X. I asked her: "What poems do you enjoy most?" and she answered with dignity: "Poems are not meant to be enjoyed; they are meant to be analysed."'[61] Graves adds that he hoped his listeners did not think he subscribed to that heresy.

That was more than thirty years ago and in the meantime the situation seems to have become worse rather than better. A few days after I happened to light upon the Robert Graves anecdote there appeared in *The Times* an interview with Professor Allan Bloom of Chicago, whose book *The Closing of the American Mind*, a hard-hitting attack on cultural illiteracy, had 'shaken America's academic establishment'. If the interview was anything to go by, it was a pity the American academic establishment had only been shaken. Stanford University had become embroiled in controversy over a decision to drop its compulsory beginners' course of Western culture, while at Duke University Shakespeare was taught as 'a vehicle to illuminate the way seventeenth century society mistreated women, the working class and minorities.'[62]

Now let there be no misunderstanding here. I am not saying that poetry should never, under any circumstances, be analysed (I am sure Graves did not mean to suggest this), neither am I saying that Shakespeare is too sacrosanct to be utilized as a source of information about the way seventeenth century society mistreated women, the working class, and minorities. Indeed, a certain amount of analysis may well enhance our appreciation of a poem, just as information regarding the way seventeenth century society mistreated women, the working class, and minorities may reciprocally illuminate Shakespeare—provided, of course, we can be sure that seventeenth century society really did mistreat these social groups as alleged. What I am saying is that literary criticism is concerned, primarily, with the enjoyment of poetry rather than with its analysis (not that the two need be mutually exclusive), and concerned with Shakespeare as an outstanding literary phenomenon rather than with Shakespeare as an important source of sociological information.

In speaking of literary criticism in this way I am of course defining it, at least by implication, and definition is no doubt premature at this stage. After all, in formal terms literary criticism is simply the criticism of literature. But what is literature? Surely it is not really possible for us to say what literary criticism is without first saying what literature itself is, and unless we can say what literary criticism is we shall not really be able to say what is wrong with it or what it ought to be doing. We shall not even be able to speak of literary criticism as being in a state of crisis, any more than we are able to speak of anything being in a state of crisis without knowing what the natural course, or the normal function, of that thing actually is.

What, then, is literature? There are quite a number of definitions, from Carlyle's 'the thought of thinking Souls' and Godwin's 'the grand line of demarcation between the human and the animal kingdoms' to Stevenson's 'the shadow of good talk' and Pound's 'language charged with meaning'. In between, chronologically speaking, we have Mackail's 'language put to the best purpose, used at its utmost power and with the greatest skill, and recorded that it may not pass away, evaporate, and be forgotten', while more than fifteen hundred years before any of these we have Lu Chi's more poetic statement, the concluding section of which reads:

The use of literature
Lies in its conveyance of every truth.
It expands the horizon to make space infinite,
And serves as a bridge that spans a myriad years.
It maps all roads and paths for posterity,
And mirrors the images of worthy ancients,
That the tottering Edifices of the sage kings of antiquity may be reared
  again,
And their admonishing voices, wind-borne since of yore, may resume full
  expression.
No regions are too remote but it pervades,
No truth too subtle to be woven into its vast web.
Like mist and rain, it permeates and nourishes,
And manifests all the powers of transformation in which gods and spirits
  share.

Virtue it makes endure and radiate on brass and stone,
And resound in an eternal stream of melodies ever renewed on pipes and
strings.[63]

Put together, and as it were conflated, these definitions and descriptions give us at least the beginnings of an answer to the question, 'What is literature?' They enable us to see that literature consists of words, that is, words as committed to writing, and that these words are organized in such a way as to give rise to feelings of pleasure and delight in the reader or listener. Moreover, notwithstanding some rather loose talk about chimpanzees and typewriters and the collected works of Shakespeare, words come to be organized in this particular way not by accident but as a result of the creative activity of the person we rather ambiguously designate 'the writer', that is, the poet, novelist, dramatist, or essayist. In organizing words in such a way as to give rise to feelings of pleasure and delight the creative writer does four things. He conveys information, he gives expression to his individual sensibility or his individual experience of life, he communicates his personal sense of values, and he brings about a modification in the being of his audience, a modification that may be either superficial or profound, temporary or permanent. A working definition of literature would therefore be that it is a pleasurable organization of words that conveys information and, at the same time, gives expression to the writer's sensibility, communicates his sense of values, and modifies the being of his audience.

This definition could of course be worked out in greater detail. It would be possible, for instance, to bring out the fact that the writer's sensibility finds expression by way of a process of imaginative crystallization, as it has been called. But the definition as it stands is sufficiently detailed for our present purpose, which is simply to make it possible for us to say what literary criticism is by giving a tolerably adequate idea of the particular phenomenon that constitutes the object of literary criticism, namely, literature in all its forms. With the help of this definition we can see that literary criticism is in fact concerned with a number of things. To begin with, literary criticism is concerned with words, though with words not in isolation but in their contextual reality. It is concerned with their meaning, down to the very finest shades, with their origin and history, and with the different ways in which they have been used, as well as being concerned with their tone quality, their weight, and their texture. We can also see that literary criticism is concerned with the feelings of pleasure and delight which arise when these words are organized in a particular way, that is, in a particular sequence. It is concerned with the principles which make such an organization of words possible, with the exact nature of the pleasure and delight itself, and with the various methods by which that pleasure and delight is produced. We can see, moreover, that literary criticism is concerned with the kind of information conveyed by a particular pleasurable organization of words, regardless of the actual nature of that information or the particular branch of knowledge to which it belongs. We can see that literary criticism is concerned with the individual sensibility or individual experience of life that finds expression in and through that same pleasurable organization of words. We can see that it is concerned with the values communicated, as well as concerned with the effect which the pleasurable organization of words produces on the reader or listener and the way in which that effect is produced.

Thus a great deal is demanded of literary criticism, or rather, a great deal is demanded of the literary critic—for in this connection it is probably better to speak in concrete rather than in abstract terms. The literary critic must be 'well nurtured in his mother tongue' and have at least a nodding acquaintance with linguistics. He must be a person of great emotional sensitivity, with an enormous capacity for the actual enjoyment of literature in all its forms, for unless he actually enjoys the poems, novels, dramas, and essays with which, as critic, he is concerned, all the scholarship and intellectual acumen in the world will avail him nothing and he will be a literary critic only in name. The literary critic must also be possessed of a wide general knowledge of the arts and sciences, especially of social, political, and economic history, and of a considerable degree of psychological penetration. What is more, he must be familiar with the fundamental questions of philosophy and religion and be sufficiently mature, both intellectually and spiritually, to appreciate the supreme values communicated by the best and greatest literature.

From all this it is obvious that it is not easy to be a literary critic and that literary critics are, in fact, less common than it is sometimes thought. Here, as elsewhere, many are called but few chosen. It is also obvious why Dryden, Johnson, Coleridge, and Arnold are generally considered to be our greatest literary critics. Above all, perhaps, it is obvious, in the light of what is demanded of the literary critic, that the terms 'literary criticism' and 'literary critic', with their unfortunate suggestion of mere fault-finding, are singularly inappropriate. As Dryden complained three hundred years ago, 'they wholly mistake the nature of criticism who think its business is principally to find fault. Criticism ... was meant a standard of judging well; the chiefest part of which is, to observe those excellencies which should delight a reasonable reader.' The mistake thus magisterially corrected arises, no doubt, from the fact of our using one and the same word for both 'the act or an instance of making an unfavourable or severe judgement, comment, etc.' and 'the analysis or evaluation'—nothing is said about the enjoyment—'of a work of art, literature, etc.' The usage is by no means universal. In the Indian literary tradition the literary critic, as we call him, is designated the *rasika* or 'man of *rasa*'. The word *rasa* originally meant sap, juice, essence, flavour, taste. In literary criticism it is used in a metaphorical sense and means the 'taste' or 'flavour' that is essential to the enjoyment of literature and which in fact constitutes literature's very essence. The *rasika* or 'man of taste' (also known as the *sahṛidaya* or 'man of soul') is the one who 'tastes', that is, who appreciates or enjoys, the unique and indescribable flavour of a work of literary art. This 'taste' of his is not a matter of aesthetic judgement (as when we speak of good taste and bad taste), but rather one of aesthetic experience, so that the best equivalent for *rasa* is probably 'aesthetic experience' and the best equivalent for *rasika* 'the man of aesthetic experience'.

According to a leading modern authority, *rasa* or 'aesthetic experience', *aucitya* or 'propriety', and *dhvani* or 'significance', form the three great contributions of Sanskrit *alaṁkāra-śāstra* or 'poetics', *rasa* being the very 'soul' (*ātman*) of poetry and drama.[64] Such being the case it is not surprising that *rasa* should have been the subject of intense discussion throughout practically the entire history of Indian literary criticism, from its beginnings in the fifth or sixth century CE down very nearly to modern times. One of the principal topics discussed was that of the number of *rasas*, for though *rasa* as such was fundamentally one different names were given to it according to its evoking conditions. These names, or these *rasas*, together with the consequent plurality and difference, were held to be ultimately unreal; or they were at best *like* parts or aspects of a whole—the whole that was the ineffably blissful *rasa* itself. Metaphysics apart, however, *rasa* was ordinarily spoken of in the plural rather than in the singular, the number of *rasas* being usually given as eight, though some authorities admitted nine or even ten. The eight orthodox *rasas*, as they are sometimes called, are love (*śṛṅgāra*), valour or heroism (*vīra*), disgust (*bībhatsa*), wrath or fury (*raudra*), mirth (*hāsya*), terror (*bhayānaka*), pathos or compassion (*karuṇa*), and wonder (*adbhuta*), and the two unorthodox ones tranquillity or contentment (*śānta*) and parental fondness (*vātsalya*). Twenty-five or thirty additional *rasas* are also mentioned, while according to some theorists *rasa*s are in fact innumerable. Be that as it may, the mere enumeration of the eight *rasa*s, whether in English or in Sanskrit, serves to give us no idea of their real nature. It is therefore fortunate that the Indian poet and dramatist Michael Madhusudan Datta (1824–1873) should have written sonnets on the four *rasa*s of pathos, valour, love, and wrath, and still more fortunate that these sonnets should have been reproduced in the first issue (November 1987) of *Words International*. The third sonnet, 'Pathos', not only communicates something of the 'aesthetic experience' of that name but also connects pathos with poetry.

I saw a graceful woman by a stream,
Grave and sorrowful as the autumn moon
When it fears eclipse. All alone she sat;
Her face was wet with softly-flowing tears.
One by one they slid from her eyes like pearls,
Fell on the surface of the stream, and there,
Floating, turned into full-bloomed lotus flowers—
Golden lotus, moist with nectar for bees
To suck, rich with scent for the breeze to waft.
Bemused, I looked around uneasily.
The land was empty; a divine voice spoke:
"That stream is poetry; that woman's name
Is Pathos, queen of rasas. Blessed is he
Who can, through meditation, conquer her."[65]

It should be noted that in this poem Michael Madhusudan does not describe pathos directly (a *rasa* cannot in fact be described) but rather paints a word picture which, of its own accord, evokes this particular 'aesthetic experience' for the aesthetically educated reader or listener. It should also be noted that like the other *rasa*s pathos is not an emotion, though like them it has a dominant emotion as its basis. If we want to apply the word emotion to *rasa* at all then we shall have to do it by terming the latter 'art emotion', as some modern authorities have in fact done. This raises the interesting and important question of the difference between emotion and art emotion, that is, between emotion and *rasa*.

The nature of the difference between the two is very clearly illustrated in the scene of a play within a play in Kshemīśvara's *Naishadhānanda*, Act VI. As A.K. Warder relates, 'Nala, incognito, is sitting with Ṛituparṇa in the audience seeing a play about the terrible experiences of Damayantī, his wife. Ṛituparṇa has an aesthetic experience, but Nala instead reacts emotionally, though Ṛituparṇa keeps reminding him that it is a play and is puzzled at his strange excitement.'[66] Here we cannot but be reminded of another play within a play, that is, the famous one in *Hamlet*, Act III, Scene 2, when the guilty Claudius, 'frighted with false fire', reacts emotionally rather than aesthetically to the play that is being performed before him. Whether in medieval India or Renaissance England, the subject-matter of the drama is human life in all its aspects, and the drama depicts human life through the medium of the characters participating in the action of the play. These characters are personated by the actors, and according to classical Indian dramatic theory (with which Indian literary criticism in fact begins) the actors represent the emotions (*bhāvas*) of the characters they personate by representing the causes and effects of these emotions as expressed in bodily movements, speeches, etc. Thus the characters represented are not, in fact, present on the stage at all, neither are their emotions present, for the actors do not experience the emotions they represent but only act them. The characters in a play are present only in the imagination of the audience, and it is the imagined emotions of these characters which are the object of the aesthetic experience. This does not mean that the aesthetic experience is not a matter of perception but only of inference and that we infer the emotions of the characters from perceiving their effects represented. On the contrary, the aesthetic experience is immediate, not indirect. It is not a matter of ordinary perception, however, but rather of a special kind of perception—the perception produced by art. In the words of Abhinavagupta, as paraphrased by Warder, '*Aesthetic experience* is not perception as in everyday life; it is detached, pure, not involved, does not arouse our everyday concerns but takes us away from them. It is universal or completely objective, not particular or subjective. Thus it does not arouse the emotions of the audience but is a detached perception of the emotions of others.'[67] Moreover, the fact that it is the *imagined* emotions of the characters in the play which are the object of the aesthetic experience means, in effect, that the difference between *rasa* and the experience of *rasa* is purely notional. The perception of *rasa* is inseparable from its existence; or, in other words, *rasa* is identical with the experience of itself.

If all this makes *rasa* sound rather 'mystical' the fact is hardly surprising, for it is obvious that between aesthetic experience on the one hand and religious or mystical experience on the other there are definite analogies. These analogies did not escape the notice of the numerous authors and commentators who contributed to the development of

Indian literary criticism. Bhaṭṭa Nāyaka speaks of the experience of *rasa* as a process of disinterested contemplation akin to the contemplation of the Absolute, while according to Abhinavagupta aesthetic experience is non-individual and transcends space, time, and particular circumstances. In it the individual forgets himself, thereby attaining the highest happiness. Many other examples could be adduced. Nonetheless, though the connection between aesthetic experience and mystical experience was widely recognized there was never any question of subordinating literary criticism to religion. In India literary criticism was an autonomous, independent discipline, and it did not depend on religion or on any other extraneous authority. As Warder points out: 'The critics in fact held a variety of religious and philosophical opinions, which did not prevent them from contributing to the common field of criticism and developing each other's views on the basis of the principles of criticism itself. Bhāmaha was a Buddhist; his commentator Udbhaṭa appears from Jaina references to have been a Lokāyatika; Kuntaka who developed Bhāmaha's theory further was a Kāśmīra Śaiva. All this seems to have no bearing on their work as critics.... The principles of literary criticism in the main tradition are derived from literature itself, from what authors do and what readers enjoy.'[68]

There are thus significant resemblances between Indian literary criticism and Western literary criticism. In Western literary criticism, too, the analogies between aesthetic experience and religious or mystical experience have not escaped the notice of the critics, particularly those associated with the Romantic Movement, such as (in England) Coleridge, Hazlitt, and De Quincey. Like its Indian counterpart, moreover, Western literary criticism has never been subordinated to religion—except, perhaps, during the Middle Ages, when the function of criticism, like that of literature itself, was severely restricted. Western literary criticism too, therefore, has been a (largely) autonomous, independent discipline, its principles, like those of Indian literary criticism, being 'derived from literature itself, from what authors do and what readers enjoy', or at least were so derived until comparatively recently. But if there are significant resemblances between Indian literary criticism and Western literary criticism there are, at the same time, no less significant differences. Only two of these differences need be mentioned in the present connection. One of them is the fact that the Western tradition of literary criticism is much less continuous than the Indian tradition, and much less progressive. The other is the fact that although Western literary criticism continues to be autonomous and independent there has been a marked change in its relation to religion, at least in principle, so that it does not suffice to say of it—as it may suffice to say of Indian literary criticism—simply that it is not subordinated to religion.

The reason for this change is that there has been a change, here in the West, in the relation of literature itself to religion. Due to a variety of causes—causes into which I cannot enter now, but with which you will no doubt be familiar—in the course of the last three hundred or more years religion has ceased to be the sole, or even the supreme, bearer of values. For an increasing number of people, indeed, religion has ceased to be a bearer of values at all, with the result that—to cut a long story short—some of the more sensitive and discriminating among them have, in effect, come to regard literature as the principal bearer of values for the modern world. In other words literature and its sister arts are now performing, for a sizeable section of the population, a function that used to be performed by religion. The church has been replaced by the art gallery and the concert hall, the Bible by Shakespeare—except, of course, so far as the Bible is read not 'as literature' but as the inspired and inerrant Word of God. Literature, in particular, is able to take the place of religion in this way because it is a bearer of values in its own right, so to speak, independently of religion, so that in performing the function of religion it is, in reality, only performing its own function. Indeed, the fact that literature has been obliged, in recent times, to perform what was thought to be the function of religion has served to illuminate literature's own real nature. Literature is no longer regarded merely as a source of information or entertainment but, instead, as a separate and independent means of access to reality.

It is because literature is seen in this way that there has been a change in the relation of literature to religion and, therefore, a change in the relation of literary criticism to religion, so that it no longer suffices to say of Western literary criticism, at least, simply that it is not subordinated to religion. As I have already pointed out, literary criticism is no more than criticism of literature, and the fact that literature has been obliged, in recent times, to perform the function of religion, and that this has served to illuminate literature's own nature as a bearer of values, must be taken into account by any literary criticism deserving of the name. Indeed, such criticism will have to take into account the analogies between aesthetic experience and religious or mystical experience, for example, to a far greater extent that was possible at the time of the Romantic Movement. It will have to recognize that there is an area where literature and religion actually overlap and it will have to investigate the nature of the area. So far, literary criticism has not done this to any appreciable extent, or rather, no literary critic has done this to any appreciable extent, except for one neglected and virtually forgotten figure (forgotten, that is, as a critic) about whom I would like to say a few words. Before doing this, however, I want to go back to the Indian tradition of literary criticism and see what it has to say about its own subject-matter. We have already seen that in that tradition the literary critic, as we call him, is designated the *rasika* or 'man of taste', the man who appreciates or enjoys the flavour of a work of literary art, and it may be worth our while to see how what we call literature is designated.

The relevant Sanskrit words here are *kāvya*, *sāhitya*, and *vāṅgmaya*. The last of these means simply 'consisting of, or relevant to, speech (*vāk*)' and therefore is not of much help to us. *Sāhitya* means 'combination' or 'alliance', the combination or alliance in question being—according to the traditional authorities—that of expression (*śabda*, literally 'word') and meaning (*artha*). 'Expression and meaning combined' has, in fact, been the standard definition of *kāvya* from the seventh or eighth century onward, though Bhāmaha, the author of the definition, qualifies it by the statement that both expression and meaning are endowed with beauty (*alaṁkāra*, literally 'ornament'), beauty itself being defined as figurative or indirect (*vakra*, literally 'crooked' or 'curved'). This figurativeness and indirectness (*vakratā*) is an important feature of *kāvya*, particularly in view of the part that effective utterance plays in the production of *rasa*. Beauty of expression includes the choice of grammatical as distinct from un-grammatical expressions, while beauty of meaning includes the various figures of speech, starting with metaphor, but is further extended to cover the literary application of epistemology and logic, much as we might speak of a solution to a problem in mathematics as 'elegant'. All the traditionally accepted figures of speech, in fact, are beautiful, and according to Bhāmaha this 'beauty in literature' is a kind of deviation from ordinary, everyday expressions, being an added expressiveness created by the genius of the author. 'Literature follows a "curved" route, so to say, instead of the shortest line, uses indirect expressions, takes in additional meanings, as it were a wider prospect of the country traversed. Thus the characteristic of all beauties of literature, of all accepted *alaṁkāra*s, is their crookedness or curvedness, *vakratā*.'[69]

From this it is clear that *kāvya* designates only a small part of what we call literature, for as Warder points out the English language has no word for 'literature' in the precise sense of literature as an art, and it is just literature in this sense that *kāvya* designates. Western scholars have in fact tended to render the term *kāvya* as 'poetry', or even as 'ornate poetry', not to speak of 'court poetry'. This has given rise, however, to a certain amount of misunderstanding. *Kāvya* is not 'ornate' quite in the sense that is implied by the English term, neither does the fact that it was cultivated, more or less exclusively, at the courts of Indian princes, really tell us very much about its actual nature. Above all, *kāvya* is not poetry as distinct from prose but poetry as distinct from metrical composition. As Sushil Kumar De comments: 'The doctrine that prose is the opposite, not of poetry but of verse, which began to be realized rather late in European critical theories, was very early admitted without question by Sanskrit authors with whom metre does not play the same part as it does in European poetry; for in India from the earliest time, it was usual to put down even the driest teachings in a metrical form.'[70] Enlarging upon this theme in a footnote, the same authority declares: 'One need not emphasize the point that Sanskrit theorists define poetry so as to include any literary work of the imagination in its scope, and absolutely refuse to make of rhyming or versing an essential. This tradition is so well established that the question is nowhere discussed and never doubted. Thus, the theorists include under the heading of poetry romances like *Kādambarī* or *Harsha-carita* which are written for the most part in prose. Vāmana even quotes a dictum which says that prose is the touchstone of the poets...' Vāmana seems to have 'flourished' around 800CE, that is, about a century after Bhāmaha and two centuries before Abhinavagupta, and the meaning of the dictum which De refers to him as quoting may become clearer if it is paraphrased as follows: 'The real poet is the one who is able to write poetry in prose'. Thus while on the one hand *kāvya* designates less than what we call literature, on the other hand it includes more than what we usually think of as poetry. In other words, *kāvya* is art literature or, as we are more accustomed to say, creative literature or imaginative literature in the widest sense (which does not mean in the loosest sense), and it is this art literature that forms the subject-matter of Indian literary criticism and is enjoyed by the *rasika*.

Perhaps the best way of getting an idea of what constitutes *kāvya* is to draw up a select list of those works of English literature which could be regarded as designated by the term. Obviously the list would have to include *The Faerie Queene, Macbeth,* and *Paradise Lost,* as well as Smart's 'Song to David', Gray's 'Elegy Written in a Country Churchyard', Keats's Odes, Tennyson's 'The Lotos-Eaters', Poe's 'To Helen', Fitzgerald's *Rubáiyát of Omar Khayyám,* and Rossetti's *The House of Life.* But it would also have to include *Areopagitica,* Sir Thomas Browne's *Hydriotaphia* or

Urn Burial, De Quincey's 'The English Mail Coach', Coleridge's marginal glosses to 'The Rime of the Ancient Mariner' (as well as the 'Rime' itself, of course), Melville's *Moby Dick*, Pater's *Studies in the History of the Renaissance*, Hudson's *Green Mansions*, Wilde's *Poems in Prose*, Synge's *Deirdre of the Sorrows*, and Lawrence's *St Mawr*. All this—and much more besides—is *kāvya* or art literature, and it is this 'English *kāvya*', therefore, that we must concentrate on if we want to know what kind of material Indian literary criticism is concerned with and what it is like to be a *rasika* or 'man of taste'.

But it is time I left *kāvya* and the Indian tradition of literary criticism and said my promised few words about the neglected and virtually forgotten figure to whom I referred a few minutes ago—the figure who, alone among the critics of his time, investigated to any appreciable extent the area where religion and literature overlap. The figure in question is John Middleton Murry (1889–1957). As my reference to him implied, though Murry may have been forgotten as a literary critic he is not completely forgotten. In some ways we remember him very well. We remember him as the friend of D.H. Lawrence, as the husband of Katherine Mansfield, and as the opponent—so far as theories of literature went—of T.S. Eliot. In particular, perhaps, we remember him as the man who somehow let Lawrence down very badly, even actually betrayed him, thus bearing out the truth of Murry's own words when he wrote, apropos of the relationship between Godwin and Shelley: 'There are few harder fates for the man of some genius than to be intimately associated with a man of more. He is remembered, but in such a way that it seems better to be forgotten.'[71] In short, Murry as a person has had a bad press, and this fact has helped obscure the importance of his contribution to English literature and, indeed, to English life. At any rate, there has been no biography since F.A. Lea's 'official biography' of 1959 and only two or three short critical studies, the most substantial of them by an American scholar. To make matters worse, all Murry's books are now out of print in England, as are Richard Ree's 1960 and 1970 volumes of selections from his enormous output, while second hand copies of *Style* and *Keats and Shakespeare* are less easy to come by than they were ten or fifteen years ago.

Nevertheless, it seems the tide has begun to turn. Now that he has been dead for more than thirty years it seems that the friend of D.H. Lawrence and the husband of Katherine Mansfield is coming into his own at last. Two years ago there appeared *Beloved Quixote*, Katherine Middleton Murry's deeply moving memoir of her father, and the fact that four or five of his best known works are currently available in American reprint (at vastly inflated prices) suggests that on the other side of the Atlantic, at least, a process of reappraisal is already in progress. If the tide has indeed begun to turn, and if Murry is indeed coming into his own, it is an occasion for rejoicing, and we must hope that there will be a process of reappraisal on this side of the Atlantic too. Looking back in 1960 on the years following World War I Herbert Read observed of him that, at his best, he was 'the most stimulating "creative critic"' of his time, and in the same year another reviewer applauded 'his insight into literature as a composite appeal to the reader's entire nature, which helped reawaken confidence in poetry and fiction, as a medium for the intelligence of the age at a time of dejection and uncertainty.'[72] It is difficult to believe that a critic of whom such things could be said has no significance for us today. Not that he should overlook the phrase with which Read is careful to qualify his praise: it is Murry *at his best* who is the most stimulating 'creative critic' of his time. But neither should we overlook the epithet with which Read characterizes Murry as a critic. As Ernest G. Griffin, the American scholar already referred to, points out: 'The epithet "creative" which Read applies to Murry is much abused nowadays, but it is useful in distinguishing his criticism from that which is found more commonly in academic circles. Murry's criticism was of a kind which led to a wider creative atmosphere for writers and to wider literary appreciation rather than to the academy. His tastes in later life demonstrated this difference: on the one hand, he had little sympathy with the scholarly critics loosely termed "the new critics", and, on the other, he was excited to discover the work of J.D. Salinger. In fact, the combination of a moral concern with society and a personal, frequently mystical, enquiry into religious values, which one finds in Salinger and other modern American writers, was just that which was basic to Murry's own work.'[73]

Murry's own epithet for himself as a critic was not 'creative' but 'emotional'. Writing to Katherine Mansfield in 1919 he told her: 'I can't treat art as a clever game, and I am (to myself anyhow) always notoriously weakest in the examination of the technical side of a work. My test is extremely simple. If a work awakens a profound response in me, then I sit up and try to find out what it is that is working on me. In other words I am an absolutely emotional critic. What may seem intellectual is only my method of explaining the nature of the emotion.'[74] It was because he was an emotional critic that Murry was able to perform what he saw as the critic's primary function. The task of the critic was to discover and work from the 'creative centre' of the writer with whom he was concerned. The greater the writer, the more mystical would the apprehension of that 'creative centre' be, since the greatest artistic perceptions were those moments of 'immediate apprehension of the unity of the world' in which the basic paradox of life was resolved. In characterizing himself as an emotional critic Murry does not, however, have in mind the usual meaning of the word emotion and its derivatives. For him emotion is not merely an immediate feeling but a 'mode of experience' based on a subtle interplay and development of original emotions with which, as the development becomes more complex, there grows a progressively acute understanding of the human situation in general.

At the beginning of his 1919 lecture on 'The Nature of Poetry' there is a passage in which Murry gives an impressionistic account of how, as an emotional critic, he approaches the task of criticism. After speaking of the 'curious exaltation that comes to a critic as he begins to disengage—as he believes—the central, golden thread of a poet's being,' and quoting the 'small wise sentence' of Anatole France to the effect that criticism is the confession of the adventures of a man's soul among books, he continues: 'Whether it is that I have some special liability to such adventures, or that my mind is such that the adventures I do have take a peculiarly exciting form—I cannot say; but the fact is that there are moments when criticism of a particular kind, the only kind I care for, utterly absorbs me. I feel that I am touching a mystery. There is a wall, as it were, of dense, warm darkness before me—a darkness which is secretly alive and thrilling to the sense. This, I believe, is the reflection in myself of the darkness which broods over the poet's creative mind. It forms slowly and gradually gathers while I read his work. The sense of mystery deepens; but the quality of the mystery becomes more plain. There is a moment when, as though unconsciously and out of my control, the deeper rhythm of a poet's work, the rise and fall of the great moods which determined what he was and what he wrote, enter into me also. I feel his presence; I am obedient to it, and it seems to me as though the breathing of my spirit is at one with his.'[75]

Murry is conscious that these are 'vague words', but though claiming to have none better to offer he does, in fact, devote the next few pages of his lecture to explaining, and enlarging upon, his approach in somewhat more analytical terms. From the way in which he does this it is clear that for Murry literary criticism is a very serious matter and that, therefore, literature is a very serious matter too. Referring to the fact that it is not in literature only but in all things that 'the directest and truest apprehension we have is a sudden communication, a sudden communion rather, between mystery and mystery,' he speaks of 'the universe of life of which literature is the symbol and the flower'.[76] It is evident that these last words, casually as they appear to have dropped from Murry's pen, are deserving of careful study. In what sense is literature the symbol and the flower of the universe of life, and what is the precise point of the distinction between literature as the symbol of that universe and litera- ture as its flower? It is also evident that in speaking of literature in this way Murry has, in fact, given us yet another definition of the subject-mat- ter of literary criticism. Not only is literature 'the thought of thinking Souls', 'the shadow of good talk', and 'language charged with meaning' and so on. Literature is also the symbol and the flower of the universe of life.

Thus we have come full circle. We have come back to the point from which we set out nearly an hour ago, that is, the point at which I raised the question, 'What is literature?' Since then we have seen the beginnings of an answer to that question, and having seen the beginnings of an answer to it, in the form of a working definition of literature, we have been able to achieve at least some insight into the nature of literary criticism, East and West, as well as some insight into what is demanded of the literary critic. We are therefore now in a position to say what would, in principle, constitute a crisis in literary criticism. Literary criticism would be in a state of crisis if it had a false, or an inadequate, idea of literature and, consequently, a false or an inadequate idea of its own function. Whether literary criticism in England and America is currently in a state of crisis *in this sense* I do not really know, even though I strongly suspect that there is, in fact, something wrong with it at present. But if literary criticism is in crisis, or even if it is just in a mess, or if it is in a crisis because it is in a mess, then the fundamental reason for its being in such a state can only be that it has a false, or an inadequate, idea of literature and, consequently, a false or an inadequate idea of its own relation to literature. What literary criticism therefore ought above all to be doing, if in fact it is in crisis, is trying to achieve a truer and more adequate idea of literature and literary criticism, such as I believe is reflected, albeit fragmentarily, in what I have been saying to you on these subjects in my capacity as an 'outsider'. How literary criticism will achieve such an idea of literature and literary criticism I do not know. Perhaps a dictum of John Middleton Murry's will provide a clue. 'The true literary critic,' he says, 'must have a humanistic philosophy. His inquiries must be modulated, subject to an intimate, organic governance, by an ideal of the good life.'[77] But even if Murry's words do not provide a clue, and even if literary criticism is unable, at this juncture, to achieve a truer and more adequate idea of literature, there are still a number of things it ought to be doing, and I shall conclude with a few words on some of the more important of these things. In speaking of them I shall not be observing any particular order.

Firstly, literary criticism ought to be concerning itself with actual concrete works of literature (that is, works of 'art literature'), and it ought to be concerning itself with them *as literature*. This is so obvious and so elementary a point that had I not come across two rather shocking examples of the way in which literary criticism does *not* concern itself with concrete works of literature I should hardly have dared to make it. In a recent article on 'T.S. Eliot, Robert Lowell and the New Critics' the poet and lecturer Philip Hobsbaum, having referred to 'scholars who wrote their doctoral theses on Lowell and devoted their lives thereafter to the study of his work' continues: 'Beyond their purview, a further school of critics has arisen which shows less and less interest in literature. Not the nascent poetry of our own time, but marginal works of the past ... are the hostages of these other critics, and the works under discussion are not so much texts as source-material for clashes among the ideologies.'[78] This is bad enough, but there is worse to come. In a still more recent article on John Buchan the critic and editor David Daniell tells the painful story of how Buchan came to be labelled 'anti-Semitic'. 'Gertrude Himmelfarb, an American historian of English life, wrote from New York in the September 1960 number of *Encounter* an article about Buchan later reprinted, with changes, in her 1968 book, *Victorian Minds*— which began this particular myth. There she propounded a racist Buchan who was grossly anti-Semitic. Most of her evidence was made up: her portrait was grossly untrue. "Buchan's Jewish villains", her invention, do not exist. She showed that she had read virtually no Buchan at all, and what she had, she had taken so carelessly that she thought Greenmantle was a woman. Yet her piece had been enormously influential, and traces of it are everywhere. Buchan, she announced—with no evidence—was the fictional "perpetrator" of the "Jewish-capitalist-communist-conspiracies." It seems difficult to get over to a large part of the public that this is a lie.'[79] Obvious and elementary though the point may be, it therefore becomes necessary to insist that literary criticism ought to be concerning itself with actual concrete works of literature, and concerning itself with them *as literature*, and that the literary critic should at the very least have read the poems or the novels or the plays with which he—or she—is purportedly dealing.

Secondly, literary criticism ought to be enjoying the works of literature with which it is concerned and which form its particular subject-matter. It is not enough that the literary critic should have enjoyed *Paradise Lost* or *Middlemarch* or *Julius Caesar* twenty years ago, when he was 'reading English'—assuming that, unlike the girl in Robert Graves's anecdote, he did in fact enjoy them then. He must enjoy them here and now, when he is writing about them, and something of that enjoyment must find expression in his criticism. By enjoyment I do not, however, mean the pseudo-aesthetic self-indulgence that Tennyson, in 'The Palace of Art', satirizes in the figure of the 'glorious Devil, large in heart and brain, That did love Beauty only.' By enjoyment I mean the self-forgetful delight that comes when one surrenders to a work of literature and allows oneself to experience it with one's whole being, emotional and intellectual, sensitive and intuitive.

Thirdly, literary criticism ought to be getting out of the universities, or at least trying not to confine itself to them. In other words literary criticism ought to be emancipating itself from the constraints which our current system of higher education tends inevitably to impose on any creative activity. It ought to be transforming itself from a profession into a vocation.

Fourthly, literary criticism ought to be widening its horizon and getting to know the traditions of literary criticism that have developed in India, in the Far East, and in the Islamic world.

Fifthly, literary criticism ought to be re-evaluating our literary heritage. As John Middleton Murry wrote in 1920: 'The function of true criticism is to establish a definite hierarchy among the great artists of the past, as well as to test the production of the present; by the combination of these activities it asserts the organic unity of all art.'[80] In fulfilling this function and establishing the hierarchy of which Murry speaks literary criticism must have the courage of its aesthetic convictions and not hesitate to put down the mighty from their seats and exalt the humble and the meek. Among the mighty I would include James Joyce, Virginia Woolf, Ezra Pound, and (probably) T.S. Eliot, all of whom I believe to be overrated, and among the humble and the meek Cowley, Thompson (the author of 'The Seasons'), Johnson, Crabbe, Scott, Patmore, Rossetti, Gissing, and Wyndham Lewis, all of whom I believe to be underrated.

Sixthly, and lastly, literary criticism ought to be pointing us in the direction of literature, even as literature itself points us in the direction of life.

DHARMAPALA: THE SPIRITUAL DIMENSION

ANAGARIKA DHARMAPALA IS BEST KNOWN to the Buddhist world as the founder of the Maha Bodhi Society, the resuscitator of Buddha Gayā, and the fearless proclaimer of the Dharma in three continents. In the course of the fifty years from 1883 to 1933 he built temples and viharas, established schools, hospitals, and rest houses, opened Buddhist centres, organized the celebration of Buddhist festivals, sponsored international Buddhist conferences, reclaimed sites connected with the life of the Buddha, revived Pāli studies in India, promoted traditional Sinhalese arts and crafts, encouraged technical education, founded and edited journals, printed and distributed Buddhist literature, wrote articles, lectured on Buddhism, politics, and social reform, corresponded with friends and sympathizers throughout the world, and did a hundred other things in pursuit of his declared objective of working—through Buddhism—for the good of humanity.

So much did he in fact do that one might be forgiven for thinking that he was no more than a Buddhist activist, of the type that was later to become only too common, and that he had allowed himself to become absorbed in external activities at the expense of his inner life. Such was my own impression, at least, until the year 1952, when the late Devapriya Valisinha, the chief lieutenant and principal disciple of the Anagarika's latter years and his successor as General Secretary of the Maha Bodhi Society of India, invited me to contribute a biographical sketch of his guru to the Society's Diamond Jubilee Souvenir. This sketch I wrote at the Society's Calcutta headquarters, where I had the opportunity of examining some of the bulky quarto volumes of the Dharmapala Diaries—

diaries the Anagarika had kept for about forty years. At the head of every alternate page he had, I found, written 'The only refuge for him who aspires to true perfection is the Buddha alone.' These were the words— originally a message from the Master K.H. to A.P. Sinnett—which Madame Blavatsky had quoted to him in 1884, when he was only twenty years old and still Don David Hewavitarne, and they had, it seems, remained permanently inscribed on his heart. This is highly significant. Going for Refuge to the Buddha (and to the Dharma and the Sangha) is the central and definitive act of the Buddhist life, and the fact that Dharmapala should have gone on writing out the words quoted by Madame Blavatsky in the way he did showed that for him Going for Refuge was not a formality to be observed on special occasions but something that had to be personally experienced—or at least called to mind—every single day. It showed that for him being a Buddhist was not something that one could take for granted. Being a Buddhist represented a commitment that had to be constantly renewed. Moreover, the Master's message spoke of the Buddha alone being the only refuge *for him who aspires to true perfection*. True perfection was ethical and spiritual, and ethical and spiritual perfection was synonymous with bodhi or Enlightenment. Since the Buddha was the embodiment of Enlightenment it followed that the act of Going for Refuge to the Buddha and the aspiration to true perfection were inseparable. It is therefore not surprising that throughout his life Dharmapala should not only have observed the basic ethical precepts of Buddhism but also have striven unremittingly for complete purity of body, speech, and mind. Nor was that all. The Buddha *alone* was the *only* refuge for the aspirant to true perfection. Though he was a man of broad religious sympathies, having joined the Theosophical Society at an early age (he remained a Theosophist, though not a member of any Theosophical organization, to the end of his life), Dharmapala was by no means a woolly-minded universalist for whom all religious teachers were equally enlightened and all religious teachings equally true. For him the Buddha was the *supremely* Enlightened One and his teaching the way to Enlightenment *par excellence*.

On examining the Diaries I also found that Dharmapala's day began at two or three o'clock in the morning and that it began with meditation. He had always been interested in meditation, and admits in his unfinished 'Reminiscences of My Early Life' that from boyhood he was inclined towards the mystic, ascetic life, and that he was on the lookout for news about Arhats and the science of *abhijñā*, or supernormal knowledge, even though, as he relates, the bhikshus of Ceylon were sceptical about the possibility of realizing Arhatship, believing that the age of Arhats was past and that the realization of nirvāṇa by psychic training was no longer possible. These mystic and ascetic tendencies were strengthened by his contact with the teachings of Theosophy, especially its teachings about the Masters, and by the fact that in the course of his travels on behalf of the Buddhist Theosophical Society—travels which took him to every corner of the island—he came across a number of palm-leaf books on meditation, one of which he had transcribed. But though he came across books on meditation he was unable to find anyone, whether monk or layman, who actually meditated or who could instruct him in the practices the books described. The nearest he came to finding such a person was when a monk told him that his late guru had practised meditation—and had gone mad! Some time in 1889 or 1890, therefore, when he had sought in vain for a teacher for several years, Dharmapala started practising meditation without the benefit of a personal teacher after making a careful study of the *Satipaṭṭhāna Sutta* or 'Discourse on the Foundations of Mindfulness', and the relevant sections of the *Visuddhimagga*. Having thus made a start he continued, and for the next forty years meditation formed an integral part of his day, as the pages of the Dharmapala Diaries abundantly testify. Shortly after embarking on the practice of meditation, however, he travelled to Adyar for the Theosophical Society's Annual Convention of 1890 and there, besides joining the Esoteric Section of the Society, had the good fortune to meet a Burmese Buddhist layman from whom he received some practical instructions on meditation. This friendly mentor appears to have been Moung Hpo Myhim, with whom Dharmapala stayed when he visited Rangoon the following year on his way back from Japan and who proved to be a staunch supporter of his work. Another significant contact, in view of Dharmapala's confessed inclination towards the mystic, ascetic life, was a female yogi known simply as Maji or Reverend Mother. Dharmapala heard of her at Benares, which he visited shortly after the Convention, and at once went to see her in her cave on the banks of the Ganges. They had a pleasant chat, he reports, and at his request she presented him with a rosary. What use he made of the rosary we do not know. Perhaps he recited on it the epithets of the Buddha as enumerated in the *iti'pi so* formula—a traditional Theravāda practice. We do not, in fact, know much about the methods of meditation practised by Dharmapala at this stage of his career or just how extensive was his experience of higher states of consciousness, though a diary entry for 17 February 1891 speaks of his experiencing, for the first time in his life, 'the peace which passeth all understanding'. What we do know is that *mettā bhāvana* eventually became the sheet-anchor of his spiritual life and that not a day passed without his consciously directing thoughts of loving-kindness to parents, benefactors, and friends and, indeed, to all living beings.

Meditation must be well grounded in ethics. It is hardly possible for one to develop skilful concentration of mind when the mind is disturbed by those unskilful states of lust, hatred, and so on which are the effect, even as they are also the cause, of unethical behaviour. As the Buddha repeatedly reminded his followers in the course of the last few months of his life: 'Great becomes the fruit, great the advantage, of meditation (*samādhi*) when it is set round with ethical behaviour (*sīla*); great becomes the fruit, great the advantage, of understanding (*paññā*) when it is set round with meditation' (*Dīgha-Nikāya* ii, 81 *et seq.*). In Dharmapala's case meditation was certainly well set round with ethical behaviour, even as understanding was well set round with meditation, and for him, therefore, the fruit and advantage of both meditation and understanding can be assumed to have 'become great'. The importance of leading 'the life of holiness, perfect and pure', formed, in fact, one of the major themes of his lectures and addresses in East and West alike. His first lecture—actually a sermon—in the United States, immediately before the World's Parliament of Religions, was on 'The Pure Life', and after a long and tiring session of the Parliament he characteristically remarked 'All papers full of Theology and Anthropomorphism but pure life naught.' Not that Dharmapala saw purity of life solely in terms of its bearing on meditation. Purity of life, or ethical behaviour, was as necessary to the householder as to the monk, to society as to the individual. 'The Buddha laid great emphasis on the moral progress of the individual,' he wrote in the *Maha Bodhi Journal*. 'The householder without morality is like a ship without a rudder.' Similarly, 'Morality is the most solid foundation that is needed to build up a lasting society. The Lord Buddha again and again emphasized that the Aryan religion shall only last so long as the disciples would strictly follow the path of purifying morality. When morality disappears society degenerates.' In the course of his travels in the West, especially, he could not but observe how many rudderless ships there were adrift on the ocean of humanity and the extent to which society had therefore degenerated. 'Slaves of passion,' he wrote in his diary during his second trip to the United States (1896–1897), 'controlled by the lower senses, wallowing in sensuality, these so-called Christians live in killing each other, hating each other, swindling each other, introducing liquor and vice where they hadn't existed. Themselves slaves of passion they enslave others to themselves and their vices.'

Dharmapala himself, though of an ardent temperament, was far from being a slave of passion. At the age of eight, he tells us in his unfinished 'Reminiscences', he was initiated into the *brahmacharya* vow by his father at the local temple, and advised to be contented with what he got to eat, and to sleep but little. What form the initiation took, and whether the ceremony was performed by his father personally, or by the incumbent of the temple, we are not told, but the experience left a permanent impression. Besides being accustomed, in later years, to satisfy his hunger with whatever food he received, and to sleep for only two or three hours at night, Dharmapala continued to observe the *brahmacharya* vow and remained, despite all temptation, chaste in body, in speech, and—to the utmost of his ability—in mind, to the end of his days. His mature commitment to the life of chastity was signalized by his adoption of the title of anagarika or 'Homeless One', an anagarika being one who, without being technically a monk, observed the precept of abstention from unchastity (as distinct from the precept of abstention from sexual misconduct) and whose life was wholly dedicated to the service of Buddhism. Prior to this he had signalized his rejection of foreign manners and customs, which were having a deleterious effect on the cultural and religious life of the nation, by dropping the Portuguese-Christian 'Don David' and assuming the name of Dharmapala, or 'Guardian of the Law'. It was therefore as Anagarika Dharmapala that he became known to the world and as Anagarika Dharmapala that he has his place in Buddhist history.

Being an anagarika, and observing as he did the *brahmacharya* vow, Dharmapala was free as he could never have been as a married house-holder. He was freer than even the monks, restricted as these then were by the requirements of the Vinaya. He was free to work for humanity; free to work for Buddhism; free to travel; free to speak his mind; free to sacrifice health, strength, and life itself for the sake of his ideals. He was also free to form friendships with men of all sorts and conditions in many different parts of the world. Dharmapala in fact had something of a gift for friendship. By nature warm-hearted and enthusiastic, he not only made friends easily but, once having made a friend, he remained loyal— even fiercely loyal—to the friendship through all vicissitudes. That he had this gift for friendship was fortunate, since the best part of his life was spent in a foreign land, working for a long-vanished faith, and struggling (in the matter of the Buddha Gayā Temple case) against powerful vested interests, and had he not enjoyed the support of friends and well-wishers he would have encountered even more difficulties than he did. Some of his closest friends were to be found among the English-educated Bengalis of Calcutta, where from the beginning of 1892 Dharmapala made his homeless home and where he lived on terms of intimacy with men who were, or who subsequently became, prominent in the life of the great city, then the capital of India. In more than one instance the friendship continued through two, and even three, generations of the same family, being handed down from father to son like a precious heirloom.

Dharmapala's gift for friendship was naturally strengthened by his practice of *mettā bhāvana*, in the course of which he sought to develop thoughts of loving-kindness towards all living beings, not excluding animals. As a boy he was revolted by the fact that one of the masters at the Christian school he attended took delight in shooting birds. It therefore is not surprising that he should have been a lifelong vegetarian (as was his disciple Sri Devapriya Valisinha), being particularly opposed to the eating of beef. A photograph taken on one of his preaching tours in Ceylon (now Sri Lanka), and reproduced in the Maha Bodhi Society of India's *Diamond Jubilee Souvenir*, shows him leaning out of the window of a small omnibus on the side of which are emblazoned, in large Sinhalese characters, the words 'Don't eat beef.'

Thus there was a definitely spiritual dimension to Dharmapala's life, and it was because of this spiritual dimension, as exemplified by his recognition that the Buddha alone was the only refuge, his aspiration to ethical and spiritual perfection, his inclination to the mystic, ascetic life, his devotion to meditation, his observance of the *brahmacharya* vow, his adoption of the homeless life, his gift for friendship, and his vegetarianism, that enabled him to found the Maha Bodhi Society, to resuscitate Buddha Gayā, and to proclaim the Dharma, as well as to engage in numerous other activities. All these activities were, in fact, the outward and visible expression of an intense inner life. His illustrious Hindu colleague at the World's Parliament of Religions, Swami Vivekananda, defined the ideal man as he who, in the midst of the greatest silence and solitude, finds the intensest activity, and in the midst of the intensest activity finds the silence and solitude of the desert. By this definition Anagarika Dharmapala was an ideal man or, in Buddhist terms, a Bodhi-sattva—the kind of being of whom the *Ratnagotravibhāga* (verse 73) declares:

Like a fire his mind constantly blazes up into good works for others;
At the same time he always remains merged in the calm of the trances and
formless attainments.

It was the life of a Bodhisattva that his father exhorted him to lead when he entrusted him, in his twentieth year, to the care of Madame Blavatsky, and it was accordingly the life of a Bodhisattva—a life dedicated to the highest good of humanity—that he endeavoured to lead for the next forty years. Consequently it would not be too much to describe Anagarika Dharmapala as 'a modern Bodhisattva', as I did in an editorial I wrote for the September 1954 issue of the *Maha Bodhi Journal*. In that article I considered his practice of the Bodhisattva ideal in terms of his cultivation of the Ten Perfections (*dasa pāramitā*) of Theravāda tradition, from giving (*dāna*) to equanimity (*upekkhā*), concluding: 'As we remember his 93rd Birth Anniversary ... we recall his practice of the Bodhisattva Ideal and are grateful for the fact that even in these dark days we have before our eyes the inspiring example of a modern Bodhisattva to follow.' Thirty-six years later I see no reason to revise that judgement, and on the occasion of the one hundredth anniversary of the Society he founded salute the memory of the great Anagarika with renewed appreciation.

With Allen Ginsberg in Kalimpong (1962)

Our first meeting with a person often seems of special significance, especially in retrospect. This was certainly the case with my first meeting with Allen Ginsberg, which took place in Kalimpong, a small town in the foothills of the eastern Himalayas, in June 1962. Allen was on his first visit to India, and had been touring the holy places of Hinduism and Buddhism and making friends with Indians of all classes and creeds. I had lived in India for more than fifteen years, of which the last twelve or more had been passed in Kalimpong, after I had spent two years in South India as a wandering ascetic and a year in Benares studying Pāli and Buddhist philosophy. In 1957 I had established, on the outskirts of Kalimpong, a small monastery which was already well known as a centre of interdenominational Buddhism, and it was in the sparsely furnished sitting room of this monastery that Allen and I had our first meeting.

Allen had already published *Howl* and *Kaddish* and was probably the most outstanding—certainly the best known—of the Beat Poets, but of all this I then knew nothing. Though I had read and written poetry from an early age, and was still reading and writing it at intervals, I was quite unaware of the more recent developments that had taken place in this field, whether in Britain or in the United States. In any case, my tastes were traditional rather than modernist, and it is doubtful if I would have felt much sympathy with the attitudes of the Beat Generation, at least so far as these were expressed in literature. Be that as it may, the fact that I knew nothing of the Beat Poets, and that Allen Ginsberg was not even a name to me, meant that when the slouching, dirty, dishevelled, hirsute figure appeared unexpectedly on my verandah one afternoon I could meet and greet him simply as a fellow human being.

How he came to know about 'the English Buddhist monk in Kalimpong' I do not remember. It may have been from Gary Snyder, with whom I had corresponded (about Zen Buddhism) in the early fifties, or it may have been from Sister Vajira, the elderly and somewhat eccentric English Buddhist nun he had met in Darjeeling a few days earlier. Most likely he had heard about me from Devapriya Valisinha, the General Secretary of the Maha Bodhi Society of India, whom he had met in Calcutta, when he visited the Society's headquarters. Calcutta had, it seemed, affected him deeply. He and his friend Peter had spent two or three uncomfortable weeks there, I gathered, but since Peter had fallen ill he had had to make the trip up to Darjeeling and Kalimpong on his own. 'Peter's my wife' he added, by way of explanation. At first I thought that I had either misheard my visitor or that Peter was in fact not a man but a woman. After all, there were female Lesleys and Robins and so on, especially in America. Why should there not be a female Peter? I had yet to discover that Peter definitely was a man and that Allen was nothing if not frank.

My initial impression of Allen, however, appearances apart, was that he was very American. That was indeed obvious as soon as he opened his mouth and began talking. Crouched uncomfortably on the edge of one of the bamboo armchairs that constituted almost the sole furniture of my little sitting-room, and glancing uneasily out of the window from time to time in the direction of the blue Darjeeling hills, Allen indeed talked quite a lot that afternoon. Much of what he said was rather incoherent, and he rambled a good deal, but I gathered that he was interested in Buddhism, especially Tantric Buddhism, and that he had come to Kalimpong—as so many other Westerners had come—in search of Tantric initiation, the more powerful the better. While we were talking Lobsang Norbu, the young Tibetan manager of the monastery, brought in the tea and started pouring it out. Allen looked up from the apathy into which it seemed he had sunk for a moment. 'Wow, he's a good-looker!' he exclaimed, goggling up at Lobsang admiringly. Lobsang, who had spent the greater part of his life in a Tibetan monastery (he was still technically a novice, though he insisted on wearing Western dress) was not ignorant of what such admiration meant, but his only response was a broad smile that showed his magnificent white teeth. I began to think that perhaps I had not misheard my visitor and that Peter might, after all, be a man.

While we were drinking our tea I gathered that the balding American hunched opposite me was interested not only in Buddhism but in poetry. In fact, he was a poet. As though to prove it, he dove into a travel-stained cloth bag that he had dumped on the floor beside him and produced two small, dog-eared volumes. These were *Howl* and *Kaddish*, the latter of which had been published only the previous year. One volume he inscribed and presented to me (which one, I can no longer recollect), while the other he offered to leave with me to read overnight since he had no other copy with him in India and was therefore unable to give it to me. From the way in which he handled the two volumes, as well as the way in which he spoke about their contents, it was clear that Allen cared very deeply about his poetry, and that in making me a gift of the one volume and offering to lend me the other he was in fact giving expression to his willingness to share with me the deepest and most precious part of himself. Suddenly he seemed very open, very vulnerable, and very human.

That night I sat up quite late, after my usual meditation and puja, reading *Howl* and *Kaddish* by the light of a kerosene lamp. Before Allen's departure it had been agreed that he should come again the following afternoon to collect the volume he had left with me, and that I should tell him what I thought about his poetry. It had also been agreed that I should take him to see my friend C.M. Chen, the Chinese Buddhist yogi, who I felt might be able to help him in his search for Tantric initiation. Poring over the two dog-eared volumes by the yellow light of the kerosene lamp, I could not but be struck by their raw energy and their directness, but I found it difficult to think of them as poetry and could not help wondering what I was going to say to Allen the following afternoon.

I need not have worried. When we met he was preoccupied (in an obsessive, unhealthy way, I thought) with the idea of Tantric initiation and on my returning the volume he had left with me the previous day he stuffed it into his cloth bag almost absent-mindedly. What I said about his poetry I do not know. Probably I got away with telling him that I found it very interesting, which was true enough. As we walked into Kalimpong along the Upper Cart Road he plied me with questions about Tantric Buddhism, especially about the exact nature of its sexual practices. I was describing these as best I could, and going into a certain amount of detail, when my companion suddenly stopped dead in his tracks, seized me by the arm, and with a voice hoarse with excitement demanded 'Say, can you do it with a *boy*?' I had to confess I did not know if you could do it with a boy, and that he would have to ask Mr Chen. I was now quite sure that Peter definitely was a man.

Mr Chen's hermitage was situated at the farther, lower end of the Kalimpong bazaar. When we reached it half an hour later, and were sitting in the tiny reception room with its numerous pictures of Tantric divinities locked in (hetero-)sexual embrace, Allen lost no time in putting his question. *Could you do it with a boy?* Rather to my surprise, Mr Chen showed every sign of extreme embarrassment. No, you certainly could *not* do it with a boy, he replied shortly, and at once changed the subject. Allen's visit was not a success. When I saw Mr Chen a few days later he referred to the strange American I had brought to see him, and to his outrageous question, in terms of horror and disgust. How could anyone even *think* of 'doing it with a boy'! So far as the Chinese Buddhist yogi was concerned the sexual practices of the Buddhist Tantra were, it seemed, essentially and unalterably heterosexual, which I could not help thinking was rather a limitation.

Nevertheless, though the visit had not been a success it had not been a total failure either. Mr Chen had advised Allen to seek Tantric initiation from Dudjom Rimpoche, who was then living in Kalimpong, and I believe Allen did in fact meet the Nyingmapa hierophant before rejoining Peter in Calcutta. Whether he succeeded in obtaining Tantric initiation, or in finding an answer to the question that had puzzled me and embarrassed Mr Chen, I never discovered, for Allen and I did not meet again for three or four years. When we did meet (in London, on the morning after the famous Albert Hall poetry reading) it did not occur to me to ask him how he had fared in Kalimpong after our visit to Mr Chen. Nor has it occurred to me to ask him since. If he reads these lines perhaps they will jog his memory.

Notes and References

Aspects of Buddhist Morality

1 *Dialogues of the Buddha, Part II,* trans. T.W. and C.A.F. Rhys Davids, Luzac, London 1971, p.97 *et.seq.* (translation modified).
2 *Majjhima-Nikāya* 24.
3 *Visuddhimagga VII*, 101–6, Harvard edition, pp.222–3.
4 See Sangharakshita, *A Survey of Buddhism*, 7th edition, Windhorse, Glasgow 1993, pp.462–3
5 Ibid., p.461 *et seq.*
6 *Paṭisambhidhāmagga* i,44.
7 *Visuddhimagga* I, 17–18, Harvard edition, pp.7–8.
8 sGam.po.pa, *The Jewel Ornament of Liberation*, trans. Herbert V.Guenther, Rider, London 1970, pp.164–5.
9 See, for example, Sangharakshita, *Crossing the Stream*, Windhorse, Glasgow 1987, p.179 *et seq.*, and *A Survey of Buddhism*, op.cit., p.92 *et seq.*
10 *The Jewel Ornament of Liberation*, op.cit., p.101.
11 *Majjhima-Nikāya* 26.
12 *Visuddhimagga I*,32, Harvard edition, p.14.
13 J. Evola, *The Doctrine of Awakening*, Luzac, London 1951, p.151.
14 Ibid., p.151.
15 Ibid., p.151–2.
16 *Dīgha-Nikāya* 31.
17 cf. *The Jewel Ornament of Liberation*, op.cit., p.165 *et seq.*
18 *Dīgha-Nikāya* ii, 86.

19 *Visuddhimagga* I,24. *The Path of Purity, Vol.I,* trans. Pe Maung Tin, Pali Text Society, London ?1923, p.12.

20 *The Jewel Ornament of Liberation,* op.cit., p.170.

21 *Dīgha-Nikāya* iii, 72–3.

22 C.D. Darlington, *The Evolution of Man and Society,* George Allen & Unwin, London 1969, p.53.

23 *Visuddhimagga* I, 34.

24 *The Awakening of Faith,* trans. Yoshito S.Hakeda, Columbia University Press, New York & London 1967, p.56 *et seq.*

THE JOURNEY TO IL CONVENTO

25 Peter Lamborn Wilson, *Angels,* Thames & Hudson, London 1980.

26 The present owner of Il Convento di Santa Croce informs us that the Convent was established in 1620 and was occupied for most of its period as a monastery by black-robed Augustinian friars. In 1790 it was taken over by Franciscans who remained there until they were turned out by Napoleon's troops in 1805. The Convent was never re-established.

BUDDHISM AND BLASPHEMY

27 Buddhadatta's *English–Pali Dictionary* does indeed give *ariyūpavāda* as the equivalent of blasphemy, but this is a recent coinage not found in the Pali Text Society's *Pali–English Dictionary.*

28 *Contra Mendacium,* 39. *Seventeen Short Treatises of S.Augustine, Bishop of Hippo,* Walter Smith (late Mozley), London 1884, p.466.

29 *Dīgha-Nikāya* 1, in *Dialogues of the Buddha, Part I,* trans. T.W. Rhys Davids, Pali Text Society, London and Boston 1973, pp.2–3.

30 Robert Burton, *The Anatomy of Melancholy, Vol.ii,* Longman and others, London 1827, p.587.

31 *De Civitatis Dei,* lib.XVI, cap.xxxi.

32 Anne Fremantle, *The Papal Encyclicals in their Historical Context,* Mentor, New York 1960, p.145.

33 Ibid., p.137.

34 Ibid., p.146.

35 Quoted Jolan Jacobi, *The Psychology of Jung,* Kegan Paul Trench Trubner, London 1942, p.88.

36 Ibid., p.24.

37 Quoted Nicolas Walter, *Blasphemy in Britain,* Rationalist Press Association, London 1977, pp.9–10.

BUDDHISM, WORLD PEACE, AND NUCLEAR WAR

38 This was his second visit. His first seems to have taken place within a year of the Enlightenment.

39 Nurse Edith Cavell was shot by the Germans (Brussels, 12 October 1914) for helping English, French, and Belgian soldiers reach the Dutch frontier. On the eve of her execution she said 'I realize that patriotism is not enough. I must have no hatred or bitterness towards anyone.'

40 According to some accounts, a remnant of the Śākyans survived the massacre.

41 *Dhammapada* 197–201

THE BODHISATTVA PRINCIPLE

42 D.T. Suzuki, *Mysticism: Christian and Buddhist*, George Allen & Unwin, London 1957.

43 Perhaps I am not being quite fair to some forms of mysticism. However, there is no doubt that *some* human experience may be characterized as 'the extreme of subjectivity and emotion', in that it does in fact seek to absorb the object in the subject, and equally no doubt that *some* forms of mysticism are instances of this kind of experience.

44 See Sangharakshita, *The Three Jewels*, Windhorse, Glasgow 1991, p.23.

45 M. Monier-Williams, *Buddhism*, John Murray, London 1889, p.111.

46 It should in any case be born in mind that the Jātakas, though very numerous, do not account for *all* the Buddha's previous existences, and that the 550 Jātakas of the Pāli *Jātaka Book* are not arranged in 'chronological' sequence but in accordance with a quite artificial principle.

47 Sangharakshita, *The Three Jewels*, Windhorse, Glasgow 1991, p.8.

THE GLORY OF THE LITERARY WORLD

48 *Dīgha-Nikāya* II, 119, trans. as *Dialogues of the Buddha, Part II*, by T.W. and C.A.F. Rhys Davids, Pali Text Society, London 1951, p.127.

49 *The Mahāvaṁsa or the Great Chronicle of Ceylon*, trans. Wilhelm Geiger, Pali Text Society, London 1912, p.237.

50 *Sutta Nipāta*, 453.

51 *Anthology of Chinese Literature*, edited by Cyril Birch, Penguin, London 1967, p.225.

52 Ibid., p.222.

53 Ibid., pp.231–2.

54 The First Part of Tamburlaine the Great, Act V, Scene 2.
55 *The Laṅkāvatāra Sūtra*, trans. Daisetz Teitaro Suzuki, Routledge & Kegan Paul, London 1978, pp.123–4.

A Note on *The Burial of Count Orgaz*

56 James A. Michener, *Iberia: Spanish Travels and Reflections*, Greenwich, Conn., p.165
57 *The Symposium*, trans. W. Hamilton, Penguin, Harmondsworth 1981, p.83
58 Ibid., pp.92–4
59 Gerald Brennan, *The Face of Spain*, Penguin, Harmondsworth 1987, p.239
60 *The Symposium*, op.cit., pp.90–1

Criticism East and West

61 Robert Graves, *The Crowning Privilege*, Penguin, Harmondsworth 1959, p.109.
62 *The Times*, 15 February 1988, p.10.
63 *Anthology of Chinese Literature*, op.cit., pp.231–2.
64 V. Raghavan, *The Number of Rasas*, third revised edition, Adyar Library and Research Centre, Adyar 1975, p.ix.
65 *Words International*, Vol.1, No.1 (November 1987), p.19.
66 Dr A.K. Warder, *The Science of Criticism in India*, Adyar Library and Research Centre, Adyar 1978, p.16.
67 *Ibid.*, pp.16–17.
68 *Ibid.*, pp.69–70.
69 *Ibid.*, p.29.
70 Sushil Kumar De, *History of Sanskrit Poetics*, second revised edition, Calcutta 1960, Volume II, p.45.
71 John Middleton Murry, *Countries of the Mind: Second Series*, Collins, London 1931, p.181.
72 Ernest G. Griffin, *John Middleton Murry*, Twayne, New York 1969, p.42.
73 *Ibid.*, pp.42–3.
74 F.A. Lea, *The Life of John Middleton Murry*, Methuen, London 1959, p.86.
75 John Middleton Murry, *Discoveries*, Collins, London 1924, pp.13–14.
76 *Ibid.*, p.14.
77 *J. Middleton Murry: Selected Criticism 1916–1957*, Oxford University Press, London 1960, p.4.
78 *Words International* Vol.1, No.3 (January 1988), p.42.
79 *Words International* Vol.1, No.5 (March 1988), p.34.
80 *J. Middleton Murry: Selected Criticism 1916–1957*, op.cit., p.9.

Also from Windhorse

Sangharakshita

A Guide to the Buddhist Path

Which Buddhist teachings really matter? How does one begin to practise them in a systematic way? Without a guide one can easily get dispirited or lost.

A leading Western Buddhist sorts out fact from myth, essence from cultural accident, to reveal the fundamental ideals and teachings of Buddhism.

The result is a reliable map of the Buddhist path that anyone can follow.

256 pages, 245 x 195

ISBN 0 904766 35 7

Paperback £10.95 / $22.00

Sangharakshita

The Three Jewels

The Buddha, Dharma, and Sangha Jewels are living symbols, supreme objects of commitment and devotion in the life of every Buddhist. To have some insight into them is to touch the very heart of Buddhism. Sangharakshita's scholarship opens the way to the immense riches of a great spiritual tradition.

196 pages, 205 x 134

ISBN 0 904766 49 7

Paperback £8.95 / $18.00

SANGHARAKSHITA

A SURVEY OF BUDDHISM

'It would be difficult to find a single book in which the history and development of Buddhist thought has been described as vividly and clearly as in this survey.... For all those who wish to "know the heart, the essence of Buddhism as an integrated whole", there can be no better guide than this book.' *Lama Anagarika Govinda*

'I recommend Sangharakshita's book as the best survey of Buddhism.' *Dr Edward Conze*

544 pages, 235 x 154
ISBN 0 904766 65 9
Paperback £12.99 / $24.95

SANGHARAKSHITA

FACING MOUNT KANCHENJUNGA

In this delightful volume of memoirs, glowing with affection and humour, Sangharakshita shares the incidents, encounters, and insights of his early years in Kalimpong. Behind these events we witness the transformation of a rather eccentric young man—as he must surely have appeared to his fellow expatriates—into a unique and confident individual, completely at home in his adopted world and increasingly effective as an interpreter of Buddhism for a new age.

498 pages, 215 x 134
ISBN 0 904766 52 7
Paperback £11.95 / $24

KAMALASHILA

MEDITATION :

THE BUDDHIST WAY OF TRANQUILLITY AND INSIGHT

A comprehensive guide to the methods and theory of meditation giving basic techniques for the beginner and detailed advice for the more experienced meditator.

A practical handbook firmly grounded in Buddhist tradition but readily accessible to people with a modern Western background.

288 pages, 244 x 175, with charts and illustrations

ISBN 0 904766 56 X

Paperback £11.99 / $22.99

For orders and catalogues, contact

WINDHORSE PUBLICATIONS

3 SANDA STREET

GLASGOW

G20 8PU

SCOTLAND